All my children,
Yoav
Shira
Tom
Guy
Yonatan

To Nina Weiner
Founder of ISEF
Israel Scholarship Education Foundation

A word from Amos Oz

Daniel Ben Simon's memoir is not only a fascinating, painful and eye-opening record of the encounter between the newly-born State of Israel and the massive Jewish immigration from North Africa — it is also the very personal, very moving story of one young intellectual who, despite of pain and insult, became a leading figure in Israel's politics, journalism and education. A touching tale of pain and love.

Amos Oz

Daniel Ben Simon

The Immigrant
From Morocco to Israel

The Immigrant/ Daniel Ben Simon

© All rights reserved to the author and publisher.
No part of this book may be translated, reproduced or transmitted in any form or by any means, electronic or mechanical, including photocopying, recording or by any information, storage or retrieval systems, without written permission from the author.

KIP - Kotarim International Publishing, Ltd

Translated by: Elizabeth Yuval
Graphic Design by: Bat Chen Nachmani

Publisher: Moshe Alon
kip@smile.net.il

ISBN: 978-965-7589-20-5

Author's Note	7
Chapter One: Leaving	11
Chapter Two: Family	36
Chapter Three: Kippa and Tsitsit	64
Chapter Four: The First Israel	91
Chapter Five: Lost in Their Own Country	122
Chapter Six: Hatred for the Left	151
Chapter Seven: Old Wounds	182
Chapter Eight: People without a Future	209
Chapter Nine: Infants Taken Captive	239
Epilogue	283

Author's Note

Of all the immigrants who came to Israel after the State of Israel was founded, no group has been considered as problematic and unsettled – and unsettling – as the Moroccans. Over the years I have repeatedly listened to unflattering remarks and "diagnoses" of immigrants from Morocco. What hasn't been said about us? We are angry all the time. Easily enraged. Refuse to integrate. Shout instead of speaking. Have no culture. Are prone to violence. Are not as well-developed as others. Primitive.

Were Moroccans like that before they came to Israel or did the encounter with Israeli society change them? While other immigrants worked their way into the fabric of the country, the Moroccans are still mired on the margins of main-steam life. That always seems to surprise people. Why did those who immigrated to France succeed so well compared to those who immigrated to Israel? Were they different kinds of people? By any objective standard, Jews from Morocco reached unprecedented heights compared with other groups that immigrated to France.

Author's Note

Within three generations, they positioned themselves at the pinnacle of French society. In Israel the situation is different. Moroccan representation in Israel's elite is negligible. A couple of percentage points, nothing more. Is it their own fault? Why did France succeed where Israel failed? To this day, many Moroccans are convinced that the state deliberately blocked their advancement and success because of their origin.

Worst of all, in many instances the marginality of their lives as immigrants was passed down from generation to generation. Chronic hardship that left three generations on the sidelines. They made careers in Israel's defense establishment and politics, but didn't penetrate other elite circles. And as if that weren't enough, the saga of Moroccan immigration has never been properly told or appreciated. Heroic descriptions of pioneering were reserved for other immigrants. Immigration from Morocco was left out of the heroic ethos of the founders and builders of the state.

This book is very personal, but it embraces all the stories of the immigrants from Morocco. Of their moments of pain and joy. All sorts of books have been written about Moroccans, the folklore, the cuisine, the superstitions, the famous rabbis and how supplicants prostrate themselves on their graves. Academics have described Moroccan immigrants as prone to political and religious extremism. Others have claimed the amazing success of Israel's right wing can only be understood by factoring in the support of Moroccans.

No serious attempt has yet been made to study or understand the sociology of the Moroccan immigration. This book is one modest step in that direction. Throughout my journalistic career I have written endlessly about Israel's peripheral communities, its development towns and the daily hardships of the people who live in them.

I have spoken with thousands of people and while it is hard to credit, most of the immigrants from Morocco still point to their arrival and reception as responsible for how their lives played out afterwards. I came to the country two decades after the great wave of immigration from Morocco and I learned of their suffering directly from them. They refused to forget. Their experiences as new immigrants changed their lives and led them down unexpected paths.

I tried to find the moderation, tolerance and restraint that had characterized them in Morocco. Where did they go? They were somehow expected to resolve the raging disagreements between the founders and pioneers. Between left and right. Between religious and secular. Between those who believed and those who didn't. Between Jews and Arabs. Between those who advocated profit and those who advocated welfare. If their faith had been turned to compromise and middle ground, they could have changed the face of the nation. They could especially have influenced the undercurrent of civil war waged by the various sectors of Israeli society. Their innate moderation and discretion should have lowered the flames of jealousy. They did not, and the fact that they did not was a missed opportunity of historic proportions.

This is a book about moving to a new country and the high price paid for it. Anyone who has made such a move knows how forceful the upheaval, the changes in passing from an old homeland to a new one, can be. In this book I recount the story of my first years and those of my family in the Israel. My brothers and sisters and I came at three different times in a program called Youth Aliyah, which brings Jewish children to Israel. After a separation of years, our parents joined us here. It turns out that even with the passing of years the sensation

Author's Note

of displacement doesn't leave, and there are dilemmas which are difficult to resolve: What do you do with your past life? Do you shake it off? Deny it? Pretend it doesn't exist? Or do you take it with you, alive and kicking, to your new country? The more integrated I became into Israeli society, the further I distanced myself from my former life. I learned that in human terms, rapid integration comes with a high price.

I'm not sure my personal experience represents all the immigrants from Morocco. But I do know it is common to many immigrants. From Morocco and from other countries. In moments of pain and moments of joy. I wrote this book for them.

***

Friends read drafts of this book, gave me advice, suggested corrections and helped make it better. I want to thank them with all my heart: Carlo Strenger, Shmuel Ben Zvi, Ehud Hazan, Danny Shek, Rami Rotholz, Emi Bouganim, Gabriel Malka, Orli Levy, Tom Segev, Ella Cohen, Israel Carmel, Yigal Bin Nun, Avi Lazimi, Yitzhak Booton, Esty Akselrad, Rivka Carmi, Zion Abu. And a special thanks to my partner Oriella Ben Zvi for her inspiration and support.

Chapter One
Leaving

One morning I was called to the office of the headmaster of the boarding school I attended in Casablanca. It was no everyday occurrence. Émile Sebban was known for his strictness, and he could look at you in a way that froze your blood. Needless to say, we called him Monsieur Sebban. We knew his first name was É`mile, but we never dared to say it aloud, not even when we were alone.

My classmates sensed something out of the ordinary was happening and looked sideways at each other, wondering what was going on. I rose from my seat and joined Monsieur Lévi, the school's senior teacher, who had come for me. It was a fairly short walk from my classroom to the headmaster's office. I didn't dare ask why I had been given the dubious honor of an audience with Monsieur Sebban. Students didn't ask why someone in authority did something. Communication was not a two-way street. When it came to authority, the student was the bottom rung of the ladder.

I was fifteen years old at the time and still afraid of those in charge. We all were. As soon as a teacher entered the room we looked up, rose and stood silently next to our seats. If the headmaster entered the room our hearts skipped a beat, that's how scared we were. And how respectful, of course.

"Sit!" ordered Monsieur Sebban. Monsieur Lévi had delivered me and he left immediately. Monsieur Sebban took a sheet of paper out of a drawer and looked at me for a long time. "I am not pleased," he said, and looked at the paper.

"About what, Monsieur le Directeur?" I dared to ask in a whisper.

"It's not good that you are planning to leave the school. It is very serious."

"But I have no plans to leave."

"You are listed here," he said, "as having registered to go to Israel."

Actually, I had been playing with the idea of immigrating to Israel for a long time, but I never thought actually realizing it would lead to something as dramatic as a call to the headmaster's office. At that time, 1969, when we wanted to talk about Israel, we called it *là-bas*, "there." Maybe out of fear, maybe out of hesitation. We didn't really know how to deal with the phenomenon called Israel. Behind closed doors, and only with other Jews, there was no problem. In the presence of Muslim friends and neighbors, we never mentioned it.

It was more than two years since the Six Day War, and Israel's stature had only grown. Our lives were divided into before the War and after the War. In the weeks before the War broke out fear pervaded the school; most of those students were Jewish. The teachers and mentors prepared us for the worst. The atmosphere was very tense and was hard to ignore. Many staff members had relatives in Israel and fatalistically assumed the coming war would mean their certain death. We usually spent our lunch breaks in the room set aside for cultural activities, where Moroccan and French newspapers were laid out. Reading them we learned the war was apparently unavoidable and could potentially annihilate the Jews living in Israel. The Moroccan papers couldn't contain their glee. The headlines predicted certain victory for the Arab armies and the collapse of the "Zionist entity." The smiling face of Egypt's president, Gamal Abdel Nasser, became a permanent fixture. We knew by heart all the names of all the important people on both sides, Arab and Israeli, in the drama that was about to unfold.

We were Jewish boys in an Arab country with a Muslim majority. We knew our lives would be different after the war. Usually, classical music was played in the cultural activities room during the two-hour breaks between morning and afternoon lessons. Now, however, tension eroded the routines of our lives. The broadcasts in Arabic stubbornly repeated that the end of the "Zionist enemy" was fast approaching. We weren't sure of the details, but one thing we knew for sure, if Israel were harmed, we would be harmed as well.

Zionism stole into our class through the back door. It simmered on a slow fire and was transmitted in whispers. However, the Six Day War pushed it into our lives straight through the front door. We felt it in every bone of our bodies. And then the great victory! It took us a few days to digest it and appreciate its magnitude. Moroccan Muslims also had a hard time understanding how it had happened: they had been prepared for the end of Israel, and instead they got the end of the Arab nation. Or rather, no, not the end, but the humiliation. All of a sudden everyone knew who Moshe Dayan was, Yitzhak Rabin, and other stars of the great victory. Dayan's eye-patch became the symbol of the victory of the Jews over the Arabs. I remember the Saturday after the war, the holiday atmosphere in the synagogue on Avenue Ferdinand de Lesseps, where we prayed.

It is hard to forget that Saturday, how joyous it was and how special. We strode to the synagogue as though we, personally, the Jews of Morocco, had won the war. We wore fancier clothing than on any other Saturday. Even those who usually didn't feel the necessity to pray came to the synagogue to show they belonged to the community. The Jewish community of Casablanca, which until only a few days before had been plagued by premonitions of death and loss, was now filled with an unprecedented pride. My father, who was far from being religiously observant and even found it hard to decipher the Hebrew letters of the prayers, pushed his way into the crowd of worshippers at the synagogue. We students got Saturday off from school to join our parents on Israel's holiday, not to mention our own holiday. The section of the synagogue reserved for women was full to bursting. My brothers and I managed to find seats in one of the back rows of benches, smiling and looking proudly at our mother. She had gotten a choice seat in the women's section, which was on the upper floor. The sound of the prayers came from afar and everyone's face glowed with both solemnity and joy.

When we left the synagogue, drunk with happiness, we could smell the familiar aroma of *defina* (the main Sabbath meal). Not far from the synagogue was the public bake house (called a *fran* in Moroccan), where we used to bring our food to be cooked. On that Saturday we stood at the entrance, looking at the enormous oven, its fire never extinguished, waiting for our pot of *defina*, which like the rest, had been cooking over a slow fire since Friday. That was the custom of the Jews of our community: bread dough was kneaded at home but sent to the *fran* for baking. On Friday, a few hours before the Sabbath began, the Jewish families would give their pots of *defina* to Muslim messengers. They would bring food to the *fran*, then return the pots and trays when the food was ready. Every pot had its owner and its special aroma. The messengers had an uncanny ability to differentiate between them. It was rare to find a pot or baking tray marked in any way. Nevertheless, the messenger boys could tell what belonged to whom by their size and lids. At noon, after the pots had spent an entire day in the oven, the messengers put them on improvised wagons and began distributing them.

We often went with them, and thus became acquainted with the hundreds of Jewish families who lived in our neighborhood. Sometimes we even went inside to see who was sitting at the table. Every family and its pot of *defina*. Every family and its own style of cooking. Some liked their *defina* cooked more, some less. Some added rice, others liked chickpeas. Some preferred beans to rice. Some put everything into one pot. There were pots that drowned in thick sauce, and others that had different kinds of meat.

On the great Saturday after the War the *defina* was also part of the victory. The tables were decorated, some people even using little Israeli flags. There had been a sharp, immediate transition from existential anxiety to pride and ecstasy. Suddenly, a frightened, submissive community openly raised its head. For the first time, the Jews felt safe, protected, that there was a strong country standing behind them. And not Morocco. Only a few days previously they had been afraid for their lives. The headlines had screamed the end of the State of Israel, and many felt the threat had been meant for them

Leaving

personally. Before the War, euphoria was the sensation felt by our Arab neighbors. The War took it from them and it now belonged of the Jews.

While Morocco was not an active participant in the Six Day War, it had been hard not to notice the pro-Arab carnival atmosphere in the streets. Solidarity with Egypt was evident in every corner of the city. The songs of Umm Kulthum, the most popular Egyptian singer, who became a national symbol, were played constantly, morning, noon and night. We became acquainted with the biographies of the members of the general staff of the Egyptian army, who were about to become the heroes of the campaign against Israel. They were commanded by the chief of staff, the charismatic field marshal Abdel Hakim Amer. He was on TV every day, his mustache impeccably groomed, his hair carefully combed, a grin of victory from ear to ear. We also knew the names of some of the heroes of the Syrian army. Pictures of the two presidents, Gamal Abdel Nasser and Hafez al-Assad, were hung everywhere next to those of King Hassan II of Morocco.

Even in our building we could sense the approach of the Arab armies, it was in the air all around us. We were the only Jewish family in a five-story building on Boulevard Moulay Youssef. Other families included petty and senior officers in the Moroccan army. Across the hall from us lived a family with a son who was an officer in the infantry.

During the days before the War my parents were invited to dinner to celebrate, in advance, the great Arab victory. The wife, whose immense proportions kept her seated most of the time – and the other family members were no different – distinguished between us and the Israelis, whom they called "Zionists." We were considered Jews but Moroccans, who for generations had enjoyed the protection of the royal family. The Israelis were of course also Jews, but living in Israel made them enemies of the Arab nation.

Their living room was hung with pictures of Amer, Nasser, Assad and the king of Jordan, and all the others who were about to decide the fate of the Zionist entity. All of my mother's family had immigrated to Israel in the early nineteen fifties, and she feared for their safety. She said goodbye to them many years ago and was afraid she would never see them again. When she wept tears for them, her neighbor comforted her, but also said that if they had stayed in their homeland they wouldn't have the troubles they had now. "Denise," she berated my mother in Moroccan Arabic, "why did they go there? We have always loved our Jews and treated them like family. They chose their fate. May Allah help them."

The atmosphere at school was the same: we felt history was being made. From one day to the next, the great victory changed our lives completely. We were Jewish students in a prestigious boarding school in Casablanca, and now we were Israeli patriots. We passed along information and traded opinions and again questioned our future in Morocco and looked for ways to express our new feeling of identity.

Before the Six Day War most of my friends had only the faintest concept of Israel. We knew it was a country where Jews lived and most of us had relatives who had immigrated before we were born. But for us the division was not between Morocco and Israel, it was between our lives in Morocco and the lives we expected to lead in France. We all knew that when the time came, after we had passed our matriculation exams, the *baccalauréat*, we would leave our parents and relatives and emigrate to France. Our new homeland.

Morocco gained independence in 1956 and France

withdrew, but the French had left behind them a modern society and a rich cultural legacy, and we naturally aspired to be part of it. Unlike Algeria, our neighbor to the east, no one in Morocco challenged the sovereign status of the French legacy or accused France of the sins of occupation. Both Jews and Arabs studied French as their first language, and some also chose to study English or Spanish.

For the Jews remaining in Morocco, the most natural next stop was France. We spoke French at home, our school curriculum was the same as France's and we watched French TV shows and hummed the songs of popular French singers.

In the meantime, there was a strong undercurrent of drama in our class. And not only ours. We didn't dare say anything to anyone in authority, but we couldn't help but notice the mysterious disappearances. From class, from the schoolyard, from the school itself. It was hard not to notice. Our school was the École Normale Hébraïque and belonged to the Alliance Israélite Universelle network. It was considered the best Jewish school in Morocco. Every year entrance exams were held for students from all over the country, and only the top twenty-four were allowed to enter its gates. The names of the happy winners were published in the newspapers as though they had been elected to the National Assembly. Every day we stood in line, like soldiers on parade, in front of the classroom. Only after we had welcomed the teacher by saying, "Bonjour, Monsieur le Professeur," did we enter the classroom and take our seats.

Now there were no longer twenty-four students in our class, only nineteen. A short time later there was one less, and then another. The school filled the vacant seats with new students, but the departures worried the school administration. David, who sat next to me for almost three years, was gone. We were in the eighth grade at the time, and one day he didn't come to class.

The empty seats saddened us deeply. Our best friends abandoned us with no explanation or farewell. We were distressed and the academic atmosphere suffered. It was one of the fruits of the Six Day War. From an anchored community that knew where it was headed we had become a community in transit with no fixed poles. Our French literature teacher noticed that no one was sitting next to me. "Where is your neighbor, Monsieur Ben Simon?" he asked. I had no answer. He turned to the class and asked, "Does anyone know?" "Non, Monsieur le Professeur," they answered. "Did he sleep here in school last night?" he asked.

I was too shocked to move. It was impossible that my friend David had been abducted by that country across the sea. Actually, he hadn't slept at school the night before. We thought he was ill or had to go home for some reason. Our boarding school consisted of seven classes of between 20 and 24 students, both boys and girls, from the sixth to the twelfth grades, living like a large family in comfortable surroundings. We always knew where everyone was almost all the time. School began at eight in the morning and ended a little before nine at night, after we had finished our homework. Then we went to the dormitory, where we slept in bunk beds.

I sat next to David in class and shared a dormitory room with him and two others. He had the lower bunk and I the upper. He was considered the best student in class. I came next, or possibly third. At the end of the year he was the top student in school, having received the highest grades in almost every subject. Every class received prizes and listed its students according to the grades they had received. David headed the list in most of the subjects, leaving me in second or third place.

Leaving

At the end of the year the teachers, students and parents met at the school for the distribution of prizes. First prize was many books, second prize was fewer books, and third prize was one book. The names of the top three prize winners were announced to the whole school. We used to joke and say that David needed a wheelbarrow for the piles of books he won. We were also jealous of him. He was self-disciplined and amiable, and came from a poor family, but when it came to achievement, he left all of us middle-class children far behind.

And then he disappeared. Without a word, without a trace. "Does anyone know if he went *there*?" asked the teacher, looking directly at me. I should have been first to know. Three years of closeness, friendship and sitting next to one another in class had made us inseparable. As soon as I heard "there," *là-bas*, I froze. No, I thought, it is impossible, he couldn't have disappeared as though the earth had swallowed him. He couldn't have gone without saying goodbye to his friends. Where was our friendship? Where were the bonds between us? He couldn't have left, I comforted myself.

A few days later we had days off from school, and I used the time to go to his house. He lived in a crowded neighborhood of Casablanca where there were a lot of Jewish families. My legs trembled when I opened the door. His mother was sitting on the floor of the kitchen, sorting lentils. Her head was covered with a scarf and she was humming parts of the Rosh Hashanah prayers, or maybe Yom Kippur. I kissed her on both cheeks and she got up to make me tea. I knew all the members of the family quite well. Every chance we got, David and I would go to his house, straight to the kitchen. His mother didn't need more than the look of expectation on our faces. She would slice bread, put a thick layer of butter on the slices, and sprinkle them with sugar. Happy, we took the bread with us and went into the street to play.

The street was our playground and our community center, Jews and Muslims alike. We knew almost no other form of entertainment. Whenever we had free time we played in the street. We played ball, sat on the curb, just hung around doing nothing and watching the world go by. We stayed at school only when we had to. Once night fell we went inside. In most houses lights were only lit when it got really dark, and sometimes not even then. Electricity was considered a luxury. Not only the young people, but adults as well spent a lot of time in the street. Women kept house in the street, doing their cooking and washing, soaping, rinsing, wringing and hanging the clean clothing to dry on lines strung outside. They set their cooking pots down at the entrance to the house, while the men looked for empty chairs in the local coffee house. They would almost always order tea, drinking it slowly to pass as much time as possible. I remember the scenes from Meknes, and then later, when my family moved to Casablanca. Many years later, when I returned to Morocco as a journalist, I again saw the scenes of my childhood, so similar it seemed time had stopped. The coffee houses were full of men slowly sipping tea, watching people and cars go by. Anyone who couldn't find a free chair leaned against a wall. Some leaned and some squatted. When the average Moroccan hadn't found anything else to do, he could always be seen sipping a cup of tea.

Because we watched all the time, we knew everything that happened in the neighborhood. Who came and where they went, who was visiting, who was quarreling, who walked in happily and who slammed the door on his way out. We knew almost everything that happened to every Jewish family in the quarter. Our curiosity had to be satisfied and it led us to the threshold of an engagement party or bar mitzvah celebration or into a house of mourning. Everyone knew everyone and everything about everyone. Staying inside, within the walls of your home, was alien to our nature and in general to the nature of all Moroccans, who were always looking for a back door to escape through. Boys even fought in public. We knew what the neighbors were eating and we could tell by the raised voices that they weren't getting along. At that time there were almost no telephones, people had almost no books except the Torah, and virtually nothing forced them to stay inside. With endless, oppressive heat and no ventilation, the street became the Moroccans' real home, for both Jews and Arabs.

"Yes, yes, my son," said David's mother in Moroccan Arabic, "David has gone." She waved her hand at some faraway place. "The ship took him *there*. They told us not to talk about it, because we were afraid the neighbors would know David went *there*." The Sionistes, that is, the Zionist emissaries, demanded she keep his departure a secret.

I tried not to show my sadness. I was so sorry he had left, and sorry at the way he had left. Three years of close friendship and such a cruel way to leave, without a word, no goodbye. We lived in a boarding school, physically separated from our family, and our friends were our only support. We were as good as dead without them. David had helped me get over my unhappiness and homesickness when I first came to the school. I was there against my will and was one of the most miserable students ever accepted. On my first day I lingered close to the gate, refusing to enter. I couldn't bear to say goodbye to my parents, who accompanied me as far as the entrance. They took my small suitcase out of the car, put it on the sidewalk and drove away. I didn't know when I would see them again.

David was barely twelve years old, but he was solid and strong, both mentally and physically. He took responsibility for the new students, most of whom were having trouble dealing with their first days away from home. The more I overcame my sadness and pulled myself together, the more thankful I was that he had come to my rescue. Every time someone was homesick, every time one of the students sobbed after lights out, David was there to ease the pain.

As those three years passed our friendship grew stronger. Now I was angry that he had suddenly disappeared. And no less, that Israel had taken him. Two weeks after he left we had a surprise test in composition. Monsieur Soli Lévi, the much-admired but very strict French literature teacher, blew into class like a storm. "All of you, choose a subject and write five pages about it," he ordered. He gave us two hours.

David's inkwell was still full of blue ink. His chair was empty and so was the drawer where he kept his books and notebooks. I was still very upset and the most natural thing was to write about my friend David who had simply disappeared, about the ship that had abducted him and taken him away. I never mentioned Israel in my composition, despite the pride I felt, but rather called it "the country over *there*, far away from us."

And now I was sitting in front of Monsieur Sebban, looking at him sheepishly. How could I justify the presence of my name on the list of students who had disappeared and were going to disappear? He did not disguise his distaste for the endless line of students sneaking away from the institution where he was head master. Jews and non-Jews knew Monsieur Sebban and admired him for turning the school into the country's leading educational institution. He too, as a practicing Jew, had accepted the fact that the Jews of Morocco did not view the country as their future homeland. He also knew that the Jews were living in Morocco on borrowed time, that they were worried and looking for a new homeland.

He admired Israel, but believed it would be easier for his students to integrate into life in France or one of the French-speaking countries of Europe, or Canada. Israel demanded too great a sacrifice, or so he thought. He had been sent to Morocco by the Alliance directors to head the boarding school in Casablanca.

He had a naturally authoritative personality and radiated strictness. He kept his hair very short, which made him look like a soldier in the Foreign Legion. He also had perfect command of the French language. Like everyone else, I revered him, and was thankful he had exempted my parents from paying for school tuition, because they would not have been able to afford it. Despite the fact that I didn't want to study at a boarding school, he kept me there. He had made a deal with my parents: excellence in studies in return for payment. Three years previously, when my parents and I sat in his office, he set down his terms. "As long," he said, "as Daniel is one of the top three students in his class, he will not have to pay tuition." Then he shook hands with them and escorted them to the gate.

I met his terms. Three years had gone by, and Monsieur Sebban could barely believe the change in me. I told him that not long ago "Zionist" emissaries had visited our house and encouraged my parents to send me to Israel. Their visits became routine. We knew they would come and expected them. They spoke fluent French and to many looked like angels of deliverance. Give us your children before it is too late, was their message. They warned of the dangers lying in wait for the Jews of Morocco, and predicted a catastrophic anti-

Jewish Arab uprising. They spoke with such authority, we didn't doubt that in some prescient way they knew what our future would be.

We knew they lived in Israel and spoke Hebrew. After the Six Day War, every Israeli who came to visit looked like a hero. We gazed at them in awe. We were certain they had participated in the great victory over the Arabs. Every time we asked, they just smiled meaningful smiles.

Our relations with our Arab neighbors remained complex. After the War, when the enormity of the Arab defeat became known, anti-Semitic graffiti covered the walls of the streets of Casablanca. The shock of defeat was so great that merchants and labor unions ordered a boycott of Jewish stores, claiming the money, or some of it, went to finance the Zionist war machine.

We were children and didn't notice our neighbors related to us differently. We knew nothing of street fights or about Jews who had been attacked because they were Jews. But there was a sense of discomfort, a lack of ease and certainty, about the existence of Jews in Morocco. Israel's victory undermined the routine of daily life. The Jews began to feel they were on quicksand and that their presence in Morocco was insecure and temporary. Towards the end of the nineteen sixties almost no poor Jews remained in the country. Most of them had immigrated en masse to Israel at various times during the nineteen fifties, partially emptying Morocco of its Jews. Those who remained belonged to the upper and middle classes and could choose their countries of immigration. Israel had attracted immigrants in distress. France, Belgium and Canada were the destinations preferred by the wealthier Jews.

One evening I was called home from school to meet an emissary from Israel. He was waiting for me in the living room, wearing a gray hat. He introduced himself as Monsieur Marciano. There was a pile of forms in front of him and my name was on all of them. I looked through them and saw my parents' signatures at the bottom. Next to them were forms bearing the name of my sister Eva, who was three years younger than I. I was fifteen years old and she was only twelve, and it was clear that our fate had been sealed. Like my two brothers and older sister before us, we were going to leave Morocco and be separated from our parents.

I couldn't believe my eyes. There had been similar visits over the years, but I never imagined I would be the object of one. Immediately after the Six Day War my two brothers and my sister disappeared from my life without saying goodbye. I was at school when it happened, and when I came home for vacation they told me that Robert, who was fifteen, and Linda, who was thirteen, and Michel, who was eleven, were no longer in Morocco. "They were taken to Israel," my mother told me. I remember the shock I felt. That was in December 1967, at the height of the immigration of young Jews from Morocco to Israel.

Not only Zionist emissaries came to our house. There were Ashkenazi rabbis from Chabad and other centers of Orthodox Jewish sects who begged to take the children to their yeshivas in New York, London, Strasburg, and who remembers where else. They promised payment in return and showed us pictures of children who over the years had become bearded rabbis in their communities overseas. Competition for the children knew no bounds. Behind it were two factors, push-pull, that made people eager to leave: the first was the danger lying in wait for the Jews in Morocco from the Arabs, and the second was the growing strength of the Jews in Israel and the rest of world. The temptations presented by the Orthodox Jews were more beguiling, because they resonated with the Jewish sentiments which were part and parcel of the very nature of every Jew in Morocco. Whenever they met a man with a hat and a beard they bowed and sometimes kissed his hand. Everyone who looked like a rabbi was received with honor. Admiration for rabbis, or people who looked like rabbis, was boundless. With no other local leadership, rabbis were perceived as the source of authority for community life. The sick went to doctors, but also went to receive a blessing from the rabbi. Anyone who was having trouble at work appealed to the rabbi – to say nothing of people with marital problems. The rabbis were the most suitable courts of appeal for quarreling spouses, because rabbis would spare no effort to prevent families from splitting up.

When my brothers and sister left I didn't know what to think or where to turn. One minute they were there and the next they were gone. They didn't leave an address or even a memento. All they did was throw some clothing into a suitcase and go. My parents walked them as far as the waiting car waiting in front of the building, embraced them briefly and said goodbye.

It had been more than two years since they left, or more accurately, since they had been forced to leave. Now it was my turn. The emissary praised Israel to the sky and gave glorious descriptions of what was waiting for us. I was especially taken by his stories about how children grew up there. He showed us pictures that left no doubt as to the great gap between them and us. While we had to dress according to European norms and our external appearance had to be impeccable, the children in Israel looked as if they had just stepped out of *The Jungle Book*. They wore short-sleeved shirts, their hair was uncombed and wild, they wore shorts. And they wore sandals. I was amazed by the sandals. We wore black leather shoes and wouldn't go to school until they were properly shined. Next to the daring, almost feral Israeli children, we looked like candidates for the *petite bourgeoisie*. In class we were careful to behave and maintain our self-control. Anyone who felt he had to laugh did so as quietly as possible, and covered his face with his hands to keep the teacher from seeing.

The photographs of Israeli children spoke of a completely different life. I fantasized about the day I would cast off my suit, stop combing my hair, and wear shorts and sandals. More than anything else, I was captivated by photographs of groups of boys and girls my age happily hugging each other. Clearly, they were pictures of a different world. At the age of fifteen we still didn't know how to approach girls. Our school was coeducational, but the separation was almost total. No romantic alliances were formed, and certainly not overt romantic alliances. All we knew about sex came from reading and rumors. The atmosphere we lived in was very conservative, and we still had no experience, not even the most passing, with girls.

That created pressure. We passed through puberty while we were awake and while we were asleep, but we didn't understand what was happening to us. Needless to say, we said nothing to the teaching staff. We lived in a country where people touched one another. We hugged and kissed each other whenever the opportunity arose, family, friends, and acquaintances. Jews and Arabs responded the same way to demonstrations of closeness and friendship. There was an abundance of warmth and love, but no sexual intimacy. We didn't know, and moreover were apprehensive, about expressing sexual desire or hinting at sexuality.

In our house, as in other Jewish homes, sex was considered a taboo subject. And at school as well. One particularly memorable incident occurred in the sixth grade during a drawing lesson. Our teacher was a Frenchwoman named Madame Kravetz, she must have been in her forties. She used to wear skirts so short her knees showed. Every time she came into class we were wildly excited. Her appearance was provocative and a whiff of her perfume almost made us faint. We were not used to such women. One day she was wearing a particularly short white skirt. She turned to the blackboard to show us how to draw a straight line between two points, picked up the chalk in her left hand and passed it to her right, and raised her arm to the blackboard. For a moment we stopped breathing. As she raised her arm her miniskirt rode up and we saw a good deal more than we were used to seeing.

I think it was the most erotic thing, the most openly erotic thing that happened to us during those three years at boarding school. Had we seen it, or was it a collective fantasy? That night we sat on our beds and refused to let go of the image. We had no idea of how to respond, how to behave with an erotic scene of the sort we had witnessed. Nothing in the conservative atmosphere of the school had prepared us for it. Even in biology lessons we didn't learn about human anatomy or the structure of the human body. Conservatism didn't differentiate between Jews and Arabs. Two Arab boys walking in the street hugging one another as if they were a couple was a very common sight. People touched each other out of natural closeness, part of a society which treated personal contact as an act of humanity.

The Israeli photographs, showing boys and girls embracing and cuddling, seemed absolutely revolutionary to me. But my parents were worried. "What about school for Daniel in Israel?" "No problem," said Monsieur Marciano. "He will be taught Hebrew and we will make sure he lacks nothing. He will receive everything he wants. Once he is in Israel he will study in a class with others his own age, and when he graduates at the age of eighteen, he will be inducted into the Israeli army."

I listened enthusiastically. I imagined the suit I always wore changing into an Israeli army uniform. Until now I had only seen soldiers in movies. The thought that I would be a soldier with a gun, maybe kill someone, never crossed my mind. Monsieur Marciano told us about many graduates of the Casablanca boarding school who had immigrated to Israel in previous years, served in the army and had been instrumental in Israel's heroic victory over the Arabs two years earlier. He even mentioned the names of some of the graduates who had excelled in the fighting.

"When are we talking about?" my parents wanted to know.

"As far as I'm concerned," he said, "the sooner the better."

"But it's the middle of the school year."

"I can wait until the beginning of the summer vacation. If everything is OK, this week I'll go to the school and update Monsieur Sebban about Daniel's future move to Israel."

Monsieur Sebban, to put it mildly, was not pleased. The day before he called me into his office he had received the list of students who were leaving in the summer, and my name was on it. He told me he had no intention of granting the Jewish Agency's request. "It's not for you," he said as though the issue had already been settled. "Israel is not for you. I know who is capable of living in Israel and who is not. It is a very difficult country. Don't misunderstand me. It's very important that Jews immigrate to Israel, because it's our country. I have relatives living there."

While he was talking, Monsieur Marciano entered the office. They shook hands like old friends. Monsieur Marciano sat next to me and smiled. After having convinced my parents, he now had to release me from the clutches of the school headmaster.

"I think it's a mistake for you to take Daniel," he said, looking very serious and adding that I had to stay at school until I finished the twelfth grade. After that I would study in France, like most of the graduates of an *école normale*. "I have," he continued, "a 100% success rate in *baccalauréat* exams. My graduates are accepted by the leading French universities. Who knows better than you how we completely changed the face of the Jewish community in France? We have first-rate physicians and dentists and university professors and senior functionaries."

"I know," said Monsieur Marciano.

"I cannot give you Daniel. He will be lost in Israel. He is a gentle boy and an excellent student. Only recently I received a report from Monsieur Lévi, who teaches French literature and composition. He said he is convinced Daniel's future as an author in France is guaranteed. How will he get by with the language in Israel? Monsieur Marciano, you know me and you know I always speak openly. I believe wholeheartedly that if you take him you will be doing him a grave injustice."

I listened to the conversation, looking from one to the other, mesmerized, watching them sitting on opposite sides of the desk and deciding my fate. Monsieur Sebban looked like a Frenchman, Monsieur Marciano looked like a local Jew: he wore a slightly threadbare suit and spoke French with a prominent Moroccan accent. He was one of a group of Jews who had linked themselves to Israel with the objective of attracting students to immigrate. Judging by the rate at which the schools were emptying out, they were very successful.

I thought about the day when the literature teacher returned the compositions we had written in class. More than a composition, I had given him several pages of my inner torment, my silent scream about my friend David, who had abandoned me for Israel and left me empty and in despair.

A few days later our compositions were returned with a grade at the top of the page. He went from one student to another, passing out the exams. I waited, but he didn't return mine. I panicked. He stood in front of the blackboard holding some papers. I recognized my handwriting. Was he going to make fun of me? I could imagine every scenario except what happened.

He demanded absolute silence, and then read my composition aloud. It seemed to take forever. As though the clock had stopped. One page, and then another page, and yet another, and I was about to lose consciousness from shock and embarrassment. Finally, he finished. He raised his eyes, smiled at me and said one word I will remember forever: "Merci."

After thanking me for "a moving composition," he told me seriously that the only profession open to me was that of author and that without a doubt writing was my purpose in life. "It is almost certain you will be an author or a journalist, possibly both. You have the necessary facility with the language as well as the sensitivity."

The forms to be filled out for leaving the school were on the desk in Monsieur Sebban's office. Tirelessly, Monsieur Marciano explained how important it was for good students to immigrate to Israel, about the shining future awaiting them, about the atmosphere of uncertainty in Morocco, about the dangers lurking for the Jews if they remained and about Israel as the haven created to protect the Jews.

Monsieur Sebban wasn't convinced. He looked at

Monsieur Marciano with an "if looks could kill" look. "Are you also talking about the Jews who immigrated to Israel twenty years ago? Look at how they are living now. We know everything about what happens there. Many Moroccan Jews were sent to places with no education and no work."

"I immigrated to Israel at the same time and I agree that it was very hard, but now things have changed for the better. Believe me, Monsieur Sebban."

Monsieur Sebban shot me a look and raised his hands helplessly. "And what does the young gentleman have to say?" he said, pointing at me. "Did you ask him? Do you ask the opinion of anyone you take? I have great difficulties with the way you do things. You cut the students off in mid-path and hurt their chances to succeed in the future."

I could see he was disappointed. He motioned for me to return to class. The other students were curious to know why I had been called to the headmaster's office. After the bell rang they gathered around me. "I may be going to Israel," I said, stressing "Israel" without fear. They looked at me, perhaps in awe, perhaps disappointed, perhaps incredulous. Two or three said an immigration emissary had visited them at home as well but that their parents sent them away. Some were openly sorry I was leaving the class and the school.

During my third year at the school I had won my place as the lead actor in the theatre group. Barely a week before I said I was leaving, we had appeared before the other students after the Sabbath meal. My acting had made my friends smile and even laugh aloud. During my years at school I made many friends and was considered popular. Now it was obvious that another parting was very close. Salomon Cohen, who sat behind me, was extremely upset. I knew him and his older brothers, who also attended the school, and were admired as leaders in the scout movement. I also knew his parents. They lived not far from the synagogue in the center of the city, and on Saturdays when the family was together we would often leave in the middle of the prayers and go to his parents' house.

Ariel Sebban, who sat one row in front of me, was considered class king because his father was the headmaster and his mother taught math. He was amazed my father had surrendered and agreed to let me leave. If I had followed the school tradition I would have finished high school with the rest of the class and then gone to study in France.

Salomon and Ariel did follow the school tradition. They moved to France, studied medicine, and when they were in their twenties were already working as physicians. Over the years their reputations grew, both in the big city and beyond. I followed them on the social networks. Our personal connection was broken the day I left boarding school, and was renewed after almost four decades. The circumstances were tragic. Salomon's email surprised me. "I want to renew our connection and would be happy to see you when you come to Paris," he wrote. I became very emotional. Some time later, before I boarded a plane for Paris, I was informed that he had succumbed to cancer.

Two years later, another email arrived. Daniel Sebban, Ariel's brother, asked all those who had been to school with Ariel to write a few words in his memory. It turned out that he too had died of cancer. I immediately thought of Monsieur Sebban, our strict, determined headmaster. How had he reacted? How had he dealt with the death of his beloved son? I was deeply grieved. Only twice had the connection between me and my old school mates, those whom I left when I was fifteen, been renewed. And twice death had intervened.

On that day, at the beginning of summer 1969, Salomon, whom we all called Charlie, and Ariel were among the schoolmates I would very soon say goodbye to. They all gathered around me. Were they jealous? Did they pity me? I didn't know where I was going or what was waiting for me there. As the day for leaving my parents and Morocco grew closer, my expectations became tinged with anxiety and fear of the unknown. To a great extent I wanted to change my fate, to slam the door on my family, I wanted to turn over a new leaf, I wanted a new life, I wanted to assault the new country, I wanted to meet my brothers and sister, whom I had not been able to say goodbye to three years earlier. I wanted to know Israelis, I wanted to touch the glory of Israel, the country that had performed magic for us, I wanted to see Israeli soldiers with my own eyes. I wanted to leave the country of my birth. I no longer wanted to come into contact with those young Muslims whose hobby was to curse and insult every Jewish child they met, I wanted to be free, liberated, I wanted to wear shorts and a T-shirt and sandals, I wanted to distance myself from the terrible distress that had oppressed my parents and relatives. And yes, I also wanted to find my old schoolmate David, who had left his friends so abruptly and left me feeling abandoned.

Chapter Two
Family

I can't recall saying goodbye to my parents or my four little brothers. Maybe I tried to wipe out the memories as too traumatic. In any event, I don't remember a hug or a kiss or a tear. I wasn't particularly excited or emotional. It was an ordinary evening in August 1969. We waited in the living room, my little sister Eva and I, for the *aliyah* representative to come for us. Our two small suitcases and some sandwiches were near the door. We lived on the fourth floor and I could hear his footsteps as he climbed the stairs. After some pleasantries he shook hands with my parents and told us to follow him. I took one last look at my mother and saw she had closed her eyes and was murmuring a prayer. That's what Moroccan women always did, both Jews and Arabs, during moments of crisis, believing that praying to God would make things better somehow. Now my mother prayed for our health and safety as we left for a new country.

Evening had fallen and our street was dark and quiet.

THE IMMIGRANT

No neighbor saw us get into the dark Renault Dauphine waiting for us on a side street. On the way to the airport I pressed my nose to the window, silently saying goodbye to Casablanca, the metropolis I had lived in for eight years. It was a city of both bright lights and gloomy areas veiled in darkness. The massive influx of people had left its mark: large parts of the suburbs had been taken over by millions of Moroccans from the regions of the high Atlas Mountains. They came with nothing and gathered in slums of tents and tin shacks. They moved to Casablanca hoping to find work and a better life for their children. Nevertheless, the influence of French rule was evident in every corner of the city: the houses were well maintained, the avenues were broad, the wealthy areas had their own special architecture, and even the plants and flowers smelled French. The store signs were still written in French, as were the street signs. Today most of them bear the same names given by the French when the Protectorate of Morocco was established in 1912.

Recently, in the wave of national pride sweeping the country, some of the names have been changed to Arabic, but that is happening slowly. Morocco of the nineteen sixties had not yet shaken off the fairy dust left by the occupying French. The primary language of instruction at my school was, as noted, French. We only studied Arabic, the official language, four hours a week, as we did other foreign languages. The situation was the same in almost all the other Jewish schools. In general, the educational system regarded French as its first language and teachers and students stubbornly spoke it to preserve its official status as the national language, even after Morocco won independence.

So on that night in the summer of 1969 Eva and I drove through the well cared-for streets of Casablanca.

Family

Many Jews lived there. There was Charlie's house, there was Joseph's, there was the home of Mardoché, all of them schoolmates left behind. It was dazzling to look at so much wealth. Enormous villas with swimming pools and great expanses of manicured lawn. Almost every villa employed more than twenty workers to clean it and tend to the grounds. When the Jews began leaving, a sector of the labor market imploded and literally hundreds of thousands of Muslims found themselves out of work. The lack of servants was one of the main factors that made the Jews miss Morocco.

The French left as well. After Morocco received independence in 1956 hundreds of thousands of Frenchmen went home. When Algeria received independence six years later, the French again left the locals to themselves. In Morocco Jews replaced the French in almost every field: the economy, the administration, businesses, higher education. The French elite that had run the country helped the Jews take over because it was the Jews who had internalized French ways and were comfortable with the French heritage. The Muslims, who technically ruled the country, also adopted the French ways, but at the same time actively worked to foster an Arab heritage. It was no secret that King Hassan II's French was better than his Arabic. His father, Mohammed V, had sent him to study in France, and he had earned a PhD in international law before he ascended the throne.

I looked at the homes of my friends one last time, my heart heavy that I might never see them again. It was practically the end of August. They were probably all somewhere at summer camps run by the scout movement. Others, too lazy for camp, most likely went to France to visit relatives, which is what wealthy Moroccan Jews usually did.

Only a few thousand Jews were left in the country during the summer, and those who had stayed could barely wait to leave their towns and villages and go to Casablanca, where they could enjoy the many possibilities of the thriving Jewish community. Leaving the city for the last time I thought about the changes that had occurred in Morocco. I remembered houses where only Jews had lived, and then Arabs moved in after the Jews left for Israel, France, Canada and elsewhere. The Jews had gone in two enormous waves: one when the State of Israel was founded, and the second after the Six Day War. The most recent wave, after 1967, shook the soul of the Jewish community and altered Morocco's Jewish landscape beyond recognition. A community of hundreds of thousands was reduced to a few thousand. Two thousand years of Jewish life in North Africa was coming to an end.

We drove to the Mohammed V Airport. The main streets along the way were named for members of the extended royal family: King Hassan II, his brother Prince Abdallah, his sisters Princess Lalla Aicha and Lalla Amina and the other princes and princesses. The king's portrait looked down at us from every utility pole and every street corner and every sign. He wore an army dress uniform or a traditional Moroccan garb. He smiled in his pictures, but the smile never reached his eyes; perhaps he was aware of the plots against him. When the Jews prayed for his health and safety in every synagogue, it was not a random or routine act. On Saturdays, after reading from the Torah, the rabbi said a special prayer for King Hassan II, who had bestowed his protection upon the Jews of Morocco. His father also received a prayer for protecting the Jews like a father during the Vichy regime in World War Two. When ordered to discriminate against the Jews and institute a *numerus clausus* to keep them

Family

out of the universities, he announced that the Jews were under his protection and he viewed them as full citizens of his country.

I was seven when he died. He was then only fifty-two years old. At home and everywhere he was called Moulay Youssef, and we called his son, who succeeded him, Moulay Hassan. The news of his death shook Meknes. People poured into the streets, frantic, sorrowful, men weeping like children and wagging their heads from side to side. To this day I can recall what I saw, what I heard, sounds of sobbing. "Moulay Youssef is dead! Moulay Youssef is dead!" people groaned hoarsely. The father of the country had died and women punished their own bodies in mourning, scratching their cheeks until they bled. Some people banged their heads against the wall. Cries of grief could be heard everywhere. The death of the king was like the death of the kingdom. It was only natural in a country where the king was identified with existence. To this day, on hills and mountain tops, the holy trinity of Morocco towers over the landscape, inscribed in enormous letters: *Allah. Al-Watan. Al-Malik* ("Allah. The Kingdom. The King"). Like our neighbors, we hung the Moroccan flag on our balcony.

Almost forty years later, the funeral of his son King Hassan II brought millions of people into the streets of Rabat, the capital city. I covered the event as a correspondent. The dozens of world leaders who walked in the cortège behind the coffin could barely believe their eyes when despite increased security, crowds of emotional mourners broke through the police lines, endangering their lives in a desperate attempt to touch the coffin of the man who was considered a descendant of the Prophet Muhammad. His father, King Mohammed V, was considered the midwife of modern Morocco because during his regime the country had achieved independence. Immediately after his death was announced, uncontrollably weeping Jews of Meknes' *nouveau mellah* (the new Jewish quarter) filled the streets. The following day we were told to stay home. The Talmud-Torah school I attended closed its doors in mourning. Stores and businesses closed their doors as well. The king so beloved by the Jews had passed away. In those days, whenever the status of the Jews in Morocco was discussed, it was always connected to the status of the king. Thanks to the king's protection, the Jews considered themselves immune to all evil. He always found an opportunity to say he considered the Jews his children no less and even more than the Muslims. His son King Hassan followed in his father's footsteps and said that before his father closed his eyes for the last time, he made him swear to protect the Jews of Morocco.

There had been a special relationship between King Mohammed and the Jews. During the nineteen fifties he felt betrayed by the mass exodus of Jews to Israel and did not hide his anger at what he considered a lack of faith. The Israeli representatives who negotiated with him for the emigration of the Jews explained it was an ancient dream whose time had come: for two thousand years the Jews had been waiting and praying for the day they could return to Zion, the land of their ancestors.

"What's wrong with their lives in Morocco?" the king asked. While at no time did he attempt to stop the Jews from emigrating, he also did not hide his anger at their preferring a distant country to Morocco, where they had been living for thousands of years. That was what he said to Joe Golan, an Israeli sent to Morocco by Nahum Goldman, president of the World Jewish Congress in the United States, to speed up the immigration of the Jews to Israel. The mission was sensitive, and assigned to

Golan because of his relationships with American Jewry and Israel's intelligence community. During 1954 Golan met with the king three times to pave the way for the Jews to immigrate to Israel. The two conducted a surprisingly frank and open dialogue. After each meeting, Golan returned to his hotel room and took notes in French, the language of the meetings. Of the first meeting, he wrote:

"We entered the villa, its floors covered with Moroccan rugs. We sat in the reception room. 'I have nothing to teach you, Mr. Golan,' said the Sultan. 'The Jews have lived in the most blessed country in the Maghreb for thousands of years, long before the advent of Islam. They have thrived, lived among us and continue to occupy a respected place in society. Why do they want to leave now, just when our country has won its independence and our people have been liberated? The Jews are an inseparable part of us. What kind of wild adventure are they going on, to a place plagued by conflict and uncertainty? What will their fate be once they leave the land that is their land?'"

Golan replied, "Your Royal Highness, a Jew leaves when he feels he must and he has someplace to go. The Jews have been promised a return to Zion, as your highness knows. The door is open, and has been since the day Israel was founded, to every Jew wanting to end his exile. There is also the unavoidable problem of militant Arab nationalism linked to the Palestinian problem, which naturally rejects Zionism... The Jews of the Maghreb are mentally and emotionally oriented to leave. Without wishing to offend Your Royal Highness, the Jews' stay in Morocco was only a long waiting period for the moment they could return home."

The king listened to Golan, whose parents had been born in Russia and Egypt. At a certain point he showed signs of fatigue and displeasure, and dismissed his visitor. Golan wrote in his diary that the king complained Israel was breaking up families and helping healthy young people leave, leaving the middle aged and the old behind. At the time it was rumored that Israel decided which Moroccan Jews could immigrate and which couldn't. There were unconfirmed but worrying stories of Israeli representatives giving priority to young people capable of overcoming the difficulties of immigration and being absorbed in their new country. The stories made it hard to ignore the tragic drama unfolding as families were torn apart and young immigrants left their parents behind.

The king had heard those stories, and others. "I have heard," he told Golan, "that the families you take are sent to stark, unwelcoming camps, most of them far from cities. I assume that the camps are temporary, and that the immigrants live there until housing and work are found for them. Life there must be very hard. The people must feel like foreigners in the country you claim belongs to them. They don't know the language or the customs. That means suffering for people who have everything they need to live lives of honor and respect... We watch them go with anxiety, and worry about their fate. May Allah preserve them and forgive them for the mistake they are making. If I stop emigration now, I will be helping to destroy families, and I am more interested in family unity. The Jews of Morocco are my children. They remain Moroccans and I will continue to protect them, wherever they may be. If they want to return, they will be able to at any time."

Towards the end of the meeting the king asked about kibbutzim. "Can Moroccan Jews join kibbutzim? Will they be discriminated against when they arrive in Israel?" he asked. Years later, sitting in Joe Golan's house in the Old City of Jerusalem, he told me he had been surprised by the king's interest in the condition of the Moroccan Jews who had immigrated to Israel. "I think he was prompted by a sense of having been betrayed," Golan said. At the time the Israeli media were full of stories and reports about the immigrants from Morocco, who were treated with contempt and ridicule and as being "primitive." "It hurt me personally," he said, "I had helped them leave Morocco, but the way they were treated in Israel made me think twice about what I had done."

An enormous portrait of King Mohammed welcomed us at the Casablanca airport. The area was crowded and there were many Moroccan security guards. The *aliyah*[1] representative led me and my sister Eva into the terminal. We entered an enormous hall. Dozens of young boys and girls were sitting on the floor. Suitcases were piled up in a corner. I recognized some of the children sitting there; I had met them in the synagogue and around the neighborhood. The Israeli representatives scurried from room to room, holding documents. I could hear people speaking French, Moroccan Arabic, Hebrew. There was tension in the air, suspense.

Others immigrating to Israel, friends of mine, also had not been permitted to say goodbye to their families at the airport. The parents stayed at home. The representatives said they were acting on instructions from the authorities so as not to arouse suspicion. It was clear to one and all that the mass exodus of dozens of Jewish children wasn't a trip to the Alps. In those days, when Jews were fleeing the Arab countries, such sights must have raised suspicion.

It was almost midnight before we left the waiting room. We took our suitcases and followed the representatives and uniformed Moroccan security guards. They seemed to be on very friendly terms. Monsieur Marciano had

---
1. Literally, "going up," it means immigrating to Israel.

also come to the terminal and ordered us not to say a word or look at other travelers. We reached the exit. The security guard looked us over carefully. He was holding a notebook with a list of names. Last name, first name, picture – and we marched to the plane chartered for our flight. Inside the plane we heard languages other than French. Someone spoke to Monsieur Marciano, addressing him by another name. Was that perhaps not his real name? We called all the Israeli representatives "les Sionistes."

I had never flown before, but the experience remains vague, perhaps because it was late and I was exhausted. Eva woke up because of the roar of the engines when we took off. I kept asking myself if I was doing the right thing by taking her away from our parents. She was silent. She seemed not to care. A little girl, suddenly ripped away from her familiar childhood and sent to another world.

She and I were not the first of our family to leave home. During the flight I thought about my brother Michel, younger than I by a year and a half, who grew up right next to me, step by step. His family nickname was Bourvil because his crooked nose reminded us of the French comic actor. It was a compliment, for him and all of us, because Bourvil and Louis de Funès were greatly admired cultural heroes.

Michel was barely eleven years old when he was brought to Israel, with no opportunity to say goodbye to us. Unlucky, he did not fly like us, but was forced to sail from Casablanca aboard the dilapidated *SS Azemmour* during a particularly hard winter. The sea was stormy and the waves reached twenty meters. He had not had the chance to find out anything about Israel, yet he already found himself en route, helpless below deck on a wave-tossed ship. Even after years in Israel he continued wondering why he had been torn, unwillingly, from his family. He was a popular child in the neighborhood, liked by both young and old for being the little Bourvil, but also because of his talent to make people laugh.

After three days below decks he threw up and stopped eating. Linda went to visit him occasionally and found him writhing, his knees drawn up to ease the pain. "I want to go home!" he begged. Years later she told me that seeing him like that broke her heart. She desperately begged the *aliyah* representative on deck to help him. He tried to comfort her by telling her that all the children were throwing up because of the waves.

Even during the worst times when she was filled with sorrow and pitied her little brother, she didn't feel homesick. She was old enough to understand the financial hardship at home, which sometimes made it difficult to feed all the children. Our mother was always there, but we barely knew our father, Haim. He was one of the few Jews who wore the uniform of the Moroccan army. The Jews of Meknes were amazed to see a young Jew wearing the elegant uniform of his Royal Highness' army. During those pre-independence years my father had joined the French army and considered himself a French soldier in every respect. He was a tailor much sought-after by high-ranking officers and had a reputation for tailoring stylish uniforms, with all their emblems and decorations. Even after Morocco's independence, he remained in the army, this time in the service of the king.

He chose to spend his days at the army base rather than at home with his family. We neither saw much of him nor were we particularly aware of his existence. He would come for short visit, riding a horse, to the amazement of the Jewish neighborhood. His life-style was light years from theirs. He had nothing to do with the Jewish community, rarely attended synagogue except for the High Holidays, did not speak the local Jewish-

Arabic dialect and considered himself a French solider somehow stuck among Jews. He was regarded as European by Jews who lived as a community, the only person who had integrated with the Muslims, a welcome guest at the parties held by the French officers. He didn't miss a single event and had a reputation for being the life of the party; the most beautiful women were eager to dance with him and competed for the privilege.

While drinking was forbidden, the army bases where my father spent his time were awash with alcohol. One party followed another, night after intoxicated night. My father was a virtuoso accordionist and played for the dancers. He went to every party with his accordion slung over his shoulder. His music swept the revelers away and he was a genuine bon vivant, he knew how to enjoy life and didn't miss a single opportunity. He only returned home in the early hours of the morning, smelling strongly of alcohol.

Only Jews lived in the *nouveau mellah* in Meknes; Muslims were forbidden to live there. The 14,000 Jews crammed into the neighborhood lived like one enormous extended family. Everyone knew everyone, all the children went to the same Alliance schools and the same Talmud-Torah. The Jews of Meknes were considered devout and as preserving the traditions of their religion. The Meknes rabbis were famous even beyond Morocco, and were known for having made important decisions about religious law. The Jewish community of Meknes zealously preserved its character until the middle of the nineteen sixties, when the city was emptied of its Jews in Operation Yakhin, which brought the largest wave of Moroccan Jews in history to Israel. In a matter of years, almost 100,000 Jews emigrated.

Nevertheless, Meknes' *nouveau mellah* was still full of Jews who wanted my father to share his life with them and allow them entry into a forbidden world. Maurice

Family

Mamane, whose family shared a yard with us, told me he would always remember how my father took him on a walk outside the neighborhood. He said at that moment he felt his life had changed. After he immigrated to Israel with his family he told me that my father "was one of the most famous Jews in the city and when he held my hand I was in seventh heaven. We were neighborhood Jews, out of touch the world at large. I will never forget that walk with your father."

My father liked to play cards and could never resist the temptation to sit down at a table with professionals. After the French left they allowed the locals to play a French gambling game called *belote*. The Jews, especially the younger ones who had been nurtured at the bosom of French culture, became addicted and spent entire nights playing the game. There was one particular coffee house that attracted the neighborhood Jews, called Puit de Jacob, "Jacob's Well." It was situated not far from where Talmud-Torah Street crosses Jérusalem Street. More than a few streets in the *nouveau mellah* had Hebrew names, especially the names of rabbis. The Puit de Jacob's owner, Jacques Dahan, had received a license from the French authorities to open Meknes' first coffee house-restaurant. He had fought with the French in the Second World War, losing a leg, and after the armistice they rewarded him with the license. On one of the walls he hung an enormous picture, the Biblical scene of Jacob drawing water from a well.

That was how my father spent his days and nights, between the army base and playing cards. Sometimes my mother sent me to Puit de Jacob to call him to come home. I would stand next to the card table until I collapsed with fatigue. The other players wouldn't let him leave. So, night after night, the card table controlled our lives. Outside of the army base and the coffee house, there was virtually no sign of my father.

Even though the French soldiers had gone home, their Moroccan heirs preserved the symbols of the French military. At the entrance of the base where my father served there was a sign bearing the slogan of the French army: *La discipline fait la force principale de l'armée*, "Discipline is the army's main force." Military instructors spoke French and military training was conducted in French. On base, senior staff members spoke French to one another. My father was perfectly at home.

Our Frenchness opened doors to us that were closed to traditional Jews and Muslims. At the end of the nineteen fifties, swimming pools, sporting venues and coffee houses still found it difficult, or perhaps didn't want, to liberate themselves from the heritage of colonialism, and anyone who spoke the language of the occupation automatically belonged to the upper class. Anyone who socialized with the occupier was envied. My father, thanks to his Frenchness, pushed us right up to the top of community status.

Status aside, however, materially speaking, he found it hard to provide for the family. There was always a shortage of something. Every time he came home from the army he brought food, enabling my mother to vary the diet. The situation became worse as the family grew larger. Reproduction didn't stop for a minute. My mother became pregnant almost every year. Within fifteen years she gave birth to nine children. Throughout my entire life in Morocco a baby was crying somewhere in the house. It only stopped when it was my turn to immigrate to Israel.

The complexities of my family life were always present in my thoughts and didn't give me a minute's rest, not even on the plane taking Eva and me to Israel. The thought I would soon meet with my brothers and sister left me very tense. The crowded plane was now silent. Almost everyone had fallen asleep, fatigue blotting out the sounds of the engines. I could see the Israeli *aliyah* representative sitting in the front row with a *kippah*, a skullcap, on his head. He was holding documents written in Hebrew. The seats were pretty much falling apart, and every movement of the plane tossed us from side to side.

The representative had thrilled us when we were in Morocco by telling us that in a short time we would be speaking Hebrew like natives. As soon as we landed, he said, we would go to a special place to learn the language. We knew a little Hebrew because we had studied it at school, but four hours a week weren't enough to allow us to speak and understand. Our Hebrew was Biblical, and sometimes, when we held "conversations" in Hebrew class, we sounded as though we had just stepped off the pages of the Old Testament. The thought that in a few months I would be able to speak Hebrew as fluently as I spoke French exhilarated me. All we had to do was to attend Hebrew classes for a while and we would come out completely different people. Not only would we be Israelis, we would have a command of Hebrew. That's what the representatives promised us.

I looked at sleeping Eva and realized I barely knew her. For the past three years I had almost not seen her at all, except for holidays and summer vacations. I lived at the boarding school and left only occasionally to visit my family. And when I did go home I shut myself in a room and lost myself reading books, morning to night. There were almost no books at home, and most of the time I read the ones I had received from the school as prizes for academic excellence at the end of the year. Luckily for me, in Casablanca there was a store at the end of the street that let you read books and comics in the store, and that way I could read to my heart's content. There were days when I sat on the floor of the store, surrounded by piles of books, and read until my head dropped. One day the owner put his hand on my shoulder and said I could take books home without having to pay, on condition I return them within a few days. I could barely contain my joy.

In 1964, when I was 10 and Eva was seven, we moved from Meknes to the big city, Casablanca. We left the building in Meknes, all of whose residents were Jewish, for a building on one of the main avenues of Casablanca where career army officers lived. We had an apartment on the fourth floor, a little bigger than the one in Meknes, but this time as well, several of us children were crowded into the same room. We had barely moved to Casablanca when my mother gave birth again, to child number eight. While she was in the hospital there was no one to look after us. We didn't have family in Casablanca and my father came and went as usual. Our Muslim neighbors were open and warmhearted and shared their meals with us. I was too young to understand the significance of another baby. When my mother came home from the hospital holding a newborn infant, neither I nor any of the other children was particularly excited.

We suffered from our routine lack of material goods in our new home as in our old, and my father's frequent absences left us in continual hardship. Whenever he came for a visit my mother would rage at him. She had inherited or learned a tendency to shriek. She and my father almost never conversed quietly. She hurled abuse at him, accusing him of being absent all the time and blaming him for our poverty, for our chronic want and because there was no money to buy clothing for the children or for enough food to feed all of us, and for all our troubles. In response he would go sit in a corner of the house, pick up his accordion and play until her anger had exhausted itself. Often he would escape to the corner coffee house he had recently left to come home.

Her screaming frightened us. We would sit helplessly next to each other, waiting for the hurricane to pass. My mother cursed in Moroccan Arabic, wishing my father all the evils in the world, and in return my father made fun of her in French. I think we must have heard every possible swear word and insult in both languages. Every year the approaching holidays filled us with anxiety because we knew the shouting war was about to begin again. We grew up in an atmosphere of anxiety and fear and emotionally it left us scarred. I was lucky because I was considered an industrious child who liked books, and was spared the fate of my brothers and sisters. In addition, I had a haven at boarding school for a couple of years, so I missed out on a lot of battles. During vacations my brothers would update me on how awful they had been and the damage they left behind. By virtue of my success at school my mother had a strict rule for the family. When I closed myself in a room to read, the house was under lockdown so that I wouldn't be disturbed.

My mother, Denise, because of the number of children or because it was just her nature, wasn't strong enough for the burdens she had to bear. My father, perhaps because of the number of children or perhaps because it was just his nature, avoided the burdens of a family, preferring to entertain himself with his friends. My mother terrified everyone around her, my father charmed everyone around him. Everyone loved him and wanted his company. He conducted his emotional life elsewhere, far from home. When he came home he sealed off his feelings towards my mother and towards us. Once he left home he was a star and the life of the party; at home he kept silent. I can't recall a kiss, a hug, or a caress from either of them. Sometimes an affectionate hand was laid on me, or something nice was said, or they showed maternal or paternal feelings.

Never having received parental love, I used to stare at demonstrations of intimacy between parents and children. In the street, on a bus, on a train, in kindergartens and schools. I was filled with an envy that refused to be assuaged or wane, even years later. I once asked my mother why it had been like that. She answered, in her defense, "And when I was growing up, did my parents love me?"

The new baby boy waited to be circumcised. Until the last minute they couldn't decide on a name. Eventually they named him after my paternal grandfather, Jacob. Grandpa Jacob came from Meknes to Casablanca to participate in the family celebration and serve as godfather for the baby who would bear his name. Grandpa Jacob knew his health was failing and that he wouldn't live much longer. And in fact, sometime after that I was standing in the street and the neighborhood postman gave me a telegram for my father. I looked at the single line: "Father died. Funeral tomorrow in Meknes." One of my father's brothers had signed it.

Immediately after the circumcision the house emptied of the few people who had come. Apparently the excessive number of childbirths in our family displeased them. I came upon my uncles speaking angrily to my father and demanding he put an end to the births. They were particularly angry because he disregarded his financial burden. My father blamed my mother. She blamed him. Both promised Jacob would be the last. Eight was enough.

During the flight to Israel I kept thinking about meeting

my brothers and sister who were already in Israel. From the few letters they had written to my parents, I knew they had been sent to religious boarding schools, where they divided their time between agricultural work and studying. My sister Linda, older than I by a year and a half, was in despair. She begged to return home as soon as possible and wrote again and again about how homesick she was. Apparently, even with the lack of parental love, my brothers and sisters had not given up on the warmth of a family. Although we were unloved, we wanted to be near our mother and father. Even after years of being separated from them and from the rest of the family, my sister still sent cries for help, begging to be rescued.

I tried to imagine what their lives were like in Israel. The thought that they spoke fluent Hebrew made me envious. How would I speak to them? Would I even recognize them? Did my two brothers miss me? While I was at boarding school in Casablanca I saw them only infrequently, and now almost three years had passed. Almost six years of distance and separation. Maybe that was why we weren't close. In Morocco I had no idea of what their lives were like, not at home and not at school, and they didn't know anything about my life at boarding school.

The hardships and shortages at home had convinced them that *aliyah* to Israel was the only solution. They didn't suffer alone, my father had his hardships to bear. As a uniformed career soldier in an Arab army he personally experienced the shock of the Arab defeat on 1967. "What do you have to say, Monsieur Ben Simon, about the war? Your Jewish state really took a punch in the teeth. The Arabs taught it a lesson, didn't they," one of the soldiers said sarcastically. The others gathered around to see what he would say. "You Arabs are pretty worthless," he answered, not bothering to hide his glee, "you just proved again that all you do is talk."

Within seconds angry soldiers assaulted him and a full-scale fight broke out. The whole base knew about it, and eventually, so did the commander. He ordered my father to leave immediately and wait until the commotion had died down. His superior officers told him it was the only way they could protect him from the hot-headed soldiers. He came home in a foul mood, and for the first time spoke about leaving Morocco, fearing for his life and those of his children.

During the days he was home friends of his, high-ranking officers, came to visit us. The fight hadn't changed the way they felt about him. Every visit was the same. Our guests sat in the living room, bottles of whiskey were opened and for hours they sat there drinking. My father sat in the middle of the group playing the accordion until the early morning, and his problem would be pushed into a corner. The officers loved the *chansons* he played and sang along enthusiastically.

I remember how surprised I was when I heard them, between drinks, criticizing King Hassan. At that time it was considered a serious crime, even a capital crime. The king's rule was strict and merciless. He was especially hard on anyone who dared to oppose him, and those bold enough to do so were sent to distant prisons, notorious for their terrible conditions and ill-treatment.

There was one young officer, Mohamed Ababou, who was a frequent guest at our home in Meknes, where he commanded the officers' training academy. When we moved to Casablanca he sometimes came to visit. Several years later he would attempt a coup against the king, shaking the country to its core and shocking it as never before. At the time of the coup he commanded a Moroccan army cadet school near Rabat, the capital city. His attempt exposed the king's vulnerability. The adulation of the people hid the dissatisfaction and unrest of the army. Colonel Ababou was a friend of General Mohamed Medbouh, and together they planned a daring coup which had it succeeded, would have ended the life of the king and turned the country from a monarchy into a republic.

The *attentat* occurred in July 1971 while the king was celebrating his forty-second birthday at his palace in Shkirat, a vacation town situated between Rabat and Casablanca. More than a thousand people had been invited from Morocco and abroad, including high-ranking army officers, businessmen, artists and religious leaders. Early in the day, Ababou, who was only thirty-six, deployed 1,200 cadets under his command throughout the palace. The official version was that they were there to provide security for the party.

At around two in the afternoon the king, surrounded by members of the royal family, held a reception in the main tent, which had been filled with food and drink. Standing right next to him was Crown Prince Sidi Mohammed, who had just celebrated his eighth birthday. He would eventually become King Mohammed VI. All of a sudden volleys of shots were fired. The guests thought the noise came from fireworks. Within seconds hundreds of cadets poured into the tent and began shooting people indiscriminately. Hundreds of guests were shot and killed. Others fled. General Mohamed Oufkir, minister of the interior, grabbed the king's hand and pulled him to the exit. They went to the royal restrooms and hid in adjoining rooms. Outside they could hear more gunshots and exploding hand grenades. The king, locked inside a toilet stall, peeped out through the keyhole to follow the slaughter.

Colonel Ababou went looking for him. It was the moment he had been waiting for. Crown Prince Sidi

Mohammed, lost and helpless, asked one of the conspirators, "What do you want? To kill my father?" They spared the child and broke into the restrooms. One of the officers broke down the door where the king was hiding. For months he had been training for the mission, the conspirators' ultimate goal: to be the one who would kill the king. All he had to do was pull the trigger. Hassan, wearing a scruffy T-shirt and a straw hat, smiled at his would-be killer. At first the soldier didn't recognize the king, because he was used to seeing pictures of him wearing a suit, not a T-shirt. Once he recognized him, he put his rifle to the king's forehead.

What happened next is a mystery, unsolved to this day. Later, the king's version would be the following: "He stood in front of me, his gun pointed at my head. He was so nervous he couldn't keep the weapon steady. Suddenly, instead of shooting me, he stood at attention, raised his arm and saluted. I immediately gave the order, 'At ease!' I understood that something extraordinary was happening. I told myself I had to persevere to the end. I stood in front of him and shouted, 'Why do you not kiss my hand? What happened to all of you? Have you gone crazy? You are soldiers in the Royal Moroccan Army, you are my children!' He dropped to his knees, then kissed my hands and my feet, rose and kissed my shoulders."

The coup failed. Colonel Ababou had failed in the greatest mission of his life, to turn Morocco from a monarchy into a republic. I remember his *joie de vivre* when he came to visit. Who ever thought that handsome young man would cause the greatest commotion in the history of Morocco?

Three days later, on July 13, 1971, twelve of the leading conspirators were tied to posts and executed in the center of the Shkirat palace. Ababou's head was covered to hide signs he had been tortured. Relatives were summoned to watch his death first hand. Thus ended the life of Little Napoleon, as he was called by the Moroccan media.

Barely a year went by and there was another attempted coup. It was led by General Mohamed Oufkir, whom I had seen when I went to military parades with my father, and when he came to the synagogue in Casablanca on some of the Jewish holidays. It was not unusual for one of the heads of state to attend one of the important synagogues as a courtesy on Rosh Hashanah or Yom Kippur. Oufkir, a war hero and admired member of the military, was considered the man closest to Hassan II.

The second *attentat*, in August 1972, was no less daring than the first. This time it was done from the air. Five F-15 war planes lay in wait to ambush the royal plane as it flew back to Morocco from a visit to France. The planes were in the sky over the city of Tetouan, near the Spanish border. They shot at and hit the royal plane, killing some of the passengers sitting near the king. Miraculously, despite holes in the fuselage, the plane could still fly. And as if that weren't enough, one of the planes went into a dive, trying – unsuccessfully – to crash on top of the royal plane. Finally the king's plane managed to land at the airport, where Hassan got into a waiting car and hid until forces loyal to him arrived. The conspirators, headed by General Oufkir, one of the most powerful people in the country, were executed. The king appealed to Moroccans in a radio broadcast, convincing them that he had been saved from evil because he had been blessed by heaven. From that day until he died in 1999, the Moroccans believed in their own holy trinity: the kingdom, the king, and God. When Oufkir died Israel was left without its closest intelligence liaison. He had been involved in Israel's activities in Morocco and in the operations to bring Moroccan Jews to Israel.

Moroccan Jews felt they were in great peril. The attempted coups only reinforced their opinion that the future did not lie in Morocco. Without the king no one could guarantee their existence, or at least that is what they believed. Yitzhak Meir, the *aliyah* representative who came to our house immediately after the Six Day War, suggested my parents send the older children to Israel before a catastrophe was visited upon the Jews of Morocco. He painted the future in particularly dark colors. "How many children do you want?" my parents asked. "As many as you can give," he answered. It sounded like a business deal, as though they were bartering us. "And what about Daniel?" Meir asked. He had been told that I went to an academically very good boarding school, and it would be better for me to stay until I graduated. So my place was taken by Michel, who was then ten years old. In that way my parents solved two problems, financial security and personal security, in one shipment of three of their children.

Meir was a representative of both the *aliyah* institutions and the Mossad. When we met him, he introduced himself as Henri Dumoulin. He spoke French with no trace of a foreign accent. He came to an Arab country for the first time in his life after the Six Day War, and to Moroccans he represented himself as a French industrialist who had come to do business. The people who had sent him told him to focus on school children. "Leave the parents," they said. The logical conclusion was that after the children had immigrated to Israel, their parents would join them, an assumption that justified itself. In most instances the children paved the way for their parents' immigration.

Like other *aliyah* representatives, Meir lingered near the entrances of Jewish schools, waiting to talk to

Family

students entering or leaving. Once he went into a school in Marrakesh and talked to some of the girls during recess. The school principal ordered him to leave and threatened to call the police. She could tell the guest was an *aliyah* representative who had come to "abduct" students and take them to Israel.

Meir, who was then in his thirties, had lost most of his family in the Holocaust and his brother in the Six Day War. To overcome the tragedy he looked for patriotic challenges that would fill his life and benefit the country. Bringing young Jews to Israel as part of the Youth Aliyah program looked like a worthy goal. He himself had immigrated from Belgium as a youth and viewed *aliyah* as a way of insuring the continued existence of the State of Israel. His fluency in French helped him become a representative in Morocco. After he had acclimatized and knew his way around, he felt he could invite himself to the homes of Jews to suggest they let their children immigrate to Israel. He didn't care what means he used. If the parents refused, he tried his luck with the children: "Hello! Would you like to go to Palestine?" or "Hello! Would you like to immigrate to Palestine?" He never mentioned Israel but used the term current among the Jews in Morocco, "la Palestine."

Such an approach from someone who looked European was so surprising it made them curious and they gathered around him. He was actually quite surprised when they replied, "Yes! Yes!" Most of them did want to go to Palestine. He asked them for their addresses and a short time later knocked at the door and introduced himself to their parents. He didn't need much in the way of introduction. The children had already told their parents about the man from "la Palestine," and they knew he would come.

So only a few months after the Six Day War, Meir

made the rounds of the Jewish neighborhoods as if he had been born there. He was invited to pray in the synagogue and dine at Jewish homes. After meeting with hundreds of families, he realized that many of them were still traumatized by the Six Day War. They told him they had feared Israel would be defeated, and that would mean the end of the Jews in Morocco and the rest of the world. Some saw him as an angel sent to rescue their children. They turned the children over willingly without knowing if they would ever see them again. Meir kept a diary in which he described the existential angst of the Jews and their overwhelming fear of their future in Morocco. The parents felt helpless, not knowing what to do, and preferred sending the children to Israel to keeping them in Morocco. "At least they will save themselves," they told Meir. Uncertainty about the future made them send off even children who were barely ten years old. Meir's superiors had instructed him not to let children younger than eleven immigrate, but he didn't always follow instructions. He wrote that he witnessed emotional separations which left him greatly saddened. Deep in his heart he knew that some of the children would never see their parents again.

My two brothers and sister left the family only a year after Peduel, number nine, was born. We called him Peddy. We were now seven boys and two girls. There had been complications during last birth and my mother almost died. When she recovered the doctor told her another pregnancy was out of the question because it might kill her. Muslims who lived in our building came to the circumcision. The same rabbi who had performed the rite barely a year before came again, the same terrifying cut and the same screams from the baby. My mother held Jacob, who was only a year old, in her arms and left the infant to the care of a Muslim neighbor. My

Family

mother looked tired and broken with no interest in the newest member of the family. On the morning of the circumcision my father still found time to play cards at the coffee house on Boulevard Moulay Youssef. Neighborhood residents and people from other quarters used to go there all the time, attracted by the chance to see members of the local soccer team, who often frequented it. WAC, the Casablanca team, led the upper league, but the FAR, the military team, threatened their first place. Television had been introduced into Morocco a few years previously and the coffee house was tuned to soccer games all day without a break. People watched the games for hours on end, holding cups of mint tea.

My father loved playing cards and thought life wasn't worth living without a card game. It was hard to drag him away from the table. Often he was the only Jew there, and felt as though he were one of the Arabs. They liked him because of his army uniform and because of his innate love of life. Even though he did not speak fluent Arabic, for them he was the Jew who had fully assimilated into the Arab environment.

My mother was isolated from her own family, all her relatives having immigrated immediately after the establishment of the State of Israel. After she married my father she decided to remain in Morocco with him. It had been more than fifteen years since she had seen her parents and her eight brothers and sisters. She was always terribly unhappy, bemoaning her loneliness and woes. We never met them because they had left Morocco before we were born. During all those fifteen years she received almost no mail from them, except for a few black-and-white pictures taken in Givat Olga, a neighborhood near Hadera in the center of the country, immediately after their arrival.

My father was also one of nine children, but at that

time all of his brothers and sisters were in Morocco. They grew up in a country that regarded itself as a suburb of France. Their children had French names, and traditional Jewish names were given as middle names that no one paid any attention to, giving way to Jean-Claude and François and Paul and Jean-Paul and Alain and Jean-Luc and Nicole. We spoke to each other in French, read French books and considered France our Promised Land, waiting to receive us with open arms. We identified with French culture and it brought us one step closer to entering the modern world. We competed with each other in our knowledge of everything French. Whoever could recite French poetry by heart walked around school with his head high.

So ends the chapter on life in Morocco. The plane carrying the young immigrants was descending for landing. Suddenly, as though by prior agreement, everyone began singing the traditional Hebrew song, "We have brought you peace."

Chapter Three
Kippah and Tsitsit[2]

Early September 1969. I was brought to the boarding school that would be my new home. It was evening, and the truck entered through a large gate, stopping at the front door after a few hundred meters. The dilapidated shacks on both sides of the dirt road made the place look like a work camp. As soon as we got off the truck a middle-aged man with carrot-red hair came out to receive us. He was wearing a large *kippah* that had fallen to one side, saved by his ear from hitting the ground. We stood next to the truck holding our suitcases, huddling together. We were a few boys and one girl, who had come to a new land to begin a new life. Two weeks ago we had left Morocco, and now it seemed we had come to the last stop on our journey of *aliyah*.

---

2. Kippah, plural kippot, are yarmulkes and tsitsiot are the visible fringes of the small tallit, an Orthodox Jewish prayer shawl worn by men under their clothes.

Around us were young boys and girls, running from one place to another, paying no attention to us. The boys were wearing khaki shorts and undershirts, and they all wore *kippot*. The girls wore khaki trousers and shirts. Night falls quickly in the Middle East, and the enveloping dusk would soon turn into darkness. There were almost no lights on the path. Nearby, some of the school employees were standing together, talking among themselves. Some of them were instructors responsible for receiving the new immigrants. One woman took Eva by the hand and led her towards one of the shacks further along the path, to where the girls lived. A male instructor asked me to follow him. We entered a large building with a red tile roof and a long row of rooms along a central hallway. Fewer than ten of us new Moroccan immigrants had come in the truck.

The noise coming from the rooms was deafening. Shmuel, the instructor, asked the boys in the hallway where there was a room with a free bed for "the new immigrant who has just arrived." When no one answered, he took matters into his own hands. He opened the door of the first room. There were four beds, all taken. He opened the door of the second room. There were four beds there as well, also taken. Dragging my suitcase, I trudged after him from room to room, without finding a free bed.

I didn't really understand what was going on. It would be night soon and I had nowhere to sleep. Shmuel began to look a little unsettled. He went to talk to another instructor, and when he returned he checked the rooms again, more thoroughly this time, looking for a bed or mattress. Finally, in the last room, a cot, virtually a mattress on the floor, was found under one of the beds. It turned out to be the hiding place for the watermelons the boys had taken, unauthorized, from the field. My prospective roommates didn't want another person in the room and the discovery of the stash of stolen fruit did nothing to endear me to them. They became very angry and began a shouting match with Shmuel. Finally, he managed to soothe their ruffled feathers: it was only a temporary arrangement, he promised, and things would soon be back to normal. He pointed at me as though I had just walked into the room. They pushed the illegal watermelons into a corner and let me call the cot my own. Before leaving, Shmuel lay his hand on my shoulder to say goodbye. "Are you OK?" he asked with a smile. "I'm fine!" I answered in Hebrew. I was proud of my first two Hebrew words spoken in Israel. It seemed like a great beginning. Shmuel didn't know a word of French. I was impressed by the way he had fought for me. It had taken him a long time to convince my new roommates to let me stay. Two of them were willing but two protested bitterly. What was I supposed to do? I sat on the cot, which was almost on the floor, trying to avoid their angry eyes.

That was my first meeting with the real Israel, my first meeting with Israelis. The loud argument between students and someone in authority was to a certain degree representative of the way things worked in my new country. He shouted at them and they shouted back. They also made threatening gestures, and treated him as though he were irrelevant, someone who was somehow meddling in their affairs.

I remember my shock and embarrassment, my confusion. As someone who later turned watching the human condition into a profession and his life's purpose, I remember the joy of watching my first debate in Israel. For me it was a watershed. Where I came from it would never occur to anyone to argue with a superior. It wouldn't matter if he were an instructor, a teacher, or any other adult. Discipline and obedience marched shoulder to shoulder together through the world I had just left, they fashioned our lives both at home and in society. We were brought up to obey and didn't know what rebellion meant. We were obedient students, we never disobeyed orders or instructions and never rebelled against authority. I had just arrived, but I had witnessed one of the most prominent aspects of life in my new country.

Becoming acclimatized to Israel was one shock after another. The immigrants who came from Morocco in the early nineteen fifties told me that their first real crisis was the loss of parental authority. In Morocco children customarily listened to their parents and responded with blind obedience. In a show of respect, many kissed their parents' hands when they returned from prayers. The first immigrants had barely arrived in Israel when the children rebelled against parental authority and began treating their parents as equals. Before their eyes, traditional family structure crashed and burned, leaving them helpless. Immigrants from Morocco, like those from other Arab countries, watched as hundreds of years of familial hierarchy disintegrated. The new country changed the balance of power within families to the point where the older generation could no longer recognize or navigate within it, and the standing of the paterfamilias was trampled into dust.

Generally speaking, coming face to face with Israel was a terrific shock for immigrants from the Arab countries. Their sense of inferiority led them to apathy, depression, violent outbursts and suicide. Shaul, the hero of the Six Day War in Sami Michael's book, *Some Are More Equal Than Others*, describes his father's shock, loss and humiliation during his first days in Israel. He writes, "My father cried! Petrified, I listened to sounds my ears could not accept: Abu Shaul was crying! After a couple of minutes my mother shook his shoulder. 'Ya'akov,' she whispered, 'enough, Ya'akov. We shouldn't mourn for what is gone.' But I knew my father would never stop mourning for the dream that had been shattered. Nothing was waiting for him on the threshold of his new love...He had entered with joy and slammed the door behind him, and now found himself in the presence of an apathetic monster...Perhaps my mother didn't understand, but I understood. My father's body was still alive – but his soul was dead. He was a new immigrant from Iraq, an old man, responsible for a family, penniless, tossed on a sea of people without the slightest ability to provide for his family...And all that was merely the foundation for a new discovery, far worse: it was made obvious to him that he belonged to an inferior race...and his soul never recovered from the burning humiliation."

    I lay on my cot, still wearing the suit I had come in, too frightened to change my clothes. I can't recall falling asleep. I dozed on and off and was brutally awakened by someone banging on the door and shouting. It was our wakeup call. A man opened the door and turned on the light, shouting at us to get out of bed. My roommates got out of bed and began getting dressed with obvious resentment. I looked at the clock. It was two in the morning. I couldn't figure out what catastrophe had been visited upon us. I remained lying in bed, hiding my eyes from the strong light. Suddenly I felt something hit my back, and the man who had awakened us shouted at me to get up. One of my roommates told him I was a new immigrant from Morocco and had just arrived. That made no difference to him. "*Slichot!*"[3] he yelled at me, "*slichot!*" Paralyzed with fear and unable to speak, I walked in

---

3. Prayers, especially those said before the Jewish High Holidays (Rosh Hashanah and Yom Kippur).

darkness to the synagogue with the other students. I was still wearing the suit I had worn when I left Morocco. The synagogue was packed. At the entrance Shmuel took a *kippah* from his pocket and put it on my head. So, in the middle of the night, I prayed my first prayer in my new country.

The prayer ended before dawn. I went back to bed. I kept thinking, why had I been summoned to say the *slichot* prayer in the middle of the night, my first night in Israel? It surpassed my understanding, literally. I had never heard of people praying in the middle of the night, what kind of custom was that? I had never heard of a prayer called *slichot*, either.

During the two weeks before we were dispatched to the boarding school we thought things would be different. We landed in Marseilles and it seemed like a new life was opening up before us. We were taken to an immigrant camp where hundreds of young people just like us were waiting, eager for the Israeli experience. They came from all over the world, leaving behind families, lives and plans for the future. Everyone spoke a different language, but nevertheless we understood each other. We didn't know what was waiting for us but we felt certain we had reached a safe harbor. Every group sang songs in its own language, while the Israeli flag fluttered in the wind and filled us with patriotic pride. Israeli songs we were hearing for the first time were sung along with songs in other languages. There wasn't always enough food in the dining room, but euphoria filled us and we felt no hunger. The beds weren't always comfortable and we didn't always sleep well, but we woke in the morning feeling ready for anything. We had shaken off the burdens of family and parents and the neighborhood and school and our old countries, and were now breathing new, fresh air. All around us we heard Hebrew spoken freely, and we drew it deep into our souls. We were full of expectation, for a new world awaited us. Of course, we didn't really know what awaited us, but we were swept away and swept others away with an inner faith that we were treading the right path. Each one of us had his own story. Each one of us and the personal and family baggage he had left behind. It is hard to believe, but cutting ourselves off from our previous lives didn't trouble us in the least. Even those who had loving parents and an easy, comfortable life didn't seem sorry to have left it all behind. We were riding the crest of a great wave of expectation and enthusiasm.

One night we were shown a short movie about our new country, only a few minutes long but exalting body and spirit. Could such a place really exist, where everyone was always smiling and happy and having a good time? When would we go there? We had a deep longing for our new home. The movie was in color, the sky was bright blue, the sun shone, fighter jets roared out of nowhere, shearing through the skies, soldiers marched in ironed uniforms, tanks charged through the sands of the desert, paratroopers drifted to earth, and then an aerial view of all of Jerusalem and its antiquities, minarets of mosques and church steeples. And above all the Western Wall in all its glory and grandeur. Its image had barely flickered on the screen and we all instinctively applauded. We knew very little about the Western Wall, but even its name had enchanted us, and for us it had become the essence of our existence as Jews living in other countries. In French we called it *le Mur des Lamentations*, the Wailing Wall. We had been told that a written request inserted between its stones would eventually be granted. We had been told that God was particularly attentive to every request, preferably from a Jew.

During the day at the camp in Marseilles it was as though we all belonged to the same extended family. We knew we would be scattered once we arrived in Israel, and each of us would be sent to the schools we had requested. We made the best use of every minute we were together. Some of us were planning to go to kibbutz schools, other wanted city schools, some to continue their studies in French and others wanted technical training. Still others had asked to be accepted into an educational framework emphasizing Jewish tradition.

We waved our new immigrant documents proudly when we received them upon landing at the airport in Lod. Such excitement! We could barely understand what they said. From the airport we were taken to Ramat Hadassah, a youth village midway between Haifa and Nazareth. From there we would be sent to other parts of the country. The atmosphere of togetherness continued in Ramat Hadassah. A few days later busses came and filled the parking lot in front of the school. We were saddened by the thought that we were going to be separated from our new friends, who seemed like perfectly good substitute for family. Bus after bus filled with new little Israelis, they revved up their motors and pulled out. Only a few of us were left, my sister Eva, myself, and two Alfassi brothers who had immigrated with us from Morocco.

I was unsettled and upset. I wondered why we had been left behind. Why hadn't we gone with the rest of the group? An open pickup truck bounced towards us and stopped. We were told to take our things and get in. Apparently the time in Marseilles and Ramat Hadassah had been good for Eva. She was the youngest child in the group had gotten a lot of attention from older children. In both places I noticed that she had joined the others as though it were the most natural thing in the world.

Kippah and Tsitsit

One of the *aliyah* representatives got into the truck with us and explained that we were now going to our new home. It was a religious boarding school called the Religious Youth Village, and it was situated in a religious settlement close by in Kfar Hassidim, a few minutes by car from Ramat Hadassah. He said once I arrived I would have to wear a *kippah*. In addition, our days would be divided between studying and agricultural work. In no scenario at any time did I ever envision myself doing agricultural work. I had no idea whatsoever of working the land, I wasn't cut out for it in any way, shape or fashion. I didn't know what to expect, and during moments when I had time for reflection I never gave it a thought.

On that first morning the sun rose and shone brightly over the school. I left the building and saw the synagogue where I had spent several hours the night before. I was about to learn the local customs. They were so very different from the customs of my former homeland! The clash would continue over the years and force me to make choices I had never had to make and never imagined I would have to make. I had been educated at an Alliance school in Casablanca, and it imbued us with uniquely Jewish values as well as the usual ethical principles. We had no experience of secular European ideologies, which were foreign to the way of life of the Jews of Morocco. We also hadn't become addicted to religion because we saw it as just another natural aspect of our lives.

In that way we had the best of both worlds. Our path led us to university educations while preserving the Jewish traditions of the Sabbath and the holidays. We were well integrated into our society but we were careful to preserve our identity. We didn't hide the fact that we were Jewish, and in fact were proud of it. Both Jewish identity and modern Moroccan identity coexisted peacefully in our souls.

Rabbis had a special status. As a child in Meknes I lived not far from the school run by Rabbi Joseph Messas. Because of his appearance I was certain he was the Messiah, or at least related to him. He wore a black robe with a gold stripe down to his feet, and it made him look like royalty. He wore a hat without a brim, the crown encircled with a red ribbon. He had a white beard, his skin was pink and he had intelligent eyes that made him look all the more holy. He was considered the greatest spiritual figure in Meknes and his presence cast a spell over all of us, Jews and Muslims. According to rumor, he was a guest at the home of King Muhammad, who regarded him as the highest religious authority of his generation. Also, according to the same rumor, the king himself received the rabbi by kissing his hand, just as ordinary people did. Having the king kiss his hand instead of the other way around raised the rabbi's status to practically divine. It was an old, established tradition that anyone who met the king bowed and kissed his hand, hoping to receive even the smallest part of the holiness of the descendant of the Prophet Muhammad. Yet according to the rumor, the king had such great respect for the rabbi that he kissed his hand.

When the rabbi left his house to go to the synagogue, we felt the *nouveau mellah* had been enveloped in holiness. He extended his hand and we ran forward to kiss it. Even as young children we knew that touching him could open the gates of heaven. As God's representative on earth he had to power to decide people's fate, cure the sick, relieve hardship, and give spiritual aid to those in need. Married couples with problems went to him and left looking like newly-weds. When I was growing up in Meknes, almost no couples got divorced. The rabbi was a life-saver, and anyone who consulted him came out

Kippah and Tsitsit

revived.

On occasion, when we were young, we used to go to his house unannounced. We exploited our friendship with his grandchildren to enter the inner sanctum. He would smile at us and extend his hand. We did not wear *kippot* and he never told us to. The members of his own family walked around the house with their heads bare. They sat at the table wearing the suits of rabbis, but their heads were uncovered. That kind of liberality was characteristic of the Jews of Meknes. There were Jews who rode on the Sabbath and those who went to the swimming pool after the Sabbath prayer. None of them felt that by doing so they had personally shattered the tablets of the Ten Commandments.

Israel changed and deepened the relations between the rabbis and their congregations, and pushed the Jews from Morocco into cults of holy men and Kabbalists the likes of which we had never seen in Morocco. The cults reached enormous proportions and had considerable power, including political power, greatly contrasting with the traditions which had existed in Morocco for generations. Here in Israel the religious heritage of the Moroccan Jews became religious fanaticism, following in the footsteps of and imitating the Jews from Eastern Europe. Given the stark geographic division of Morocco, the holy men in the Jewish towns of the Atlas Mountains were venerated, while in the large cities the rabbis played a lesser role. The entrance of France into Morocco had a strong influence on the lives of the Jews and weakened the traditional status of the rabbis. Choosing between the charms of the rabbis and the wonders of the modern world, most of the Jews rushed toward modernism. In the high Atlas Mountains, where French influence didn't penetrate, abject veneration for the holy men flourished. Regarding adoration and veneration of the rabbis, Tel

Aviv University Professor Gabriel Ben-Simhon, upon returning from a visit to the scenes of his childhood, wrote: *"They suspended daily life in favor of eternity, forgot the present for the sake of the future, traded life for the raising of the dead, gave up their days in favor of Judgment Day, traded the love of a woman for the love of the Creator, traded the Shulamite Woman of the Song of Songs for the Divinity. They formed a strange community of men who devoted their lives to prayer, a community that wiped out the history of thousands of years while waiting for the Messiah. Until then they had hidden themselves from history in remote villages in the Atlas Mountains and villages in the Sahara. So that history would not see them, would leave them alone, would not trouble them. As soon as the Temple was destroyed they began quarreling with life, and perpetuated the pain, the weeping, the destruction."*

On my first morning in the youth village I was summoned to the home of the director, Yossi Cohen. That morning as well his crocheted *kippah* fell to one side, stopped only by his ear. I eventually learned that the position of his *kippah*, so far from the crown of his head, was not a matter of chance. Cohen, who was red-haired and rather plump, radiated paternal warmth. Like the others, he was innocent of any knowledge of French, and I knew only a few words of Hebrew. A French-speaking teacher was called in to translate for the new immigrant. Mr. Friedman had immigrated to Israel from Strasbourg and taught at the school. He wore a large *kippah*, and a thin, well-tended beard covered the bottom half of his face. Speaking for Mr. Cohen, he told me that as soon as I entered the grounds of the school I had to wear a *kippah* all day. I had to go to the synagogue three times a day to pray. I had to be observant and carry out all the *mitzvoth*, the religious precepts of the Bible. I could not meet with the female students after dark. I could not go to the girls' quarters to visit. I had to say a blessing before every meal. I had to say a blessing after every meal. And of course, he reminded me, I had to go to the synagogue that night to say *slichot*.

I couldn't believe my ears. I carefully told Mr. Friedman that I was not strictly religious. I had never made a point of carrying out all the *mitzvoth*. I had faith, I explained. He translated for Mr. Cohen. Mr. Cohen turned to me, a kind but resolute expression on his face, and said that wasn't the way things worked at the school. The school's customs were what had just been explained to me, and I had to respect them. He added that my status as an immigrant student meant I had no choice in the matter. He spoke in a very friendly way. It seemed to me that they were both very forgiving. "Where would you go?" asked Mr. Friedman. He added that the school was fully responsible for me. "Don't forget," he said, "that you are a Jew. I know that the Jews in Morocco led a religious life. Why should it bother you do be a religious Jew?"

"I don't understand you," said Mr. Cohen. "You have to decide if you are religious or secular."

I had never heard the word "secular" and I didn't know what it really meant. I don't think it existed as a concept among Jews in Morocco. Mr. Friedman asked, "*Vous êtes laïc?*" ("Are you secular?"). I didn't understand what he was talking about. He explained that in Strasbourg, where he came from, there was a clear distinction between secular Jews and religious Jews. "The secular Jews are Jewish, but they don't carry out *mitzvoth*."

I said, "I really am a believer, but I am neither secular nor religious."

"There is no such thing!" said Mr. Cohen. "You have to decide what you are, religious or secular."

"I am a Jew just like you."

"That is correct, but a Jew is either religious or secular. You have to be one or the other."

"In Morocco I was both," I said.

"Daniel, I can see you are a good boy. I want you to know that Israel is different from Morocco," Mr. Cohen said with a big smile, trying to remain patient with the confused new immigrant. Mr. Friedman took a colorful *kippah* out of his pocket and fastened it to my hair with a bobby pin. It immediately made me look like the other students. "As long as you are with us, you have to behave like everyone else," said Mr. Cohen, and stood up. I got to my feet as well. So did Mr. Friedman. Three *kippah*-wearing Jews. Mr. Cohen took a small *tallit* from a drawer and asked me to put it on over my undershirt.

Without my suit, with a *kippah* on my head and a *tallit* under my clothing, I felt as if the transition I had yearned for had occurred, from Moroccan Jew to Israeli. I was of course a little far removed from the suntanned boys with their wild hair, the ones I had seen in the Jewish Agency movies that had enticed me, but still, it was a new beginning. Although, in reality, not terribly thrilling.

Two weeks later an Israeli representative came to the school to meet the new immigrants in their new home. I was angry almost as soon as the meeting started. It was evening and we were sitting in an empty classroom. I asked why I had been sent to a school attended only by religious students. The representative, who was wearing a black *kippah*, said my parents had been worried we would lose touch with tradition. Therefore, they had requested we be sent to a "traditional" place. The Youth Aliyah representatives had interpreted their request with a certain amount of flexibility, and sent the "traditional" students to strictly orthodox religious institutions. For me it was a dramatic change. From a mixed life style I now lived in what was almost a religious dictatorship.

Aliyah representative Yitzhak Meir had sent hundreds of Moroccan youths to Israel immediately following the Six Day War. By chance, or possibly not by chance, most of them found themselves in religious frameworks. Almost five decades later he still remembered the details of those children who came to Israel with the Youth Aliyah program. Before they said goodbye to their children, many parents insisted their children be sent to "traditional" institutions. They had no knowledge of the strict divisions in Israel. That unlike in Morocco, there was no overlapping. Meir remembered how surprised he was by what he saw in the Jewish households in Morocco. "On the Sabbath eve they said the blessing with special melodies," he wrote in his Morocco diary. "They sang Sabbath songs and the next day the entire family went to the synagogue. It was exhilarating. The way they prayed and sang was breathtaking."

Full of preconceived notions of the Jews in Morocco, like most of the other *aliyah* representatives, he was surprised by the lives they led. The people he worked for in Israel, the Mossad and the Jewish Agency, had prepared him by telling him it was not an easy population to work with and that he would need all his diplomatic skills to carry out the mission entrusted to him. "I apologize for the sin I committed," he said when I met with him much later at his home in Kochav Yair, in the central part of Israel. "I found people who were smart and whose company I enjoyed, who preserved their Judaism while leading completely modern lives. French culture was natural for them and they were like fish in water. Everything I had been told in Israel was as far from the truth as east from west."

Meir sent the young Jews from Morocco to religious boarding schools in Israel. That was not what most of the parents had intended. They didn't fully distinguish between secular and religious in Israel, and wanted the representative to make sure their children were not cut off from Jewish traditions. "They used the word *traditionalistes*, that is, those who followed tradition," he wrote. "I thought they meant religious institutions, while what they meant was for their children to preserve their Jewish identity. Just as it had been in Morocco."

Meir, who was himself religious, also came from a world with a division between secular and religious. In Antwerp, where he was born and raised, observant Jews and non-observant Jews who had assimilated into non-Jewish society, led different lives. They all met once or twice a year at the synagogue for the Rosh Hashanah and Yom Kippur services. That was the extent of the secular Jews' Judaism. As a man who performed *mitzvoth*, Meir interpreted *traditionalistes* in its wider meaning. As a representative of the Mizrachi movement, he acted like the rest of his religious comrades, and sent the young immigrants to Mizrachi boarding schools to strengthen the movement. In his diary he wrote that he had been convinced that every Jew in Morocco was Orthodox, and that they spent their days and nights studying the Torah. Imagine his surprise when he discovered things were not quite what he had assumed...

"I explained to the parents," he wrote, "that there were two categories in Israel, *religieux* [religious] and *général*. Actually, I decided where to send the child according to what I saw in his home. Parents were afraid of completely religious institutions, so I devised a new category, calling it *religieux modéré* [moderate-religious], even though I knew there was no such thing in Israel. Everyone in Israel was angry with me. The left-wing organizations and the proselytizing religious right-wing organizations and all the organizations in between. They all wanted to get their hands on the new young immigrants. I divided them as I saw fit and sent the immigrants from Morocco to both sides, as seemed best to me at the time. Most of them, of course, I sent to religious institutions."

So, that's how my sister Eva and I wound up at a religious agricultural boarding school. The representative who sat with me in the empty classroom that evening explained that the school would help me achieve my aspirations. Naturally, we spoke in French. When asked in Morocco how I saw my future, I said I wanted to be an author and a journalist. Before I immigrated to Israel, I was supposed to leave Morocco for France. Now I had immigrated to Israel, but I still had the same aspirations. Instead of writing in French, as soon as I had command of the language I would write in Hebrew. What could be easier, I asked myself. I kept seeing the world through rose-tinted glasses. In reality, however, things were more difficult than expected. Unexpected developments were like a fist in my stomach, and they were threatening to break me.

The representative remained completely tranquil when I mentioned the language barrier. Unable to speak Hebrew, helpless to halt the unending treks to the synagogue, and with no background in or knowledge of agriculture, I was afraid I wouldn't find the strength to continue. Two weeks had passed and I was still unable to say two words to my new roommates. Trying to communicate using sign language embarrassed me. Even the few Hebrew words I had learned in Morocco somehow evaded my attempts to recall them.

Almost all the students at the school had some kind of connection to Morocco. Most of them were second-generation Israelis. Their parents had immigrated to Israel in the first waves in the early nineteen fifties and been settled in development towns and immigrant settlements. Some of them had been one year old, or two, or five, when their parents immigrated. Some were older, and could say a few broken sentences in French. For me, those words and sentences were like a lifeline. They let me open my mouth and speak. Their parents, sent to settlements in the Galilee, had become farmers overnight. They sent their children to a religious agricultural boarding school, hoping to see them inherit their fields and chicken coops when the time came. Studies were far less important for the parents than working the land. Maybe that was why most of the students in the school didn't take, or it wasn't suggested that they take, courses that would prepare them for future academic studies.

As we became more friendly and I learned more about them, I felt that most of them had been done a grave injustice. Some of them were very talented, but had been stuck in a religious agricultural school instead of being sent to a good academically-oriented school in one of the big cities. There had been no one to guide them or their parents, who had been sent to live in crowded apartments in development towns without learning of the academic possibilities more suited to their talents. What a waste! I thought to myself. Who knew what heights they could have reached if someone had paid attention to them and given them guidance.

They were "traditional" like me, not Orthodox religious. Their parents had immigrated from Morocco and could not speak Hebrew well. No one told them about the better education their children could receive. I thought, how many promising careers had been buried under the fields and cowsheds and metal-working shops and cleaning shifts. After graduation and after the army, almost none of them worked in agriculture.

With time I became one of them. Our common

backgrounds turned us into an alternative family. Friendships were formed that have lasted through the years. As my Hebrew improved and friendships strengthened, my situation also improved. In the twelfth grade I felt like a member of the boarding school family.

On the first nights, before I got up in the middle of the night for the *slichot* prayer, I was alone with myself and my misery. I lay on my cot, wondering about my loneliness. Until recently, language and my ability to use it were my strengths against students who were bigger and stronger than I. More than once they had come to my rescue in my school in Casablanca. More than once they had given me a special status, especially when my teachers had me represent the class to important guests from France and French-speaking countries. Thanks to my command of the language, I was appreciated by my teachers, and even by my classmates.

Now everything was different. Only a few weeks of forced silence had undermined my self confidence. I had no language and I was like a lion whose teeth had been pulled. How could I, who had been famous in school as someone whose fluency in French would some day turn him into a leading author in France, become speechless? How could I, who had recited by heart long passages from Molière and the poems of Victor Hugo, have become as silent as someone whose tongue had been cut out? Within a week my previous world, my previous life, had collapsed. I might have been sixteen years old, but I regressed to being a baby learning how to speak. I had to struggle with all my might to utter a correct complete sentence. When my classmates went to work I stayed in my room and conducted long dialogues with myself. Then at least I could make mistakes and speak incorrectly without fear of being mocked or having my accent imitated. I wrote down the key words I kept hearing in conversations to keep myself from forgetting them.

The representative who sat across from me was the link to my old world. As far as I was concerned, he was responsible for what was happening to me. I told him everything that was bothering me and making me miserable. Why had he separated me from the French-speaking friends who had immigrated to Israel with me? Why had they been sent elsewhere? Why hadn't I been sent to study in French, like many of them? I asked him all the questions that had troubled me for so long. He sat across from me without reacting, as though the scenario was familiar and he had heard the same words many, many times before. He said that every child was sent to the institution that was best suited to him, and that immigrants from Morocco were sent to religious institutions to prevent them from becoming separated for their old way of life. There were immigrants from Europe who were sent to secular schools because they were not religious. To my surprise, he told me that *aliyah* representatives who were sent to Morocco had been reprimanded in the past by rabbis for cutting young Moroccan immigrants off from religion and sending them to secular schools.

It became clear that the political parties in Israel worked tirelessly outside the country, energetically trying to recruit new immigrants into their ranks. The target locations for *aliyah* to Israel were divided, like the spoils of war, according to party affiliation. The left, which was in power until the rise of the right in 1977, got the largest share. The Mizrachi movement, which was part of the coalition government, also got its share of immigrants, although smaller and of "lower quality." Immigrants from North Africa were mostly left to Mizrachi representatives. All the political parties waited for the day they could turn the young immigrants into foot soldiers in an army of voters for the next election.

"There is nothing for you to worry about," he said in his *basso profundo* voice. "In no time at all you will become accustomed to the prayers and your new friends. Everyone goes through a crisis at the beginning, but after that everything is OK."

The meeting ended with a promise that time would be the great healer. I told him how difficult it was for me to hold a conversation in Hebrew. "Everyone here speaks Hebrew, and I can't." When he understood how really distressed I was he embraced me and promised he would come visit me again in a few weeks. Before immigrating to Israel I had been told about intensive Hebrew instruction held in special classes called *ulpanim*, where they worked miracles: the new immigrant joined an *ulpan* and a couple of weeks later he walked out speaking Hebrew like a native. I had also expected to be sent to an *ulpan* to learn the language. It turned out that the Religious Youth Village did not have an *ulpan*, and the immigrants had to learn the language themselves.

Going to meals was daily torture, especially lunch. At one o'clock the high school students descended on the dining room like the horde of Attila to find seats at the long tables. Within seconds all the food had disappeared. The famished children grabbed for food to fill their plates. Whoever was faster got more food. Before I knew what was happening there was nothing left. When they had finished eating they said the blessing and left. I often found myself sitting in front of an empty table, hungry and helpless. I was too polite and weak to participate in the daily war for food. Luckily for me, weekends were different. On Friday evening and Saturday, food was served to each student, so I could eat without having to fight for my meal.

At my previous boarding school, the École Normale

Hébraïque in Casablanca, students entered the dining room three times in a day in perfect, silent formation. Three courses were served by waiters. There was no need for guerrilla warfare to get food. We all marched in together and an hour later we all marched out.

After one month at the Religious Youth Village I had lost a lot of weight. I was so skinny that one of the instructors had me examined by the school nurse. She had immigrated from Germany and knew a little French. She weighed me and apparently I had lost five kilograms since joining the school. I didn't dare tell her the truth, I was too embarrassed. I was ashamed of not having the strength to fight for food and I was embarrassed that you had to go to war to eat.

I was weak. In both body and spirit. One day I was send to a Gadna training camp. The Gadna was a program for high school students, preparing them to join the army when they finished high school. We were given long rifles and spent the day training. Everyone else could hold them in all kinds of positions, except me. I failed at everything. My arms were too thin, and after a few seconds the rifle fell to the ground. The instructor yelled at me, threatening that until I held the rifle as ordered, all my comrades would be punished and ordered to hold their rifles longer than necessary. He was furious. He calmed down and left me alone only after my situation was explained to him. I was ashamed to show my naked body in the showers. Those around me could be proud of their muscles, but I was skin and bones, my ribs stuck out and could be counted.

My sister Eva's situation was even worse. She suffered enormously. For days and nights she stayed in bed, refusing to leave her room. She said she couldn't stand it any more. She stopped going to the dining room, because the girls had to be as aggressive as the boys if they wanted to eat. Like me, she let herself be bullied, and watched while others ate, unable to get food. She was little and ignored by everyone. She told me that one of the educators screamed at her because one morning she put on long pants. She was reprimanded in front of everyone and sent back to her room to put on a skirt. Like me, she hadn't said a word in Hebrew since arriving at the school. A doctor was sent to examine her and he immediately sent her to the school infirmary. It did no good. She had become totally apathetic. I was summoned to the infirmary to be with her. She looked at me with no expression in her eyes. I was shocked by how pale she was. The doctors tried to get information about her. They learned almost nothing from her medical records and couldn't get her to talk about what was bothering her. One doctor, who knew a little French, tried to speak to her, but without success. Her pale face and sunken eyes worried them.

I was helpless and there was nothing I could do to help her. Two people, suffering and in distress, my sister and I, colliding in unexpected circumstances. I tried to talk to her but she didn't respond. I could imagine perfectly well what she was going through but I didn't dare tell the doctor. I knew for certain that the loneliness and separation from the family were too much for her. When I visited her in her room in the infirmary she told me she felt she was standing on the outside looking in. She didn't understand a word of what was said, not in class and not in her room, she hadn't been sent to an *ulpan* to learn the language and she felt she had come to a place that was killing her. "What do you want?" I asked. "I want to go home," she mumbled.

A child who had been ripped from her foundations. Sitting next to her bed I desperately needed my parents. She wanted to go home. She wanted to be with our parents. What was I supposed to do? There was no telephone and no way of contacting Morocco. I was in such distress myself I didn't have the strength to rescue her. I was afraid the worst was about to happen. She had been connected to a saline drip and the school's head nurse tried to get her to eat something. Unsuccessfully.

The doctor asked if we had family in Israel. I said yes, two brothers and a sister, but I didn't know where they were. "How is that possible?" he asked. I mixed Hebrew and French and did my best to tell him that there were also in boarding schools and we hadn't managed to contact one another. He looked at the head nurse as though he couldn't believe what he was hearing. I told him we hadn't seen one another in three years. The doctor demanded the *aliyah* representative come to the school so he could explain the seriousness of my sister's condition. He especially didn't understand what such a fragile child was doing in an agricultural boarding school. Eugene Michaelis, the director of the school, came to take a look at my sister, and tried to talk to her. I remember him as an impressive figure who inspired respect. Everyone became attentive when he appeared. He had immigrated to the Land of Israel from Germany when he was young, just after the Nazis came to power, and was one of the Youth Village's founders. He was sent to head the school in order to take in religious students from the pogroms in Germany. He had a skin condition that made him lose his hair, and he covered his baldness with a large black *kippah*.

It was the first time I had seen him since coming to the school. He asked me about myself. He didn't hide his surprise when I told him I had gone to the École Normale Hébraïque. Yes, he had heard of the schools, both in Paris and Casablanca, and how successful their graduates had been throughout Europe. And Israel.

Kippah and Tsitsit

He told me my sister was very ill, and that once she recovered he would send her to a different school with better conditions. It seemed to me he knew the pain of emigration and parting from one's parents. "I know what you and your sister are experiencing," he said, "it is very natural. I am old, but I still miss my parents and my family." A few days later he invited me to have lunch with him and his family at his house. It turned out he had done me a great honor.

My sister was moved to Achuzat Sara, a religious boarding school in Bnei Brak, just east of Tel Aviv. I was informed she had recovered and was surrounded by girls who spoke her language and helped her feel better. I also tried to move to another school, but to no avail. The days passed, the weeks passed, the months passed. Finally I got a decent bed, the *kippah* was a permanent fixture on my head, I could stumble along in Hebrew and the other boys began acknowledging my existence. Because I was the right age I had been put in the tenth grade, but I didn't go to class often. I had skipped the entire ninth grade. Being in class made my foreignness worse. I couldn't understand a word the teachers were saying. They came into class, taught their lessons and departed as soon as the bell rang. I sat in the back row and was exactly like one of the chairs. The rapidly-spoken Hebrew of both teachers and students made my head spin. Here and there I could catch a word or two, but their fluency and speed filled me with despair. I was convinced I would never understand Hebrew.

There was no lack of difficult moments. I never imagined that moving from one country to another could be so painful. It was easy for me to say goodbye to Morocco, but I couldn't relate to Israel. I felt I was drowning. I felt bad about myself. I was angry I had left Morocco, angry about the boarding school, deeply frustrated by not being able to learn the new language. My French was useless and unnecessary. I was embarrassed when I made mistakes. I felt different. I looked different. I looked foreign. I sounded foreign. Depression made it impossible for me to learn anything in class. In any case, none of my teachers was aware of my existence, of the new face trying to become one with the other faces. My extreme sensitivity made me internalize every event, every detail, everything that went wrong. It was very difficult to come to terms with being totally ignored. I suffered from extreme loneliness. My sister had been sent to a different boarding school. My brothers and sister had still not come to visit. I had barely had time to spend time in Morocco with Michel, who was a year and a half younger than I. Now he was fourteen. I wondered what he looked like. Would I recognize him? Would he recognize me? Would he still speak French? What if he only spoke Hebrew? Where was he, anyway? I had no idea.

At night my former life in Casablanca came back to me forcefully. My distress in the Religious Youth Village painted my memories a bright, rosy pink. I imagined myself returning to my many friends, to my former happiness, the times we spent in the room set aside for cultural activities with classical music playing softly in the background, the shows we put on for the other students, the gymnastics lessons with Monsieur Bilal, the Muslim sportsman who taught physical education and became a national Moroccan hero when he won the long jump, more than seven meters. I remembered the basketball games and how well the court was maintained. We played together, new students and old, and with our teachers, and on rare occasions the strict boundaries separating us were erased. On more than one occasion I found myself playing on the same team as the school director, Monsieur Sebban. Every time he threw the ball to one of us we were so thrilled our hands shook. Once I almost fainted when he embraced me after I had scored a point. After the games we would sit around and talk about the future. It made all of us sad to think we would be forced to leave Morocco when we were eighteen. We were residents on probation, living in Morocco on borrowed time. We counted how many years were left before we would emigrate to live in France. Some of us even talked about immigrating to Israel, but very few.

It was clear to all of us that one day we would have to close the door behind us and leave Morocco. We didn't devote much thought to the idea, perhaps fatalistically. How sad it was that all of us, Jews and Muslims, could not continue our lives together. We lived together for hundreds of years, perhaps more. Without our choosing, the situation forced us into a kind of double loyalty. We lived in Morocco and were an integral part of it, but our future lay elsewhere. The duality was never given a moment's thought and seemed perfectly natural.

Chapter Four
The First Israel

Before the Hanukkah holiday, that first year in Israel, other students at the Youth Village were making plans to spend the vacation with their families. Red-headed Shmuel asked me if I wanted to join one of my classmates, but I said no. I preferred to be alone to wallow in self-pity and misery, so I decided to stay at the school, the only hand on deck, as it were. I didn't care that everyone knew how unhappy I was. Somehow pitying myself made me feel better. Shmuel was the first "real" Israeli I had met. Unlike the other people who worked at the school, he had nothing of the otherness that distinguished immigrants. He was a genuine Sabra, born to parents who had come from Europe after the Second World War. He spoke Hebrew like an Israeli with an Israeli accent, or rather, with no accent, his loud voice branded him as Israeli, and his physical strength and self-confidence only made him seem even more Israeli.

One day some of us were gathered around him. He

divided us into teams of two and then tossed out, "You, Danny Ben Simon, who do you want to partner with?" I was shocked. No one had ever called me that before, I had never had a nickname, Daniel was never Danny, and no one had ever spoken to me so directly. With so few words. Like an Israeli. Like an Israeli speaking to an Israeli. I have to admit, for the first time I felt something was happening, to me, around me. Was it a good omen? Was I beginning to be accepted? Did I already belong? Dramatically, in the blink of an eye I had gone from Daniel to Danny, a different person with a new identity. At school in Morocco we were addressed formally, like adults, "Monsieur" and then our last names. I liked my Israeli nickname. Everyone called everyone else by their first names, it was a refreshing change!

An *aliyah* representative came to visit me a few days before Hanukkah and found a very gloomy Danny. For the first time since coming to Israel, I genuinely wanted to return to Morocco. I had been in Israel for three months and felt exactly as I had when I came. I still had not joined the class for studies; actually no one had even told me to go to class. No one cared, no one had any interest in me. I walked around the Youth Village free to do as I pleased.

I changed my mind and told Shmuel I was going to spend the vacation with a family. He didn't ask me which family or where they lived. The day all the other students left for home, I packed a little bag and made my way to Givat Olga. I knew it was somewhere near Hadera. I remember my mother always talking about her older brother Shlomo, who was in the Israel Police Force. She even had a picture of him in uniform, it was in a drawer with all the other family pictures. So, equipped with his name and the memory of a picture, I was on my way to meet my family for the first time since coming to Israel.

THE IMMIGRANT

I changed from one bus to another, and after a journey of several hours I got off at the central bus station in Hadera. Now all I had to do was go to the local police station. I had no idea how to get there. I had never met my uncle, I didn't have the faintest idea of what he looked like now. I didn't even know if he was still a policeman – perhaps he worked someplace else. It was noon on Friday and the streets were crowded. Many of the people in the street carried plastic mesh shopping baskets of food for Shabbat. I watched them for a long time. It had been nearly four months since my arrival but I had never been in an Israeli city. It was also the first time I saw people who weren't from the Youth Village. I was very surprised to see that most of them weren't wearing *kippot.* There were soldiers in uniform, most of them with large backpacks hanging off their shoulders and wearing berets of all different colors.

I had left the Youth Village wearing my *kippah* and I took it off as soon as I was out of sight. I still felt strange wearing it, even though I hadn't taken it off for four months. That would eventually become my modus operandi: when I was at the school I wore the *kippah*, as soon as I left I went bareheaded.

I walked around the city, looking for my uncle and taking in Israeli life. After a few hundred yards I saw an ugly building, its façade faded, and a giant sign over the front door reading "POLICE." I walked forward hesitantly, to where police cars were parked, apparently at random. Should I enter or not? I stood there for a long time. Finally, in a sudden burst of courage I went into the building. There were a lot of policemen in the corridor and I ran back out, my heart thudding. What if he wasn't here? What if he didn't work at this police station? What if he wasn't still a policeman? In another hour or so the Sabbath would begin and bus service would stop. How would I get back to school if I failed to find him? Where would I spend the Sabbath? Where would I sleep? I sat on a bench in front of the police station. I looked at every policeman who came out of the building, trying to catch his eye. Who knew, maybe my uncle would recognize me – even though he had never seen me.

I found the courage to go into the building again. A middle-aged policeman walked over to me and asked me what I wanted. "I am looking for Monsieur Toledano," I said confidently. "Shlomo Toledano."

"And who are you?"

"He and my mother are brother and sister."

"Is he expecting you?"

"No."

"Where are you from?" he asked.

"Morocco..."

"So am I. I meant where are you from here in Israel."

I told him I had immigrated a few months ago and since then I had been living at the Religious Youth Village in Kfar Hassidim. I told him I didn't know my uncle and he didn't know me. The policeman looked at me, bemused and perhaps amused, and led me to the last room at the end of a long corridor. A tall man was standing in the middle of the room, his hair going gray and his face red. His uniform had a lot of stars on the shoulders.

The policeman who brought me whispered something in his ear, and the tall man looked at me in surprise.

"You are Denise's boy?" he asked in French.

I said I was.

"You are Daniel?"

"Oui."

"*Bienvenue*! Welcome!"

He drew me to him and hugged me. I had never seen him before and he had never seen me, and here we were, hugging like relatives! It was a very intimate family moment, the first since I had arrived in Israel. He looked at me and I looked at him. The other policeman looked at both of us, incredulous.

My uncle took me to his car. We were going to drive to Givat Olga, the perhaps-neighborhood-perhaps-*ma'abara*[4] where the family had been sent in the nineteen fifties. In a few minutes, for the first time in my life, I was going to meet my grandparents. On the ride from Hadera to Givat Olga I looked around. Neglect, indigence and poverty cried out from every corner. It was a ghost town that reminded me of the miserable *mellah* where the Jews lived in Morocco before they moved to the big city.

Was this the Israel promised by the *aliyah* representative? The Israel I knew was bounded by the fence of the Youth Village. It presented only a partial portrait of the country, and very different from what I had imagined. Years would pass before the all the aspects of the real Israel would reveal themselves to me. Only after I was drafted into the army would a different world open up, completely different from what I had known at the school. On my first day at the IDF induction center I looked around me, watching the thousands of young people who had barely said goodbye to their families and were already standing in line to pick up uniforms. A few days later I joined a group of new recruits from kibbutzim and *moshavim*[5] for basic training in the Golani Brigade (the infantry). I had no idea why I had been put with them. Kibbutzim and moshavim are agricultural settlements but they are collectives. These young people were very different from my schoolmates at the agricultural Religious Youth Village. Here and there I did

---
4. Hastily-built absorption centers for new immigrants which were supposed to be transit camps on the way to permanent housing.
5. Cooperative but private agricultural settlements.

see a couple of boys wearing *kippot*.

The Hebrew of the soldiers sounded nothing like the Hebrew I heard at school. I was embarrassed every time I said something. I could barely understand these new recruits. Their rapid-fire speech undermined my confidence. For three years I had toiled ceaselessly to achieve a command of the language and I thought I had succeeded. Until I met these other Israelis, that is, who spoke with a fluency I could only envy. While I was, by then, able to speak Hebrew fairly well, I had a prominent foreign accent that clearly revealed my origins.

From the moment I began speaking Hebrew I found it difficult to get rid of my strong French accent. Most of my schoolmates' families had Moroccan Arabic as their first language. Even after years in Israel their parents did not speak Hebrew. They had been sent to moshavim and development towns established especially for and inhabited only by them. When I went to visit the homes of my schoolmates I felt I was back in Morocco. Their families spoke Moroccan Arabic and many of them wore traditional Moroccan dress and the black hats of the Atlas Mountains Jews.

During my first months at the school I was assigned to work in the cowshed. I began my days before dawn, working the milking machine next to Mr. Pedazur, who was in charge of the cows. Like most of the people who ran the various agricultural branches, he had been born in Germany and immigrated to Israel as soon as the Nazis came to power. He spoke Hebrew with a German accent, as did Mr. Guttman, the biology teacher, and Mr. Reis, who taught chemistry. To say nothing of the Hebrew of the director of the school, Mr. Michaelis.

I found myself on the horns of a dilemma. Which way to go? Which Hebrew to speak? With which accent? Which was the correct language? Which was the correct accent? I really had no idea. I was taking my first steps in the foreign language I was going to adopt as my own. Was I supposed to choose, or do what came naturally? I had no idea. I spent several hours a day with Mr. Pedazur. Did he and his comrades, who had immigrated from Europe, speak Hebrew correctly? Or maybe my friends, with their North African accents. There was no way to know. The radios were never turned off. I was amazed to hear French singers I had just left being broadcast all day long. I was equally surprised to learn how popular they were at school. The radio programs broadcasting popular songs became a kind of campfire where everyone met. Most of the students counted the days and hours, waiting for the programs. The dormitories were on a kind of military high alert. No one was allowed to speak or make a disturbance until the songs had been played, both in Hebrew and other languages.

My Hebrew was superimposed on French and it came out sounding French. Instead of speaking I was engaging in simultaneous translation, thinking of what I wanted to say in French and saying it in Hebrew. That was a different time, when new immigrants made every possible effort to be accepted by Israeli society. Despite all the personal difficulties involved, they wanted to become Israelis and were willing to pay whatever price necessary. In those days new immigrants wanted to jettison their old world, shake it off like an unwanted cloak. Their great dream was to enter Israeli society and become Israelis. As the years passed the wheel turned in the other direction, and the immigrants became less eager to abandon their old lives. The desire to become Israeli was no longer all-consuming, and new immigrants began wanting to preserve their pasts and languages, and even regarded their accents as an integral part of their Israeli identity. The country acted accordingly, that is, it adapted and gave them the freedom denied to the first immigrants.

I came to Israel during the interim between the melting-pot policy and the policy that enabled the immigrant to act as he pleased. During the nineteen fifties the new immigrants starred in an unprecedented human drama, sometimes a cruel human tragedy, which forced them into a new way of life, one for which they were unprepared. Very few passed the entrance exams of Israeli society as fashioned by its founders. And very few of the founders tended to cooperate with the newcomers. The sociologists called it "resocialization," and it was a process undergone by immigrants young and old who had to learn new modes of behavior in order to conform. Anyone who was successful entered mainstream Israeli life. Those who lagged behind were tossed aside.

I wanted to become accepted as an Israeli regardless of the cost. My internal conflicts, as I leaned first to one world and then the other, made it difficult for me to acclimatize. Clearly, I had to choose. So I did. From now on I would not speak French. I distanced myself from the French-speaking students at school. They spoke to me in French and I answered in Hebrew. They couldn't understand my behavior. I could see no other solution, except to finally shake off Morocco and abandon everything I had brought with me to Israel. First and foremost that was the language I grew up with, the foundation of my existence. The decision had far-reaching consequences. Distancing myself from French meant distancing myself from my past, and would eventually lead to a break with my family.

Without an *ulpan* or any other formal framework for learning Hebrew, I had to learn it by myself. Every day brought new words. I knew that without a command of the language it would be hard for me to assimilate. Despite the difficulties and despite my loneliness, I decided to become an Israeli. Even before I saw myself as someone from here, I threw off the life from there. It was an exhausting internal struggle, between the new immigrant and the young Jew who had grown up in Morocco.

Those were days in a different Israel, at the beginning of the nineteen seventies. An Israel sure of itself to the point of arrogance. Everything foreign was considered irrelevant. Everything that had the faintest whiff of not being purely Israeli was regarded as coming from the *shtetl* or *mellah* and beneath contempt. Being a Sabra was a great victory. During my first year in Israel, Sabra status was sky-high. Everyone born in Israel felt he was one of the masters of the universe. The founders of the country and their offspring represented themselves as the best role models. We, who were born in an Arab country and spoke its language, and who had not yet proved ourselves on the battlefield, were considered inferior. Even though I was new to Israel I could not help but sense that my school friends and I were different from the people born in the country. It became evident that coming from Morocco was an impediment. It marked me even before I crossed the threshold. We looked different in the Youth Village, with our tattered work clothes, our unnatural piety. We looked like Jews, we spoke broken Hebrew, and we knew no great future awaited us after graduation. Very few of the Youth Village graduates went on to university. The Israeli ethos blew through the school like a gale-force wind, and we openly admired it. Almost three years had passed since the Six Day War, and all around us were signs of glory and heroism. Anyone with any connection to the great victory and the myth that grew up around it didn't want to let go. Everyone looking in from the outside wanted to link his fate to the myth. We were living in a young, vibrant, exhilarating country, you could see the signs everywhere. And I, the young boy who had just arrived, yearned, with all my soul, to be part of it.

At that time Israel drew everything into itself. The young men and women who immigrated to Israel wanted nothing to do with the customs of their own country, only to blend in. Their overwhelming desire was to know Hebrew, and even those who had trouble speaking it. Maybe it was because they desired to belong. Israel in the post-Six Day War days swept away cultures, languages and identities. Immigrants wanted desperately to change, to be able to unite with the model created by Israel's founding fathers, and that meant speaking the language.

The first test my newly-acquired Hebrew had waiting for me came quickly. One day, while I was in the dormitory, one of the students called me out of my room. There is a soldier here who is looking for you, he said. I looked down over the railing of the second floor and saw a uniformed soldier. I caught my breath. It was Robert, my older brother. It was almost three years since we had seen each other. I walked down the stairs with faltering steps, my whole body trembling. I didn't know what to do. We didn't embrace, only kissed each other on both cheeks, as was customary in our family. I was filled with immense pride. I think it was the first time since I had come to the country that I felt I belonged. Here, look, I too had stock in the company. An outsider wouldn't understand, but at the time every contact with the "real Israel" reinforced the sense of belonging. A brother in the army, wearing a uniform. What more could anyone ask?

I wanted the other students to see us. Maybe now they would take me more seriously and be nicer to me. We sat on the stairs between the first and second floor so that everyone would see us and ask me who the visiting soldier was. I didn't know what to do. The last time I saw my brother he was fifteen. Now he was eighteen and wearing an IDF uniform. He started telling me what he had done since leaving the family, about my little brother Michel, about my older sister Linda. The last time I saw Michel he was eleven, before he left for Israel. Now he was fourteen. What was he like? Tall? Short? Which language did he speak? Did he remember me? Did he know I had immigrated to Israel? How had he been able to stand it for three years without the family? How was he? And what about Linda, two years older than I? She was almost eighteen, how was she? Did they often meet?

There were so many questions I wanted to ask. Robert asked about Eva. I told him how hard the first days had been for her and that she had been sent to a different boarding school. All I knew about it was that it was in a place called Bnei Brak. I didn't know anything about it or its address. I couldn't tell him where she was, I had no contact with her, as I had no contact with him or Michel or Linda. It is hard to believe. Five brothers and sisters in Israel, one of them a soldier, four spread around the country in boarding schools without being able to contact one another. We had all immigrated with the Youth Aliyah program, but no official way had been found for us to join or even meet with each other. How could they know that I was here? How could they not know? This was in 1970, and Israel was already a modern, organized country.

In my heart of hearts I had hoped Robert would speak to me in Hebrew. So we could feel that from now on we belonged to the same tribe. However, he spoke in French. In one meeting, unexpected, the first time we saw each other, we returned to our childhood. We returned to being Robert and Daniel, two brothers, as we had been in Casablanca. For some reason I was determined to converse in Hebrew. Robert preferred French, as if he wanted to bridge the three years that had separated us and reunite in the Morocco we had left behind. How very strange and ironic was the meeting I had wished for so ardently! My "Israeli" brother spoke the old language, while I – who had just arrived – was determined to speak the new one.

Even as the years passed Robert always spoke French before Hebrew, as if refusing to come to terms with the dramatic change in his life. I couldn't know how the scales would tip. Towards him, who wanted to preserve his far-off childhood in Morocco, or towards me, who had firmly decided to cut the cord linking me to my past and assimilate. That fault line would separate us for years without resolution. Robert was determined to preserve his French. I was determined to replace it with Hebrew, with the result that he always addressed me in French and I always addressed him in Hebrew.

Hebrew, or more accurately, the determined use of it, became my mission. Results came quickly. In my second year of classes I joined my classmates in the eleventh grade. An entire year had passed at the Youth Village. I had worked in the cowshed, milking and generally helping out. I buried the calves that had not survived birth, distributed fodder and knew the name of every cow. The supervisor of the cowshed, Mr. Pedazur, didn't converse much with the students who worked with him, but had a personal relationship with the cows. He knew the name of each one, its past history and family tree, he comforted them when they were upset, stroked them when they needed a reassuring hand, got them moving when they felt lazy, stood by them when they were about to calve and gave them his unreserved love. They knew the touch of his hand and didn't balk when he put their teats into the milking machine.

He said almost nothing about himself and his relatives, some of whom had stayed in Germany. Sometimes he would volunteer a bit of information. Clearly it pained him to speak about it. We were two emigrants whose lives had been joined by fate. He had a foreign accent, but less pronounced than mine. I was comfortable in his presence; his foreignness comforted me. I thought about how hard his life had been. He had left his entire family behind, immigrated to Israel and built a new life. He seemed fragile and that made me like him. While still young in Morocco I had made a conscious decision to avoid aggression and aggressive behavior. However, when I came to Israel I became acquainted first hand with the excessive dose of aggression built into the Israeli temperament. Israelis have a horror of weakness, politeness, hesitation, refinement, foreignness and difference. Even then it was obvious that a country surrounded by enemies had to live with its sword drawn and could not allow itself any other kind of behavior. Being in his company helped me understand the Holocaust and how all-consuming it had been.

I grew up cut off from Jewish life outside Morocco. The director of the Youth Village, Eugene Michaelis, told me about what had happened to his family during the Holocaust and the systematic extermination of the Jews of Europe. It was when I had been invited to his house for dinner a short time after I arrived at the school. Afterwards, when I returned to the dormitory, I felt the hardships of leaving one's country were not mine alone. Almost all the people working in the Village carried within them the same trauma, the separation and longing and sleepless nights and lonely lives. So much agony. So much loss. A scarred country whose inhabitants had been rescued from certain death. I hadn't felt that way in Morocco. We felt secure around Arabs. We lived with them, grew up with them and went to school with them. I couldn't recall an existential danger. No one close to me had ever been harmed, that I knew of. The tension began after the Six Day War. It was the first time we had to be careful around the Arabs.

Even though he was no longer young, Mr. Pedazur's face still bore signs of distress. Unlike me, he wore a crocheted *kippah*. Maybe because of what had happened to him he was more forgiving and understanding of weakness. Whenever he could, he made it easier for me to assimilate. In my previous life I had never washed the udders of cows, never pushed my hand into a cow's uterus to tie the legs of an unborn calf together. For the first time in my life, I had calluses on my hands. After milking we would sit, the old-time immigrant from Europe and the new immigrant from North Africa, and exchange childhood memories. Even so many decades later he still enjoyed remembering his youth in Germany, before the darkness descended.

One morning, while we were sitting on bales of hay in the cowshed, the wail of a siren broke the silence. I froze. I was certain something terrible had happened. Mr. Pedazur immediately rose to his feet and stood without moving. Without thinking I rose and stood next to him. His gaze was fixed somewhere on the horizon, looking at something I couldn't see. I tried to understand what was wrong, and then I saw tears in his eyes. He started crying. The siren died down and stopped. That was my first Holocaust Remembrance Day in Israel. It was my first siren. Later on, sirens would become an Israeli trademark, signifying one thing or another.

It was years before I could grasp the enormity of the catastrophe of the Holocaust and its traumatic influence on the soul and mindset of Israel. If I hadn't stood next to a Jewish refugee from Germany, I doubt I would ever have understood the nature of the moment. Years later the siren would sound for two minutes instead of one, and standing motionless would become existential. Holocaust Remembrance Day would not only be the memorial for the Jewish victims, the Holocaust would shape and fashion the nation itself. Israel would reach a crossroads at which many Israelis chose not to see the Holocaust as a unique episode in history, but rather as a clear and present danger that could repeat itself at any time. As the intervening years grew in number, awareness of the Holocaust grew in intensity. Peace and war were painted in the same dark colors. Was the next Holocaust coming closer or getting further away?

Holocaust remembrance became the lens through which the Israeli right viewed the world – I wrote extensively about it as a journalist. I met with former Prime Minister Menachem Begin, I met with political leaders from both the right and left. Yitzhak Rabin, Shimon Peres and Ehud Barak nurtured in the bosom of the Zionist revolution, represented the Israel of Theodore Herzl. They wanted to see Israel as a full member of the family of nations. Yitzhak Shamir and Benyamin Netanyahu saw themselves first as Jews and then as Israelis, and along with Menachem Begin, devolved their political theories from the Prophets and forefathers of Judaism. The Holocaust played a main role in their worldview. It was particularly obvious in the way they related to the neighboring Arab countries and their willingness to sign peace treaties with them. Shamir and Netanyahu did not believe for a second that the Arabs wanted to live alongside Israel in peace, and regarding the ongoing Palestinian struggle as another way of persecuting the Jews.

Neither I nor my family had experienced the

Holocaust, and I was surprised to find it was always on the national agenda. Not during my first years in Israel, then it was barely mentioned. A siren and minute of silence on the eve of Holocaust Remembrance Day, and the next day life went on as usual. There were almost no government-sponsored events and the country's leaders were not required to put in appearances at one ceremony after another.

As the years passed and the right wing became firmly entrenched and then led the government, the memory of the Holocaust took center stage. Yad Vashem, the Holocaust memorial in Jerusalem, became a national symbol and going there became a kind of ritual first stop for visiting world leaders. Remembering the Holocaust became important for Israel's future. No political act of the past decades was detached from the Holocaust, as though it were a control tower directing our lives.

I had met Robert and I was going to meet Linda and Michel. I knew nothing about Eva, and had heard nothing since she had been sent to Achuzat Sara. She was surprised to learn that Michel was next door, with only a wall between Achuzat Sara and the Ponevezh Yeshiva.

Taken that Friday before Hanukkah by my Uncle Shlomo, I spent my first school vacation in Givat Olga in the home of my maternal grandparents. Linda and Michel came from their schools and we had the first extended family meeting since coming to Israel. Givat Olga was an outlying neighborhood of Hadera, where I first became acquainted with the hardships of Israel. Here and there I had had glimpses into Israeli life beyond the Youth Village but now I could see the poverty with my own eyes. Givat Olga looked like the *mellahs* in Morocco where the Jews lived before immigrating to Israel. All that was lacking was Muslims in the surrounding neighborhoods. Prompted by curiosity, I walked around the streets and alleys. I couldn't believe it. Only a few streets had names. To get back I had to ask for the people I was looking for. Ah, the Toledanos? Straight ahead and turn left, the second set of buildings, first floor. An enormous network of two-story buildings that looked like the aftermath of an earthquake. The street was barely paved, the sidewalks hadn't been repaired in a long time, mailboxes had been ripped out, stairs were broken, windows looked like slits for archers and white plastic shutters had turned black with grime. The poverty was straight out of the third world. People were hanging around, standing, sitting, not waiting for anything.

Was this the new Israel? Maybe I was in its vacant lot. During my first years in Israel I spent a lot of time in that vacant lot and became very familiar with it. The development towns in the north; the moshavim in the Galilee; the agricultural settlements in the Taanachim region near Afula; Afula itself; Migdal Haemek, a development town on a ridge on the way to Nazareth (home to several of my schoolmates), Qiryat Shemona in the far north, the Yemenite moshavim of Eliakim in the north and Elyakhin south of Hadera. Most of their residents came to Israel in the mass waves of immigration from the countries of North Africa. Two decades in Israel had changed nothing. Immigrants who imbibed the dream of Israel along with their mother's milk and prayed for the day they would realize their longings for the land of their ancestors – even after twenty years, had still not reached the Promised Land.

It was the same in Givat Olga. Wagons drawn by horses and mules went around the neighborhood offering fruits and vegetables, their owners touting their wares in Moroccan Arabic. The scenes I saw remained firmly implanted in my memory and years later led me, as a journalist, to write about poverty and hardship. The ills and suffering of society drew me like a magnet. As I wandered around the country I became acquainted with not the scars but the open wounds of Israelis who had been caught in the trap of the settlements on Israel's periphery. To a great extent their misery would dictate the country's political future. Ignoring them and their problems would make them change the political landscape. The mass waves of immigration during the nineteen fifties would lead to the resounding defeat and fall from power of the movement that had founded the country.

Sometimes my accelerated plunge into being an Israeli was an impediment. It became an impassable barrier in my renewed relationship with my family. I felt I had chosen a side, as though I were looking at Israel through Israeli eyes, while they were still living their previous lives. They didn't feel they had to choose sides. Since arriving in Israel my brothers and sister had been surrounded by people who spoke French. They had been enrolled in religious boarding schools affiliated with the Youth Aliyah program and created a Moroccan society of their own inside their Israeli environment.

More than once I suspected I had chosen to become a "real" Israeli for the wrong reasons. Maybe less out of joy and hope and more out of anger and disappointment. I was angry with myself because I hadn't realized how difficult it would be to live in another country, I was even more angry with my parents for creating the conditions that would force us to part with our childhoods overnight. That anger, how cruelly ironic, helped me lop off my past.

During a period of self-enforced reading in the school library I became acquainted with the exceptional undertaking of the first Jews who left the countries of their birth to build the new land. Young, fervent, enthusiastic, they came from Germany, Russia, Poland, the Ukraine and many other countries. I was entranced by the intensity of their personalities and the heights of their daring. I was enchanted by the romantic path they had taken in order to realize the ancient dream of the Jews, who yearned of Zion, the land of Israel, and to restore its glory. I was humbled by the hardships they had endured and overcome to build communal settlements, the kibbutzim and *moshavim*. So many weren't strong enough and surrendered to despair. Some even committed suicide.

The anger inside me distanced me from my family. My parents were far away, still in Morocco, and that enraged me even more. One day the director of the Youth Village told me my parents were on their way to Israel. I was happy, of course, but also sad. I was happy I would see them again, and see my little brothers. I was sad because I felt their coming would return me to where I had begun. Being separated from them had motivated me to assimilate into Israeli society and feel like part of it. When I heard the ship bringing them to the port of Haifa was about to dock my heart went cold. I was afraid it would mean going backwards.

I often felt we had been abandoned by our parents and were paying the price. Separated from the family I felt orphaned even though my parents were still alive. The physical and emotional distance, the separation, devastated me. I also felt I had become responsible for my own life at a very young age. I had been at the Youth Village since I was fifteen and learned how to survive. I knew I had to take care of myself and live on my own.

The day I was supposed to meet my parents I left the Youth Village early in the morning and made my way to downtown Haifa. It was the first time I had walked alone and unfettered through the narrow streets, filled with shops stocked with goods brought by sailors, selling almost everything. I found the main entrance to the port. I didn't know exactly when the boat would dock. Suddenly there were sounds of a ship coming into port. Hundreds of people crowded the dock, waiting for their relatives. I looked for my brothers and sisters. They had all come from their boarding schools for the great meeting. I identified my parents among the hundreds of immigrants pressed against the railing. Everyone was waving. Those on board the ship and those standing on the dock. Among those waiting I spotted my older sister Linda. She seemed very tense and expectant. The moment she had been looking forward to had finally arrived. She raised her arm to wave and began crying uncontrollably. Somewhat later she told me, "I didn't believe they would come. I didn't believe Dad would leave Morocco. When I saw them my legs shook." The others were there as well, waiting behind a barrier. Michel looked indifferent, not the least bit excited. It was only years later that I understood that leaving home as such a young age had been traumatic enough to repress his emotions and make it impossible for him to react.

Passengers started slowing debarking. My father approached us. He looked around, searching for his children. My mother walked behind him, four small children next to her. Robert looked at them as if he couldn't believe his eyes. When he left there had been two babies in cradles. Now they could walk, but didn't understand they were meeting brothers and sisters they had never known.

There was Gabi, the oldest of the four young brothers left behind. Next to him, Naphtali. The long sea voyage had exhausted them. The loud, emotional crowd stunned them. Here were Peddy and Jacob, the two youngest. They looked at us without knowing who we were. Suddenly they were faced with older siblings they had only heard about. The four youngest children were wearing little suits. It was the first time since the exodus from Morocco had begun that the family was together. It wouldn't often happen again. Gabi was already a big boy. He was the family's most active and impetuous child, talking to his older bothers like an equal. He hadn't seen them in a long time and after an instant it was as though all the lost time had been found again. Naphtali had changed from the infant I remembered. We older children had always pinched his cheeks because they were round and full, just begging to be pinched, and he babbled all the time, which amused us.

My father walked towards me, wearing a gray suit. I remember it as a difficult moment. We shook hands. We hastily kissed each other on the cheek. My mother could not stop crying. Everyone hugged and looked at each other. I couldn't overcome my restraint and inhibitions. I couldn't find my way into the emotions engulfing everyone else. They looked at each other carefully, searching for signs of change. I don't know where my restraint came from during times like these.

Where on earth had it come from? Had living in Israel distanced me from my family? Did I find this family reunion embarrassing? Did it return me to the childhood I sought to flee? Was I angry because I felt my parents had abandoned me? All that and more fought for expression inside me. Linda hugged her mother and didn't want to release her. Uncle Shlomo, the policeman from Hadera, also came to meet the sister he hadn't seen for more than fifteen years. His little sister was now the mother of nine children. My four little brothers were wearing winter clothing and looked puzzled by the commotion around them. My parents were only two of the hundreds of immigrants from Morocco and

Europe who had come down the gangplank. Their Israeli relatives were waiting for them on the dock. The joy and emotion of the meetings made it clear that years had passed since their last meeting. With tears in their eyes they continued holding on to one another. A man waiting on the dock told me that he hadn't seen his parents for more than fifteen years. They all stood there for a long time, sobbing in French and Arabic, but in Hebrew as well.

We stood on the dock for more than an hour, sharing memories and trading stories. French, which I had repressed, resurfaced. I felt strange, because throughout my stay in the Youth Village, in the worst moments of loneliness, I desired nothing more than for all of us to be a whole family again. And now, when the moment came, I wanted to return to school, to my friends. As soon as possible. I felt the separation had demanded a high price, and that I especially had paid it. I didn't have much to say to them. A family of nine divided by three separate immigrations to Israel, doing its best to bridge the gap of time lost. We didn't even speak the same language. My mother mixed Arabic and French, my father spoke only French and I spoke Hebrew.

And then we had to separate. Again. My mother's parents had prepared a party for the daughter they hadn't seen for almost twenty years. Uncle Shlomo took the family to Givat Olga. We stood there on the dock, several "Israeli" brothers and sisters, not knowing what to do. Robert went back to the army. I took the bus from downtown Haifa to the Yagur junction and from there a bus to Kfar Hassidim and from there I walked the two kilometers to the Religious Youth Village, my new home.

The expression on my father's face pursued me even after I entered the Village and would continue to pursue me for years. He was in his late forties when he had no choice but to immigrate to Israel. All of a sudden the ground on which he had grown up vanished. He lived in his new country for eighteen years, refusing, perhaps unable, to part with his old life in Morocco. The coffee house where he used to spend his time had gone up in a puff of smoke. The life he shared with his army buddies had gone up in a puff of smoke. His ability to speak fluently and express himself had gone up in a puff of smoke. The scenes of his childhood had gone up in a puff of smoke. Even his younger brothers, whom he loved and was loved by in return, were left behind, in Morocco and France. Until their dying day, his brothers could never understand how a man rooted so deeply in the French-Moroccan experience could exile himself to another country.

He told anyone willing to listen that he had had no choice and immigrating to Israel was the only way to unite with the children who had left. He was sent to live in a government-built apartment in a neighborhood of Moroccan immigrants to the north of Haifa Bay. The lives of the residents revolved around the local synagogue, which was always open. From a place of worship it had become, for the immigrants, a place of entertainment and refuge. They came in the very early morning for the first prayer and stayed when it was over. They sat on a wooden bench outside and told stories about their former lives. Occasionally I saw my father blossom when he remembered other days. With time that faded. My father, who had known life's pleasures so well, became a dismal shadow of himself. Not knowing the local language separated him from the local experience. For hours he would sit in front of the TV, trying desperately to understand what the news broadcasters were saying. To no avail. Once a day the news was broadcast in French. That was how he found out about his new world.

To break out of the loneliness closing on him he often went to the synagogue, where he found others like him, people whom fate had brought to Israel at an advanced age.

He had never been religious, not even traditional, like most of the Jews in Morocco. His work for the army turned Saturdays and holidays into regular working days. In Israel he clung to the synagogue as if it were a bulwark against loneliness. He could barely read Hebrew, but during the prayers he mumbled along, pretending to be just another man who had come to the synagogue to pray.

Our relationship never returned to what it had been before. We represented different worlds. The break had demanded too much, and had weakened the natural bond between father and son. My father never stopped longing for his old world and I never stopped making my way through the new one. Two fateful journeys with such different consequences. Our relationship was tragic. During the years I worked as a journalist he only believed that really was my job when he saw me on television. It was absolute proof that I was, in fact, a journalist in Israel. He never read one word of the hundreds of articles I wrote. When my first book, *A Different Country*, was published in the mid-nineties, he looked at it for a long time. He could read my name on the cover and he was so proud and happy his eyes filled with tears. The man whose reputation as a sophisticated bon vivant preceded him in the Jewish community in Meknes had become diminished in his own eyes and in the eyes of others, to the point where he felt his existence was superfluous.

One thing that lit his life was when Israeli television began broadcasting international programs, including French channels. The Moroccan channel, which played

THE IMMIGRANT

a lot of Arab music known as "Andalusian," made him feel a little less lonely. But without language he had no life. Only other immigrants like himself understood him and his suffering. His perfect French was useless, unnecessary and unwanted.

Only on the day he died did I finally have a flash of understanding of how much he had suffered, and it broke my heart. He was waiting to watch me be interviewed on a French TV show. He had gotten up early in the morning and planted himself in front of the TV, waiting impatiently for me to appear. He knew that a few minutes later the phone would ring and some of his brothers in Morocco and France would congratulate him. No one was happier than he. On many occasions I accepted invitations to be interviewed on European shows because I knew seeing them would raise his morale. For the sake of a few minutes of mercy. On that morning he sat in the living room next to my mother in their tiny apartment, waiting for me to appear on FRANCE2, France's second TV channel. Six minutes before eight in the morning the French interviewer introduced me. My face appeared on the screen and my father's head fell to one side. My mother told me he had seen what he was waiting for, and at that moment went into cardiac arrest.

We had let one another slip away in death, not only in life. At the very end I learned how much the family fabric had unraveled. A few hours after he died relatives gathered around his grave in the cemetery next to Kibbutz Afeq, north of Haifa. The rabbi from Qiryat Shmuel asked if anyone wanted to deliver a eulogy. Not one of my brothers volunteered. Their faces remained impassive. Naturally, they looked at me. I couldn't meet their eyes. I didn't know what to say. I didn't have anything to say. Actually, there was nothing to say. How could I explain the great waste of his life? How could

I talk about the agonies he had suffered since moving from Morocco to Israel? How could I describe the great blow to his standing in the eyes of his children and those around him once he had immigrated? It had very quickly become obvious that Israel was a country without a hierarchy and without respect or honor. Everyone went his own way, everyone led his own life. The language spoken was not his. His children spoke Hebrew among themselves and he didn't always understand them.

I felt confused and embarrassed, but not sad, not sorrowful. Rabbi Avraham Belahssan, who taught at the Qiryat Shmuel yeshiva, took the microphone and talked about moments he had shared with my father in the synagogue. He only mentioned things that had happened here, in the synagogue, my father's former secular life was forgotten as though it had gone up in the same puff of smoke as all the rest. If my father had heard the eulogy he would have thought they were burying a rabbi who had memorized the Torah. He most likely would have gone back into the ground laughing. My father's funeral was simple and modest. He wasn't eulogized properly and we didn't part from him or mourn him the way we should have. A few days before he died I went to visit him in the hospital, where he was going to have a cardiac catheterization. "I want to die," he said, "I have no desire for this life. I am alone without my brothers." Old as he was, he felt alone after having left his family. He loved them and they loved him. His joy of life returned only when he went to France to meet them or when they came to visit in Israel. It was the last time we met and the first time I heard he wanted to die. He was seventy-four years old.

I wondered what caused my siblings' behavior. Were they angry at him for cutting their lives in Morocco short and sending them to Israel? Did they blame him for the failure of their lives? Robert, Linda and Michel lost their way as soon as they immigrated. They spent many years at their various boarding schools but dropped out of high school before graduation. Without parents there was no one they could turn to for help in times of crisis. Like me, they had been sent to religious institutions. Unlike me, they hadn't had the strength to cope with a new life in a new country, and collapsed under the weight of the struggle.

After the funeral I left the cemetery as quickly as I could. I was heartbroken. Not only because I had lost my father, but for everything he had missed in life. The senior army officers he had frittered his time away with had been replaced with immigrants from Morocco, depressed and bent under the burden of their new existence. His distress knew no bounds and made it clear how hard and painful it had been for him to leave the land of his birth.

Before he was buried his face had the tranquility it had lacked during the last part of his life. One of the cemetery employees asked me to identify the body, a common practice at Israeli funerals. He lifted the sheet and exposed my father's face and carefully combed white hair. I never saw him looking more handsome. If I hadn't known he was dead I would have thought he was resting, saving strength for another night of dancing. "Do you recognize him," asked the employee, "is that your father?" I said it was and left the room. I only saw the death notices tacked up around the neighborhood[6] when I returned to my parents' house that evening. They bore my father's name, final proof to me that he was dead.

---

6. In Israel, when someone dies, it is customary to tack up small black-bordered death notices indicating the time and place of the funeral and address of the family where the week of mourning will be held.

My father
(Casablanca, 1968)

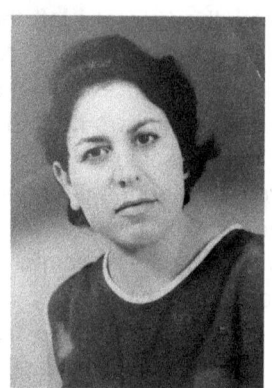

My mother
(Casablanca, 1969)

Joint bar mitzvah with my brother Michel (middle). At the left is my father

On my first journalistic assignment to Morocco, 1987.

With my brothers and sisters (Tel Aviv, 2015)

Israeli President Rivlin holding my latest book (2016)

The Talmud-Torah in Meknes (2016)

On a visit to Chefchaouen (2017)

Chapter Five
Lost in Their Own Country

Years passed and at the beginning of my career as a journalist I found myself In the living room of Amos Elon in Jerusalem. It was 1987. I had been trying to get his attention for a while because I regarded him as the uncrowned king of Israeli journalism, and for me he symbolized the professional heights to which every journalist should aspire. No one was better than he at describing Israel's complexity, or writing about it with razor-sharp clarity. I kept wondering how on earth I was going to find a way to meet him.

I had just finished a series of articles about Morocco for the Saturday supplement of Davar, the Labor Party-leaning morning daily newspaper. The series had given me a certain status and I had won some fans. Most people liked the descriptions of life in exotic Morocco and the personal tone. After my first trip back to Morocco

I wrote three long articles accompanied by color pictures. Reacquainting myself with the country after seventeen years filled me with both curiosity and longing. And a certain fear. Did the world I had known still exist? What would I find? What was life like in Morocco now? What about the Jews who were left behind? Who was still living in my old neighborhood? Who had my seat at the boarding school in Casablanca?

A short time after I had been hired by Davar, Hannah Zemer, the paper's editor, invited me to her office. We had never met before but we took to each other immediately. Tuvia Mendelson, the editor of the supplement, had asked me to write for him. One day I met Hannah Zemer in the editorial department. "Are you Danny?" she asked. Her voice was personal and unpretentious, as if she were speaking to her own child, and I was instinctively drawn to her. I was new at the paper and looked for something to make me feel more secure. Her rivals were very uncomplimentary, criticizing her as uncompromising and calling her a fighter who left wounded on the battlefield. We walked to her office at the far end of the floor. "Thank you, Ms. Zemer." "Here," she said, "everyone calls me Hannah." She smiled and put her hand on my shoulder. "We are a socialist paper, no one has a title. We are all comrades. You are comrade Danny and I am comrade Hannah." She moved off a little and said, "Don't misunderstand, I mean it of course in the Histardrut [labor movement] sense..."

During all the years I worked at Davar I was conscious of how meticulous she was about her appearance. Every day she came to work looking as though she had just stepped out of a beauty parlor, clothing perfect, hair perfect, makeup and bright red lipstick perfect. Many other journalists and public figures regarded her as the first lady of the Israeli media. She was an editor-in-chief in a profession that was exclusively male. Her close relations with the ruling elite made her even more powerful. People whispered about her and the heads of Mapai[7] and about her mysterious romantic liaisons with members of the economic and financial power elite. Her address book, never far from her side, contained the numbers of all the country's leaders, except those of the right-wing camp. She couldn't stand Israel's right-wing ideology and called it fascist. As a Holocaust survivor she abhorred aggression and arrogance, and believed in the wise, universal Jew. Everyone obviously respected her and wherever she went, she always got the front seat. In the macho male world of the media at that time, she did not hesitate to flaunt her femininity.

I sat across from her in her office, which was fairly dark because the curtains had been drawn to keep out the sun. Her desk was large and covered with newspapers and articles written by staff writers; she read every article before it went to press. Computers were just beginning to make their way into the world of the media, and most of the writers typed their articles and submitted them for editing. Comrade Hannah chain smoked and the ashtray on her desk was full to overflowing with old butts. She lit a cigarette and looked at me for a long time without saying anything. Then she praised an article I had written and said, "Danny, tell me, I have to ask you and don't be offended, but why are Moroccans so noisy all the time?"

I smiled. I was so embarrassed I may have laughed a little. Soon I would have been in Israel for seventeen years, but my Moroccan background always came to the fore and never stopped being a topic of conversation. "The first time I saw you," she said, "I wasn't sure you

---

7. Ben-Gurion's left-leaning political party and the ruling party in Israel until 1977.

were Moroccan." I was embarrassed and she noticed it. "I am telling you this," she said, "because in the first place you don't look Moroccan, and because you are refined and cultured. But that certainly must be because you grew up in France."

I said she was mistaken and I that I had been born and raised in Morocco.

"Don't be offended, but admit that you don't look like a typical Moroccan. And you have a very strong French accent."

We spoke for about half an hour. Even at such times, something drew you to her. Indefatigable, she kept asking about the lives of Moroccans and said she was surprised by the differences between the Moroccan Jews who had immigrated to Israel and settled in the development towns and those who had emigrated to France. She had an intense dislike for the former and regarded the latter as progressive and European. "It drives me crazy," she said, propping her chin on the heel of her hand. What she found particularly inexplicable was the cultural dissonance between the two communities. On trips to France she had met Moroccan Jews who had attained great status. With others she formed close friendships. The Moroccan Jews in France spoke French, acted like Frenchmen and were sophisticated. She told me about the Ashkenazi immigration to Israel and emigration to other countries, and said she had not found a great difference between the Jews who had gone to New York or Melbourne or London and those who had immigrated to Israel. In her opinion, they had all succeeded thanks to their innate talents and intelligence. She hadn't found anything similar in the Moroccan Jews in Israel, it was as though they were two different peoples.

While in France she had been invited to dinner at the home of a Moroccan Jew who was a leader in medical research. He told her that ideologically the Moroccans in France identified with equality and justice, and therefore all voted for the socialist party. She admired François Mitterrand, the socialist French president, and thought him a model of leadership, reminiscent of David Ben-Gurion. She told her hosts about the rise of the Likud (Israel's right-wing party) in 1977 and the choice of Menachem Begin as prime minister, two events she rated as catastrophes. "Did you know," she asked them, "that it was the Moroccans in Israel who put him in power? Why do you vote for the socialists here in France while in Israel the Moroccans support the right wing?"

Years later she was still troubled. Her disgust with the Israeli right wing was overpowering and she accused the Moroccan immigrants of the "catastrophe" visited upon the country. At one point she got up, or rather jumped up out of her black leather chair, and stood in front of me. "I have a terrific idea for you! A delegation of Histadrut members is going to Morocco in a few weeks. I want you to go with them. I want you to write articles for the paper, a series. I want you to explain to Davar's readers what the difference is between the Moroccans who went to France and those who immigrated to Israel. Why the Moroccans here make so many problems and are unsuccessful, while those who went to France succeeded so well. Danny, this whole business troubles me a great deal and I can't get it out of my head. I don't understand what happened. I want you to write about the Moroccans. Explain why they are so quiet in France and make so much noise here."

She accompanied me to the door and down the long corridor to the elevator. She linked her arm in mine affectionately and again said how important it was for her and the paper that someone like me was working there. Before we parted she told me again about her first years in the country. We stood in the corridor in front of the elevator and she talked about her struggle to make her way in Israeli society. People laughed at her accent and kept spreading rumors about her romantic liaisons with famous people. They couldn't stand it, she said, that a new immigrant like her, not a Sabra, had outwitted everyone and now sat in the chair of Berl Katznelson, no less, one of Davar's founders. "Moroccans could succeed as well," she said, "if only they put in a little more effort. I think they don't have the mentality for work, and I think they are lazy."

My path through journalism became other people's obsessive study of my Moroccan background. During my first years in Israel I was unaware of the charged emotions surrounding Morocco and Moroccans. My coming from Morocco made them curious. Sometimes I was surprised, sometimes I was disappointed. It was often difficult for people to find the connection between me and where I came from. Most of the people in my profession had strong opinions on the subject, and in most cases their opinions weren't particularly favorable. They didn't always manage to bridge the gap between me and where I was born. A cultured person, educated and refined, who had come from a country whose inhabitants were evidently not cultured, not educated and not refined. In most cases they suspected I wasn't a real Moroccan because I was so different from the stereotype and was nothing like the Moroccans who had immigrated to Israel from the Atlas Mountains in the nineteen fifties. Having immigrated much later, I was unaware of how deeply they had shocked Israeli society when they came en masse in the first great wave of immigration.

I became painfully acquainted with the stereotype

when I went to Haifa University to study sociology. We studied the era of the *ma'abarot*[8] and the hardships of the people who lived in them. For the first time I learned about the sociologists, journalists and politicians who described the immigration from North Africa as a disaster for Israel. I was embarrassed by the cruelly negative terms used to describe the immigrants. Sometimes I felt they were talking about me. I came from the same place and I also sought to find my way in my new country and I also had problems. If the studies were true, then I was also a millstone around the country's neck. My fellow journalists went out of their way to assure me I was different, but the awful feeling remained. I had to fight from the beginning of my career as a journalist. I didn't allow myself to sink into gloom and despair. I heard harsh and for me unrealistic descriptions about the country I came from, its culture, the violence of its people. I didn't have the strength to defend Morocco, it was easier to keep quiet.

The date for the Histadrut delegation's trip to Morocco approached. I wasn't particularly thrilled about the idea. Friends recommended that I keep as far away as possible from the subject lest I be tainted with "ethnicity." As if I couldn't be a fully functioning Israeli journalist and also write about Morocco. A prominent Morocco-born member of an academic faculty warned me not to fall into what he called "the trap the newspaper had set" for me. He was convinced it was a plot to make me look bad. While I regarded a trip to Morocco purely as a journalistic assignment, he and his friends were certain that from now I would be known as a "Moroccan journalist." I

---

8. A ma'abara was an absorption center for newly-arrived immigrants, a transit camp where they were sent to live before they were allotted permanent housing. The plural is ma'abarot.

knew people who had changed their names to disguise their origins, I knew people who had married Ashkenazi women to hasten their acceptance into society. The advice didn't work. The more they tried to keep me from going, the more determined I became to go.

I joined the delegation of Israelis who were exploiting the unusual openness of relations with Morocco, an Arab country, to pay it a visit. The previous year there had been an embarrassing diplomatic incident between the leaders of the two countries that threatened to end the easy relations. In July 1986 Israeli Prime Minister Shimon Peres paid a state visit to Morocco that was extensively covered by the media. He met with King Hassan II at the summer palace in Ifrane. It was to be his last official visit as Israeli prime minister, since the "rotation" of the national unity government was about to go into effect. Yitzhak Shamir, minister of Foreign Affairs, and Shimon Peres, Prime Minister, were about to trade places.

The meeting with the king ended badly because the king felt Peres had not kept his word. Before going, Peres sent the king messages indicating he was going to announce "political gestures" to the Palestinians during the visit. Ahmed Reda Guedira, the king's personal counselor, told him Hassan II expected to hear a clear statement about the PLO. "*Aucun probleme*" ("No problem"), Peres assured him. Based on that assurance the king prepared a royal welcome. The beginning of the visit as reported by the media was nothing like the end. The king hoped for practical measures and was surprised to discover that Peres' promises were empty.

"I speak to you as a brother, I didn't lose territory in a war and all I want is to prevent further bloodshed," said the king, speaking to Peres in French. He ended the discussion about the Palestinians and asked Peres two questions: would Israel agree to negotiations with the PLO and would Israel agree to withdraw from all the territories occupied in 1967 in return for a comprehensive peace? "Since 1967," said the king, "one hundred thousand Palestinians have been born in the territories occupied by Israel. They have no memories of the past, they have no national identity or flag. They live among Jews but most of them speak Arabic. Their frustration is liable to push them to acts of violence... I know you. You are a democratic country, a country with principles. You will not want to take away the Palestinians' fundamental rights and their right to choose. Their rate of birth is far higher than yours. Therefore, you have to find a solution that will be consistent with your needs for security and the Palestinians' national aspirations."

The king stopped talking and indicated he wanted Peres to respond. Perhaps Peres thought he was at a Labor Party meeting or a Jewish Agency rally. He began with a long lecture about the economic situation in the Middle East. The king understood Peres was playing for time and leading him on, and silenced him. "Mr. Prime Minister, your coming to Ifrane was an unfortunate waste of time..." Peres answered, "Yasser Arafat cannot be a partner in peace negotiations. He is so self-centered he has forgotten the reasons for his struggle. The PLO is an obstacle to peace."

Seven years before Israelis went to Norway to sign the historic Oslo Accords with Arafat, Peres was still stuck in the Jordanian option as a solution for the Palestinian problem. Hassan II lost patience, rose and exited. Peres closed himself in his room, concerned about the consequences of his failure. Crisis was in the air in the corridors of the summer palace, and rumors reached the Arab states. The following day General Abdel Haq Kadiry, head of the Moroccan Secret Service, paid Peres a visit in his suite. On his way there he met Knesset Member Rafi Edri, who held the Moroccan desk and answered to Rabin. Kadiry told him the king was very disappointed and convinced that Peres had "exploited" him for Israel's political needs. He hinted to Edri that the king wanted to know what Peres' plans were, a clear indication he wanted Peres to leave the country immediately. Ephraim Halevy, at the time senior member of the Mossad and who had accompanied Peres to Morocco, wrote to his superiors in Israel that Peres and his entourage had been "more or less expelled from the country."

All Peres wanted was to have his picture taken with the king, so that the Moroccans in Israel, who customarily voted for the Likud, would see that as opposed to its image, the Labor Party had a connection to the country of their birth. The king had looked forward to a political breakthrough in the Israeli-Palestinian stalemate, Peres was looking forward to winning the Moroccan vote. Interviewed by the BBC, the king was exceptionally forthright, saying, "Of course the visit disappointed me. I am disappointed because I am a Semite. We, the Semites, Jews and Arabs, when we are invited somewhere, customarily bring a gift and do not come empty-handed. I had expected Peres would bring me a gift. He didn't bring what I was hoping for..."

Back to my trip to Morocco. The members of the delegation had been born in Morocco and immigrated to Israel in the nineteen fifties and sixties. For most of them it was their first visit back. I told the story in a series of articles for Davar's Saturday supplement. After they were published I called Amos Elon. I introduced myself and told him the last article I wrote on Morocco had been published. He said he had read them all. "Would you like to come visit me?" he asked. "I would be happy to talk to you about Morocco. I am quite familiar with it. Do you know that I also wrote a series of articles about Morocco?"

I did know. In truth, I had read them with great initial interest and had been horrified. Our articles were poles apart. Perhaps because as a child in Austria he had received a colonialist view of underdeveloped Arab countries considered part of the third world. Or perhaps the appearance of the Jews from the Atlas Mountains made him think progress had passed them by. Or perhaps he was expressing the primitive fears of what the arrival of those Jews to Israel was liable to do to the young "Western" country.

In April-May 1953 Elon had written a series of eight articles about North Africa, five about the Jews living there. He had been to Casablanca, Marrakesh, and the Atlas Mountains. All he saw in Marrakesh was "thousands of Jews living in a crowded, narrow space of little alleys with raw sewage flowing through them." All he saw in the Atlas Mountains were Jews who were "very primitive and whose outward appearance and standard of living were no different from those of their Arab neighbors... They have an eleventh century mentality...You see horrible sights on all sides: children with swollen faces and inflamed eyes, half blind, and the brown skin of babies is covered with rashes...The children play outside in garbage and dust...There were two tiny children who looked about six months old but I was told they were three and four. They were eating lentils from a broken piece of a tin can. One of them had a running sore on his bald head and the other kept blinking, his eyes hidden by a curtain of dark mucus..."

He went to the *mellah* of Casablanca, which he described as "a concentration of filth, stench, poverty, degeneration, disease and perversion hard to find in the *medina* [quarter] of the Muslim Moroccans....We had barely crossed the high wooden barrier hiding the

[Jewish] ghetto and were hit by a wave of smells, a stench hard to define. As though not only onions were rotting, but the leather soles of shoes, clothing and scraps of meat...and also people."

At that time, in the middle of the nineteen fifties, Israelis argued passionately about the immigration of Jews from Morocco. Some people supported the continuation of mass immigration, others were convinced it had to be limited before the young country was overrun by the types described by Amos Elon. Every side used the arguments best suited to its purposes. Elon's articles supported those who regarded Moroccan immigrants as ticking time bombs from North Africa who would blow up the Middle Eastern dream of the Zionist founders from Europe. Elon wasn't alone. Before I went to Morocco I looked through old issues of the daily Haaretz about the immigration from Morocco. Most of them were the epitome of evil and nastiness. Haaretz actively encouraged immigration, but not for everyone, only for the worthy few, those with proven capabilities who would contribute to the new society.

Back to 1987. After my articles had been published in Davar's Saturday supplement I was invited by both radio and television to speak about my trip to Morocco. In those days trips to Arab countries were rare and aroused great curiosity. The people who interviewed me sounded like employees of the Jewish Agency. They had no interest in the conditions in Morocco, the lives of the Jews living there, the relations between Jews and Muslims. They wanted to know if the Jews were planning to stay in Morocco, and if not, when did they plan to immigrate? Despite the fact that I had described at length the good lives led by Jews who had remained, the people who interviewed me wanted to talk only about when they were going to immigrate to Israel. They envisioned their lives in an Arab country as being at risk, and staying in an Arab country as tantamount to committing suicide. Their questions were based on the well-rooted Israeli view that Jews were not safe in any country other than Israel.

Maybe it was patriotism, maybe deep fear of the Arabs, but many readers could not accept that Jews could live side by side with Arabs. Most of them were convinced that as soon as the opportunity presented itself, the Arabs of Morocco would rise up against and slaughter the Jews, as others had done throughout history. Even the Israelis in the delegation, who had been born in Morocco, were afraid for their own safety. How sad it is, I thought, that it seems perfectly natural that Jews can live in peace with Christians all over the world, despite the horrors of the Second World War, while coexistence with Arabs seems like an anomaly. What is a greater expression of peace than coexistence? The lives of the Jews and Israelis in Germany during the past few decades still seem like an enviable privilege for the few, while the lives of the Jews in Morocco, pleasant as they may be, are considered in existential danger.

And something else about our trip to Morocco: during the first days the Israelis belittled everything they saw. They compared everything to Israel and found everything wanting: Israel was better and more advanced. They were so patriotic they judged their native land like a third world state. There were those who made a point of showing how Israeli they were by not speaking Moroccan Arabic, lest someone mistake them for locals. They only thawed after a few days. It took time for them to come to terms with their Moroccan identity. Some of them wore *galabiehs*, some suddenly "remembered" how to speak Moroccan Arabic, even speaking it with one another. Mayors, public figures, members of the

Knesset and businessmen rediscovered and fell in love with the country of their birth. Fascinated, I tracked the resurfacing of their deeply-hidden Moroccan identities. Now they could love Morocco without a guilty conscience or feeling they were betraying Israel.

They stopped making comparisons. They all wanted to visit the cities of their childhoods. Their initial alienation turned into emotional tears, and some of them even broke down and cried when they saw places or met people from the past. They talked about the first days of their immigration, the separation from their families, lives in the *ma'abarot*, the hardships of growing up in a new environment where their origin was considered threatening and a drawback. I saw them fall into the arms of their old Muslim neighbors. Psychological barriers fell, one after another, liberating them.

I was the newest immigrant in the group. Only seventeen years previously I had been a young Jewish boy in Morocco. Visiting Casablanca and other cities, I felt I was coming home. Most of the delegation didn't know Morocco the way I did, but felt a great closeness. Perhaps life in Israel and its difficulties had filled them with longing or fantasies. Even those who had left when they were only five or six years old remembered every detail and their eyes lit up when they came across a house or location or person they thought they remembered from childhood. Watching them, it seemed to me that their initial alienation had been replaced by idealization. The change was dramatic. They walked along the streets deliberately speaking Moroccan Arabic so that people would stop and talk to them.

And in the midst it all the dead reappeared and came charging to the fore. The visiting Israelis were attracted to the cemeteries like moths to a flame, every city and the Jews buried there. For most of them it was the first meeting with relatives who had passed away. The teary-eyed meetings recalled the faith in the power of the dead as I had known it as a child. Every time a tragedy occurred an urgent pull was felt to visit the grave of one of the famous rabbis. Every overdue or complicated birth, every out-of-the-ordinary event in human life, every desire for more material possessions, every plan gone wrong, and the desire to realize every fantasy led the Jews to prostrate themselves on the graves of one or another famous rabbi. Not that there was any lack of them. An endless number of rabbis with all sorts of names and nicknames are buried across the width and breadth of Morocco. Jews and Muslims had the same eagerness for their healing power. They touched the grave, muttered a prayer, raised their palms to the heaven and kissed them, hoping the rabbi would intervene and help God open his heart to them.

The Israeli visitors ran willy-nilly around the cemeteries, looking for the graves of relatives. Three of them located the graves of their parents and grandparents in the cemetery of Fès (Fez). They had said goodbye to their parents, expecting to see them again, and immigrated to Israel as children with the Youth Aliyah program. That never happened. The reunion brought them to tears.

Maybe because of my own history, I kept thinking about other children whose childhoods had ended without their knowing where they were going. They were ten years old, eight, and even younger. One of them was Yamin Ouaknine, who had also immigrated to Israel with two siblings. I met him through a Jewish Agency made-for-television movie about the courage of the children who had immigrated from Morocco without their parents. Yamin was only seven years old when an *aliyah* representative knocked on the door of the Ouaknine household in Marrakesh. It was in 1961, during Operation

Mural, a clandestine Mossad operation to bring more than five hundred children from Morocco to Israel in one wave. The operation was headed by a Swiss Jew named David Littman, whose urgency to save the Jews of Morocco had been inspired by the Holocaust. He had never met an Arab but was convinced the Jews lived "like prisoners" in their own lands and that a Holocaust like the one that annihilated the Jews of Europe was about to be visited on them. Years later he and his wife Gisèle, whose pen name was Bat Yeor ("Daughter of the Nile,") became famous for having included the term *dhimmi* in the Jewish lexicon to describe the Jews of Morocco. Literally it means "protected person," a non-Muslim who pays a head tax for protection from the government but has no rights. Gisèle, who was born and raised in Egypt, watched as the property of the Jewish families was stolen by the Egyptian regime. The trauma turned her into a well-known authority on Islam. She became absolutely determined to rescue the Jewish children of Morocco.

As Ouaknine neared his fortieth birthday, and had filled a number of senior positions in Israel's defense establishment, he was asked to tell the story of his *aliyah*. He had been adopted by an Israeli family and his last name was now Kanaan. He told the director of the movie about his last moments with his parents, and his voice broke. "I look at myself today as a father," he told the camera, "and if people from the Mossad were to come to me and say, 'Give us three of your children for the State of Israel...' I'm not saying... but the people of the Mossad are good. And I'm not saying anything about David [Littman] here. Their mission was to take five hundred children and bring them to Israel. They carried out their mission... There were nine of us, and my mother had to decide who would go and who would stay." [His voice broke and he tried to hide his tears.] "My whole life I tried to understand what my mother had been thinking and I never dared ask her. I was afraid she would say I was a wild child... 'Take Yamin'... It has bothered me my whole life. Why, of the nine of us, did my mother say 'You and you and you' will go to Israel, how did she pick? They took a little wooden suitcase and packed some shirts and pants and sandals for me. I didn't understand what they wanted, what was expected of me. It was before dawn. It was still dark outside. That made the greatest impression on me, the dark... My sister said that when we were on the boat I wanted to jump into the water to go back to my mother. It was hard for me, I was a child... I had never said I wanted to immigrate to Israel. I was seven years old. I wanted my mother... It is the most natural thing in the world to want your mother. My sister was afraid I would really jump into the water to return home. No one prepared us for anything. The people who came to take us were very mission-oriented."

The visit to the cemetery in Marrakesh of one delegation member was dramatic. The Muslim guard remembered the funeral of his father. As soon as he heard the name his eyes opened wide in surprise. He was in his seventies and had known the so-called Golden Age of the Jews in Morocco, before they left the country. From the age of fifteen he had worked with his father and helped him bury the Jews. He remembered the names of them all. All he needed was a name to navigate to the grave.

He had been working with the dead for more than five decades, in a small room near the entrance to the cemetery. His life had recently improved thanks to donations from Jews of Marrakesh who had emigrated to America. He used the money to buy a radio and television and other electronic appliances, ensuring he would maintain the graves of their relatives. Every donation improved the cemetery's physical appearance. The graves of rabbis and religious authorities and Kabbalists stood out prominently from the others.

The visitor from Israel became very emotional. "You remember my father?" he asked, looking at him closely. "*Bismillah* [in the name of Allah]," he swore, "I buried your father." He laid his hand on the Israeli's shoulder. "I helped my father bury him. Your mother cried a lot. So did your uncles." The Israeli broke down in tears and embraced the guard for a long time, as though holding him would hold his memories. He was eight years old when he left Morocco with Youth Aliyah in the nineteen sixties. He barely had time to say goodbye to his father, and he remembered the last long hug and the tears and the silent prayer his father mouthed for the safety of his son. They never saw one another again. That was twenty-five years earlier. The Israeli held a high position in his new country and had filled many important public functions. He asked the guard if anyone had eulogized his father. Speaking Moroccan Arabic, the guard told him the head rabbi of Marrakesh had said he was a wonderful person and that everyone loved him. He praised the help his father had given the Jews of the community, and his charity. The Israeli sat next to his father's grave for a long time before he could bring himself to leave.

Fez made a particularly strong impression on the visitors from Israel. They waited anxiously for the moment they would see the house where Maimonides[9] had lived. The newer section of Fez was very different from the old city, especially its architecture. Several thousand people lived in the crowded old city, whose area was only two

---

9. One of the most prolific and influential Torah scholars of the Middle Ages. In his time, he was also a preeminent astronomer and physician.

square kilometers, building almost touching building. The labyrinthine streets were so narrow two people could barely walk abreast. Both sides of streets were lined with houses and the small shops of the artisan occupied with his craft and the shopkeeper with his wares and the tradesman with his merchandise. There was a wealth of delicate wooden objects for sale, copper vessels of all shapes and sizes, textiles and rugs, aromas and flavors, spices, traditional caftans, embroidered shoes for men and women. Crowds, deafening noise and sometimes the passerby had to press himself to the wall to let a laden donkey pass. Pedestrians made their way with endless patience through the crowded streets, their faces stoically calm. There was no place to rush to and no reason to hurry. Time was flexible. The way the locals kept time was one of the things first noticed by visitors to Morocco. People walked towards an undefined goal, nothing was urgent, nothing had to be done immediately. In any case, we all die in the end. Here no one looked at his watch and no one walked quickly. Only the visitors from Israel kept looking at their watches, what time was it and when would they arrive and would they arrive in time, exactly as in Israel.

In any case, with no discernible expression on his face, Elon led me to the sofa in his living room. He kept looking at me with no emotion and spoke slowly, as though all pleasure and reasons for living had been drained out of him. He radiated gloom, his words were wrapped as if in sorrow, and he viewed the world with despair.

I, on the other hand, had taken my first steps as a journalist and had been in the country for less than twenty years. My view of the world was more positive and I had an unquenchable zest for life. My name had appeared on published articles and I felt as though my rite of passage towards being an Israeli was proceeding smoothly and without obstacles. I felt I had complete command of my new language and that gave me confidence. What could be more Israeli than to speak fluent Hebrew? And what could be more Israeli than to write for an Israeli newspaper? And what could be more Israeli than to sit in the living room of the most prominent Israel journalist of his generation? What a feeling! Only a few years ago my hand shook when I dared to write. Now I felt I belonged!

Visiting Elon seemed to me like the official stamp of my professional status. I imitated him and had learned from what he wrote to look at the world as he did. With a critical eye, with doubt and with infinite curiosity. "I liked what you wrote, I liked it a lot," he said suddenly. "I especially like the way you write. You show a sensitivity that few Israeli writers show."

I thought I was going to faint. My God, how often had I puzzled over how to find the right words to describe the human condition! Writers struggle to find the exact words all the time. At that embarrassing moment Elon offered to show me his books. He had shelf upon shelf of books in many languages, he was beyond a doubt a universal Jew. Theodore Herzl, the founder of Zionism, must certainly have dreamed of someone like Elon when he fantasized about the people of the new country. He took a thin book from one of the shelves, the poetry of Ezra Pound. "I want to read you one of my favorite poems," he said. He looked at me and said, "Will it bother you if I read it in English?"

We stood next to each other while he read. When he finished, the sorrow had returned to his face. He invited me to sit again. He asked me what I thought of Israel, and before I could answer, he asked me if I thought the country had a future. Before I could say anything, he began a sad monologue about the steep slope down which Israeli society was sliding. Our situations were polar opposites: I had joined it and he apparently wanted to leave. He had traded his audience of Israeli readers for an international audience, and felt more comfortable in languages other than Hebrew.

I tried to inject an optimistic note into the conversation. Elon looked at me, and I couldn't tell if he was amused by my naiveté or even listening to me. He lectured me for an hour about the hopelessness of Israel, the lack of courage of its political leadership, the Israelis' unwillingness to make peace, Shimon Peres' path of deception, Ariel Sharon's overriding use of force, the disappointment of the generation of the founding fathers, the lack of mercy towards the Palestinians, Israel's lack of desire to integrate into the Middle East, the lack of vision among the Israeli leaders, the rampant nationalism, the people's adoration of the rabbis, the admiration for the settlers and the resources the government showered on them and the day they would change the face of the nation, the indefatigable Israeli patriotism, the disproportionate place the memory of the Holocaust occupied in daily life, and the strong desire to remember the Holocaust and the strong lack of desire to forget Germany's Nazi past, even for a minute.

The journalist I admired so much couldn't find his place in the country of my recent immigration. Nor could he find any reason to write for the newspapers. He had been writing a great deal about the Messianic Judaism spreading through the settlements in the West Bank. He felt it was a danger to the entire country, and also felt his articles hadn't changed anything. It had been ten years since the rise of Menachem Begin, and Elon saw the strengthening of the right wing as what he called "Jewish fascism." Interviewed by Haaretz, he called the country "fascistoid" and narrow-minded. He added, "I am not surprised by the population. We know where it came from. Eastern Europe or the Arab countries."

He was curious about the Arab states. He went to Morocco to see them first hand. From the first instant he recognized the Messianic glint in the eyes of the Jews. His instincts told him things would go badly. He was concerned that if they immigrated to Israel, one day they would change its face and character. He looked at them with the eyes of a liberal Western-European Jew and saw a black void. When they did immigrate to Israel, he saw the first signs of their love affair with Menachem Begin, the leader of the Likud movement.

That was in 1977. Elon watched as the immigrants from the Arab countries joined forces to overthrow the regime of the founders. He said the rise of Begin to power took him back to the days when nationalism spread through the streets of Vienna. He had left as a small child, but the aura of nationalism continued to pursue him. He was now convinced that everything he wrote had been justified. If they came to Israel, they would turn the country into something unrecognizable.

Everyone wanted to know if people were nice to me. If they treated me the way they treated "other" journalists, that is, Ashkenazi. Did they pay me the same salary? Did they print my articles or toss them into the wastepaper basket? Did they talk about me behind my back? Did they laugh at me behind my back? The fact that I was writing for Davar and Haaretz, both papers of the Ashkenazi elite, made them worry about me even more. "Never forget who you are and where you came from," warned David Levy, a Moroccan who was a minister in the early Likud government. "Because they will never forget where you came from. You will always be an anomaly for them. Someone who doesn't belong, not one of them."

Over the years I became an expert on David Levy. We had countless long, intimate conversations. With me he felt unconstrained. He liked to call me "Danny the Red"[10] because I seemed to him to have a naturally rebellious streak. He was always aware of his origins. Awareness became pain when he engaged in political activity. He bore the burden of having turned into a national joke. Every time he felt depressed he would wait for me in the Knesset hallway and motion for me to sit with him. I wrote about him countless times until I was seen as the David Levy expert. Every time he caused a disturbance in the government or at a Likud meeting I was summoned a TV studio to explain how he was going to make political capital out of it. Every time he reacted to an insult or slur, it seemed to the media he was making a bid for attention. That was particularly true when he was apparently fed up with the Likud. And when he was reportedly going to join Ehud Barak's Labor Party. And when he went to war against Benyamin Netanyahu. And when he refused to join the Israel delegation that went to the Madrid Conference. There was no lack of episodes in which his name appeared. And every time it happened, I was called in to explain.

One day, in the early nineteen nineties, when David Levy was foreign minister in the Likud government, Prime Minister Yitzhak Shamir asked me to join him in the Knesset cafeteria. He rarely ate there, preferring to go home for his wife's cooking. Shamir, who had chalked up more David Levy hours than any other senior Likud figure, put his head next to mine and smiled a little smile. A slightly unkind little smile. He told me about

---

10. Daniel Cohn-Bendit, "Dany le Rouge," led the student unrest in Paris in May 1968.

his long political romance with David Levy, its few ups and many downs. He wanted to finally understand what made him tick. "You know," he said, "he has never once picked up the phone to call me. It is beneath him. He lives for a display of respect, and nothing interests him beyond how much people respect him. Tell me, Daniel, explain to me, *please*, what is this obsession Moroccans have with being shown respect. I, for example, have no problem with calling him when I need to. I am, after all, the prime minister. He comes back from a trip to Europe and doesn't even bother to tell me how it went, because it is beneath his dignity to pick up the phone...I always have to call him. Even though I am the prime minister."

Shamir was exceptionally frank with me. He was especially angry because Levy, his foreign minister, had cancelled his participation in the Israeli delegation that would leave for Madrid in November 1991. Shamir found out that Levy had cancelled because he was offended the prime minister had decided to go and head the delegation. "But I am the prime minister," he said, "why would that offend him? This respect nonsense hurts no one but himself."

Shamir was particularly concerned by the rumors rampant in the Likud that Levy was debating his political future with the party. He wondered how a man who had come out of nowhere and reached such political heights could surround himself with what Shamir called "criminals" and "people without culture."

Levy felt his identity as an Israeli was disputed because of his origins. As time passed and more and more David Levy jokes were told and as they became increasingly unkind, he became strongly suspicious of Israel's elitism, which he described as the wellspring of anti-Moroccan racism, both overt and covert. Every time I tried to calm him, he reminded me that my acceptance into Israeli society would not help me. He didn't like the articles I wrote for Haaretz, seeing them as a desperate attempt to assimilate, regardless of the cost. The paper seemed anti-*mizrahi* (immigrants from North Africa) in general, actively complicit in anti-Moroccan racism and prejudice.

For whatever reason, I felt perfectly comfortable working for Haaretz. Nevertheless, relations began to falter. I went back to Haaretz ten years after having been told I was unsuitable. Before I was hired by Davar I had tried my luck with Haaretz. According to my agreement with Uzi Benziman, who edited Haaretz' weekend supplement, to be hired I had write two articles on topics of his choice. "If you succeed, you sign a contract." Both articles, both long, were printed as leads in the supplement. I met with Benziman and he suggested the trial period be extended to include one more article. I agreed and wrote it. It was also printed as the lead article.

He praised the articles and invited me to his home in Jerusalem; I was overjoyed. I had grown to like him and was very grateful to him for having given me the opportunity to publish. He knew my biography and how much I wanted to write for Haaretz. I felt I had passed an entrance exam and was making the trip to Jerusalem to formalize joining the Haaretz staff. He was waiting for me in his living room.

The expression on his face didn't bode well. Had something happened? Had something gone wrong? Looking at his face, my hopes plummeted. We sat facing each other on the sofa. He talked and talked, but it was hard for me to listen. He explained and explained, and my thoughts wandered. He said he had agonized all night long and hadn't been able to fall asleep. He had even asked his wife, who was a psychologist, what to decide: should he hire me or not? The question had troubled him all night, he said. He told me everything he had thought about, and I hung onto what he had said before he began having doubts. "The contract was ready," he said, "but..."

I sat there, hiding what I felt. He was very fair and noble, and told me what his doubts were, all of them regarding my degree of acclimatization, my ability to understand life in my new country, my ability to write about what I saw. Could I write about a Boy Scout trip even though I had never been a Boy Scout? Could I write about the lives of people in a village in the Galilee despite the fact that I hadn't grown up in Israel? And again, how many years had I been in the country? To improve my chances, I added a year or two. I was terribly upset and stood up to leave. I was in the situation I had feared the most: a Sabra versus a Moroccan immigrant. I felt as though I had reached the head of the line at the door to Israeli society, and at the last minute the ticket had been snatched from my hand. I felt I was the victim of injustice, that I had not been treated fairly, and that he had violated our verbal contract.

I could see that my obvious foreignness made him uncomfortable. Three of the trial articles I had written had been the supplement's lead articles and two of them had been featured on the cover. In a moment of frankness he admitted never having seen a more impressive new writer. He also said the editorial staff had had very positive reactions. But "something inside me", he said, was getting in the way. He squirmed, looking for words to justify himself. However, he didn't manage to find them. There was no need for him to say anything more. I hadn't been born in the country like the rest of the paper's staff. I wasn't an expert in the ways of the country. Still standing, I shook his hand and went out into the cold Jerusalem night air.

Even after I had breached the journalistic fortress and had become another Israeli newspaperman, otherness continued to dog my footsteps. Friends of mine who had immigrated to Israel were at peace with their otherness and were determined to preserve the values of the countries they had left. They were also determined to speak their own language whenever possible. All I wanted was complete assimilation. I suppressed my old world to be accepted by my new society. So in a way I was not so surprised when my first assignment at Davar was to write about Morocco and find out why the Moroccans in France had achieved more than those in Israel.

As the years passed I softened towards the land of my birth. I no longer made an effort to prove I has assimilated. To a certain degree I was at peace with being different. I was proud of my acquired Israel identity but was also proud of my roots. I didn't always know where to draw the line between them. "You will never be an Israeli like the others," Elon warned me once, "so preserve your uniqueness. Don't speak out of turn because you will immediately be identified with the masses of your former countrymen who brought Begin to power."

Once he asked me why I didn't write for his paper. He believed that having someone from Morocco join the staff of Haaretz would change its monolithic Ashkenazi image. He viewed himself as a European aristocrat and despised the masses who followed the sensationalist evening papers. "How in the world did you get to Davar?" he chided me, "it's the socialist party's paper, and they screwed the Moroccans more than all the others."

There was no way I could tell him that the door to Haaretz had been slammed in my face only a few months previously. I worked for Davar because to a large extent I had no other choice. I simply couldn't tell him what had happened. Being rejected unjustly had rattled my self-confidence and I kept it to myself. I was especially concerned that I was running out of time. I was 32 years old when I published my first piece in an Israeli newspaper. That is a late age for a fledgling journalist. I believed I had to show all my talents before I began. After graduating from Haifa University with a degree in sociology and political science I studied for my master's degree in journalism at Boston University. Only when I received it did I feel I was prepared to face professional challenges.

When I returned to Israel with my wife and the two children who had been born in Boston I officially applied for work at the supplement and represented myself as journalist like any other. Benziman replied politely and asked me to contact him when I had settled in, and I did.

Public figures born in Morocco monitored me and my professional career. David Levy, scarred from being laughed at and ridiculed, made certain to urge me not to keep my head down but to show respect for my Moroccan heritage. I think there were very few other Moroccans working in the written and broadcast media. "They will always try to step on you and diminish you," he would say. "Learn from me, *habibi* ["my friend"]. I overturned tables right in front of them. I made sure they feared me. Otherwise I would have been lost. What didn't they say about me? They said really terrible things. But if I had been polite and refined like you, would I have become Israel's foreign minister? Who would have paid attention to me? In Israel politeness is interpreted as weakness. All it does is invite trouble. Learn from me. Keep your head high and raise your voice when you have to. If you want to succeed in this country, shout so that everyone can hear you. That's the price."

Two main protagonists in the drama of my professional life, Amos Elon and David Levy. Two poles, two paths going in different directions. One the prince of quality journalism, the other the prince of the oppressed proletariat. Each one and his Israel. I felt close to both. Especially to David Levy, who came out of nowhere and made his way along a path very few had trodden before. Once he told me tearfully that he had had to sacrifice himself for the sake of others. "I sat on the barbed wire fence of Israeli society so that people like you wouldn't have to suffer what I had."

Chapter Six
Hatred for the Left

During my entire career as a journalist I found myself writing about hardship. We seemed to have a mutual and natural affiliation for one another. The elections held in 1996, or more accurately, their results, made me return to the "social problem" I had tried to avoid during my first years as a writer. The day after the elections, expert analysts said most of the residents of the development towns and slums had voted for Benyamin Netanyahu, the right-wing candidate. For ten years as a writer for Davar I dealt with a broad scope of national and international issues. I had distanced myself, with a fair amount of success, from everything that had to do with misery, need, poverty and squalor. Maybe I was afraid I would see myself back in the world I had come from. All of the above were prevalent in what people called "the Other Israel." The people in the development towns and slums lived in another world, physically close and at the same time metaphysically far away.

The Other Israel frightened many journalists. Every time something newsworthy happened there, I hoped they wouldn't send me to write about it. When I looked at the Other Israel I saw masses of Israelis to whom fate had been cruel. To a certain extent I was one of them. They had immigrated to Israel like me, and many of them looked like me. They spoke Hebrew with thick accents that revealed their origins. They lived under the burden of living in a new country, like me. Many of them found it difficult to leave the trauma of emigration behind. Like me. Many of them still had not mastered Hebrew and could only speak their native language. Many of them felt betrayed because Israel had not opened its arms and accepted them, regardless of their efforts. Most of them felt like second class citizens and were alienated, living their lives feeling unwanted and out of place.

When I visited the Other Israel as part of my job, people never saw me as a newspaper man like the others. I was immediately one of their own, their prodigal son, a survivor. They expected me to understand what their lives were like and what their children's lives were like, and how they had sunk to the very bottom and how it happened that they had not succeeded in building a new life here, and why they were described in such unflattering terms. They spoke to me as Moroccan to Moroccan. They mixed French and Arabic and told me what was troubling them without reservation, safe because they felt I was one of them. Some thought I had crossed impossible lines in the media, that exclusive Ashkenazi province, but there were those who were displeased by what they considered my distancing myself from my Moroccan heritage.

THE IMMIGRANT

For them I represented secular journalism, which was the habitat of the wealthy and connected. And completely Ashkenazi. Almost every time I went to the Other Israel I was accused of the greatest sin of all, of having joined the enemy camp, the people that "don't like us," as they would say. It was the first time I had met hatred for the Left, face to face. I met it again at the beginning of the nineteen eighties, when I covered the emotionally-charged elections. One evening I went to Beit Shemesh, a city west of Jerusalem, where Shimon Peres, the Labor Party candidate, was paying a political visit. It was 1981, soon elections would be held, and Amram Look, head of the local municipal council, had sent Peres to drum up votes in the city, which was considered a Likud fortress. Look, who had been born in Morocco, symbolized the last of the Right wing who had been attracted to Ben-Gurion's party, regarding him as the reincarnation of King David. Over time the others left the founding party, but Look remained loyal. The residents of Beit Shemesh liked him, but not his party. The rumor that Peres was coming to visit was enough to kindle their simmering hatred into flames. No one from the Left stirred up the resentment of the immigrants more than Peres. More than anything else, he symbolized the Left, which they despised, because it fawned on the Arabs, was willing to make peace from a position of weakness, was both secular and Ashkenazi, and had no pride in being Jewish.

The evening was unforgettable. I went out of curiosity. I had never been at a political event so frightening. The local residents came with murder in their eyes. No swear word was too taboo to utter, no insult too awful to hurl. What surprised me was that almost all of the adults kept repeating the stories of their arrival in Israel and agonized over memories of how they had been mistreated. Almost all of them spoke about the contempt and arrogance and disrespect and discrimination they suffered because they had come from Morocco. The younger generation was angry about the way their parents had been humiliated. For them Peres' visit was like a criminal returning to the scene of the crime.

Once in Israel they developed a deep hatred for the Left which had no natural connection to the overall issue of the Palestinian territories. Two years previously Prime Minister Menachem Begin had signed a treaty to return the Sinai Peninsula to Egypt and no popular anger had been voiced. Maybe the opposite. Begin's daring decision only served to increase his support in the development towns and made people admire his leadership. Barely two decades had passed since the waves of immigration from the Arab countries, and for their hardships the immigrants blamed the pioneering State of Israel that had taken them in. They took revenge mercilessly. With almost no connection between the way they voted and how they felt about the territories, they took revenge on those in the leftist parties who preached peace. I came to Israel more than a decade later and hadn't had the traumatic experiences they had. I hadn't experienced stinging insults and offensive behavior as they had. They were determined not to forget the *ma'abarot* and the shortages and what seemed to them a clear preference for immigrants from Europe. The attack on their self-respect was more than they could bear.

More than anyone else, the politician David Levy symbolized the disconnect between the immigrants from Morocco and the Israeli establishment that received them. During the years I was close to him it was not hard to see he was a moderate when it came to the Arab-Israeli conflict. I once asked him privately why he had

THE IMMIGRANT

joined Herut, a right-wing party that joined the Likud in 1988. He was a political moderate, regarded himself as a socialist and believed in the fair division of the country's resources. In other circumstances, perhaps in another country, his political opinions would have paved his way to the Labor party.

One day we were sitting in his office in the Knesset and he began talking about his first days in the country. Hung on the wall behind his chair was a very flattering picture of Menachem Begin, the Ashkenazi who, like the Pied Piper, drew after him masses of *mizrahis* and turned the despised Herut movement into their new home. Especially David Levy. "You can't understand the twisted political structure of Israel without going back to the years of the first waves of immigration," he said. "How can I forget those days? I arrived in Beit Shean with my family. It was the dead of night. Total blackness. I thought that in the morning I would see houses, streets, people. We slept in an open tent. It was the middle of summer. Beit Shean is hot in the summer. I think it must have been 45 degrees... It was impossible to fall asleep. In the morning we looked around and there was nothing but desert. There was nothing at all...

"But the worst thing was trying to find some way to support the family. At four o'clock in the morning my friends and I went to a collection point where trucks from the kibbutzim in the Beit Shean Valley came to pick up workers. The kibbutz masters stood there and handed out slips of paper to those who were entitled to work. There were hundreds of us and we knew only half of us would find work that day. The expressions on people's faces when they closed the back doors of the pickup trucks and said, 'That's it, no more,' – those expressions were excruciatingly painful to see.

"We would watch the departing trucks with tears in

our eyes. We were jealous of those who had found a way to earn money to buy food for a day. It is hard to describe the feeling, and it was the same every day. Some of us pushed and fights broke out to get on the trucks, and all the time the people from the kibbutz were watching us. My god, it was so humiliating...

"And even those who got work weren't happy. We were driven to the fields to spend eight hours bent over thinning out the crops. After an hour it was hard to straighten up. The heat was inhuman, 45 degrees, 50 in the sun. We needed to stop and drink all the time. We used to beg our kibbutz masters to put the water in the shade to keep it cool. Would they? Absolutely not. It was inhuman, purely evil treatment. They left buckets of drinking water in the sun and the water got so hot we couldn't drink it. I kept thinking, what kind of Jews are they? Where does this evil, this cruelty come from? Why do they hate us so much? We came to Israel out of love for Zion, and we are being treated like slaves. I discovered a new kind of Jew, evil, remorseless, hard-hearted."

The Other Israel was alive and well inside me even though I didn't live in a development town. As a journalist, I spent my time with mainstream Israel. Finally, since fate does play tricks, I returned to the Other Israel and it became my main area for investigation and coverage.

"What are you going to write about?" asked Hanoch Marmari, the editor of Haaretz, after I joined the paper.

"The peripheral communities," I answered.

"We don't have a desk for that," he said with a smile.

"I want to write about the development towns so readers will know how people live there and what they feel."

By the time elections were held in 1996 I had a certain amount of seniority as a journalist. I was about to finish my first decade as a newspaperman, most of it spent working for Davar. The day after Netanyahu won the election, one of the papers printed a map showing the results of the voting. Netanyahu had carried practically the entire country. The color used for the Likud covered almost the entire map. Here and there in the Rabin-Peres strongholds the Likud had been defeated. The map showed two distinct sectors. Israel of the Left, which had shrunk considerably, and Israel of the Right, which had grown to cover most of the country. The division reflected the division in Israeli society. The rich had voted Left, and the poor and traditional religious and ultra-Orthodox religious and residents of the slums and development towns had voted Right. Demography had played an important role. The *mizrahi* voted Right and the Ashkenazi voted Left.

The elections were personal, and the two candidates were the two faces of Israel going their separate ways. Peres represented the Israel of the founders, the secular, the bourgeoisie, satiety, the Left, which regarded Zionism as the natural bond to the universal and wanted to see the homeland of the Jewish people as just another country. Netanyahu represented the Other Israel, more religiously Jewish, a strand in a Gordian Knot of the history of the Jewish people, traditional religious, ultra-Orthodox religious, the people living in the settlements. Netanyahu's Israel was poorer, mostly *mizrahi*, and living in development towns and slums.

Such a drama could only play out in Israel. While in Europe the less economically-advantaged naturally turned towards the Left and the bourgeoisie elites to the Right, in Israel it was the opposite. In Israel socio-economic status isn't the only influence on voting preferences. Right and Left in Israel are also influenced by the disagreement over religious and secular identity.

Hatred for the Left

The Zionism of the Left, which of its nature is secular, never found a place in the hearts of the *mizrahi*. They loyally preserved Judaism in the countries of their birth and continued to do so in Israel. Voting for the Right was related not only to the insults from and rage at the Left, but also to Jewish tradition and its values. The Left offered a new and secular Israel, the Right fostered Jewish identity.

The map of the election results showed a new division. In the years before those fatal elections I followed Yitzhak Rabin closely. Like many, I wanted him to win. I remember the night he was sworn in as prime minister and I remember how he sat in the prime minister's chair. I was in the press box and I watched as he and outgoing Prime Minister Yitzhak Shamir changed places. Then I rushed to the hospital. It was the evening of July 13, 1992. My wife was about to give birth to our third child. She was in the delivery room in the hospital in Jerusalem and I was waiting for a different birth in the Knesset. Two births on one evening, I thought, and both of them delayed. It was after midnight and time was short. I missed the sight of Rabin taking the chair at the head of the government table because exactly then my son Tom was born. The doctor who delivered him went from my wife, who was giving birth my son, to the birth of the new Knesset on the TV in the next room.

The years Rabin was prime minister changed the face of Israeli society. I followed him and his boundless enthusiasm for getting things done. I had the feeling that because of his age, or in spite of it, he was trying to get as much done as he could. His genuine concern for the ills of society could not be ignored. He had spent most of his life in the defense establishment and knew almost nothing about the poverty and need that had spread through the peripheral areas.

I covered his visits to the settlements in the south and the north and the Arab settlements and the slums. He was impatient, he wanted to know what the bottom line was immediately. How much money would it take? That was always what he asked the heads of the local municipalities. He was especially sensitive to educational problems, always asking what could be done. Wherever he went in the peripheral areas he was always surprised by the low percentage of high school graduates who had completed their matriculation exams, one of the qualifications for university admittance.

Only one student in ten in the southern town of Yeruham had a full matriculation certificate. In Ofakim, another southern town, only two out of ten. The situation in the other development towns was similar. Academic experts told him that education was the basis for social change, the dominant factor. Peace with the Arab world, which he aspired to promote, now seemed like a direct consequence of the right kind of education.

In those days, at the beginning of the nineteen nineties, the development towns lagged far behind the rest of the country in all areas of life, especially education. Children in the eighth grade could barely read, children in the tenth grade wrote with terrible mistakes and those who had just finished the twelfth grade failed when tested in reading comprehension, mathematics and English. The number of students who were accepted by universities was very small. Only a few miles separated them from people who lived in the center of the country and who had no idea whatsoever of what life was like in the periphery. Even when the children did receive matriculation certificates, in most cases their exam scores were too low for university admission.

The 1996 elections came after years during which Rabin's government had showered the weaker settlements with financial benefits and bonuses. Rabin orchestrated a change in priorities previously unknown in the country. Under his administration economic growth boomed and millions of shekels were diverted from security to social initiatives. For the first time since the establishment of the state priority was given to societal needs instead of defense.

Rabin was received with enthusiasm wherever he went. Even though he was extremely introverted and closed off, the heads of the peripheral communities made a supreme effort to show him how grateful they were for his help. From street lighting to extra tutorials for weak students, Rabin filled every empty space he saw. His greatest miracle was Yokne'am, a poverty-stricken community located about 15 miles southeast of Haifa, where most people worked in one factory, Soltam, which was founded in 1952 and made various metal products, such as kitchen utensils. For years the children growing up in Yokne'am dreamed of one thing, the day they could join the Soltam workforce. At its height, in the nineteen eighties, the factory employed about 3,000 people, the overwhelming majority of whom came from Yokne'am.

In 1990 the dream of Soltam's employees crumbled. The factory stopped receiving orders and the board of directors announced they would have to fire hundreds of employees. The workers knew they had no place else to work and in response barricaded themselves inside the factory and locked the gates. The company directors didn't hesitate. Even though Soltam belonged to the Histadrut they recruited thugs who rushed the locked gates with Rottweilers in the dead of night to evict the workers. "What a night," said Simon Alfassi, head of the Yokne'am municipality, years later. I had gone to interview him about the miracle of the new Yokne'am which had sprung up on the ruins of the Soltam factory.

One day Prime Minister Rabin went to visit the city. "Simon, what can I do for you?" he asked. "I want to turn Yokne'am from a development town into a first-class city," said Alfassi. "OK," said Rabin, "let's see what can be done." Rabin arranged tax benefits that would extend for several years, with the result that the city attracted dozens of high-tech companies, which turned Yokne'am from a development town to one of the country's leading technological centers.

When the map of the 1996 elections was published, Yokne'am was a solid Likud red. It fell like ripe fruit into the hands of the Right, regardless of what the previous government had done for it. More than eight out of ten residents voted for Benyamin Netanyahu. Almost every development town did the same. The election results hit Simon Alfassi, who admired Rabin in life and even more after he was murdered, like the proverbial ton of bricks.

That the election results would be what they were wasn't a scenario I could have imagined, and it plagued me for a long time. In Israel, but in the rest of the world as well, people found it hard to believe that a government that had had unprecedented achievements for four straight years had failed to win over the most important segment of the population. No one could understand the failure of the Labor Party, even after the man who had headed it for three and a half years was assassinated by a killer who was avowedly affiliated with the Right. Was there another reason for the results? Was it possible that the Left really hadn't understood the mindset of the voters? Or, more accurately, hadn't read the map correctly? Did the election results herald a clash of cultures in Israeli society?

During the months before the elections public opinion polls were held one after another, almost daily. Never had there been so many in such a short time. Most of them focused on routine election issues and dealt extensively with personalities and the chances of the two main candidates to win. Every day the Israeli man in the street was asked who was more photogenic, who would be more unyielding in negotiating with the Arabs, who would be able to stand up better under pressure. People were also asked who was more experienced, who was nicer, who would promote the economy more, who would get rid of poverty, who would bring peace, who was more convincing.

All the surveys missed the main issue. They didn't examine the despair and anger bubbling and seething under the surface. Admittedly, it wasn't easy to notice when Israeli life was better than it had ever been before. In every field the progress of the four years before the elections had been breathtaking. Never had life in Israel galloped at such a pace, never had there been so many changes in such a short time, and for many it was hard to keep up. Sometimes it seemed the changes were too extreme, too frequent, too fast.

The beginning of the Rabin government in 1992 looked very promising. Four years later Israel was a different country. For the first time in its history, Zionism seemed to have come to terms with the Palestinian nationalist movement. After a year, a peace treaty was signed with Jordan and embassies were opened, ending more than forty-five years of conflict with Jordan. Countries in North Africa and the Persian Gulf opened their doors to Israeli tourists and Israeli commercial legations were opened. Economic agreements worth tens of billions of dollars were signed. The economy boomed in a way Israel had never seen before. Investments poured into the country, the infrastructure was strengthened, the scenery changed and the standard of living almost rose to that of Western Europe. Per capita income rose to $17,000 and was slightly less than that of Britain and France. They were years of constant production and industry. Wide-eyed, the international business community followed the rate of growth of Israel's economy. The future seemed rosy and promising.

And then Rabin was assassinated, and for a short time everything came to a standstill. The assassination shook Israeli society to the core, polarized it and made it unrecognizable. Yigal Amir, a law student at a religious university, shot and killed Israeli Prime Minister Yitzhak Rabin. The man who had transformed life in Israel for three years fell victim to a young religious man who felt he had been victimized by the transformation.

The assassination made Israelis anxious about the future and it polarized public opinion. Some of the population regarded it as a spiritual last will and testament to continue making peace with the Arabs, and even to accelerate the process. Others hoped it would decelerate the process and give the country time to heal, and others hoped it would end the process completely. No one imagined the political map would look the way it did in the 1996 elections. No one imagined the religious and ultra-Orthodox parties would double their strength at the expense of the secular parties. The two large parties, Labor and the Likud, which had always received more than 70% of the votes, found themselves with about 50%. Israel's political establishment collapsed under the wave of small parties which represented special interest groups which had previously been considered marginal. Shass (Hebrew acronym for Guardians of the Sephardim), the party of religious Sephardic Jews, doubled its number of Knesset members. The National Religious party became significantly stronger. The party of new immigrants, which had been formed only months before the elections, won seven seats.

During the year after the elections Israel established a tribal federation, joining hands to bring Benyamin Netanyahu to power. For the first time since the founding of the state the Left had no say in the government. Begin's surprise victory in the 1977 elections had left a few remnants of the founders in the government, such as Moshe Dayan and the Dash party (Hebrew acronym for the Democratic Movement for Change). Perhaps because he was afraid of looking like an extremist, or perhaps seeking legitimization from the Israel he had defeated, Begin surrounded himself with prominent figures from the old establishment.

The results of the 1996 elections reflected the ultimate revolt against melting-pot Israel. Israel no longer had a unified identity, and the New Israeli had to make way for the Other Israeli, who was tired of aspiring to another identity, who was perfectly content to be less of a Sabra, less Israeli and more Jewish, more religious and more nationalist. About a month after the elections I met with Shimon Peres, who had been roundly defeated, to hear how he explained the results. He had just lost an election he thought he had in his pocket, and had already gotten over it. At that time I was writing a book about the elections, and I didn't understand what they meant until I met with Peres early one morning. He valued the potential of a book more than anyone, because he believed history would be more merciful to him than another article in another paper.

His openness surprised me. It helped that I was considered one of his confidants. During the days of merciless struggles between him and Rabin, journalists had access more or less depending on how close they were to either one. My articles were considered as being favorable to Peres.

"What happened in the elections?" I asked.

"We lost," he answered.
"Who's we?"
"We is Israelis, like you and me."
"And who won?"
"All those who don't have the Israeli mentality."
"And who are they?"
"You can call them Jews."

I was surprised and it took me a few minutes to digest what he had so offhandedly tossed off. It was the first time since the elections I felt I was really seeing the heart of the new Israel. Israelis vs. Jews. And that from someone who was never defined as a Jewish Israeli. His rivalry with Rabin only served to point out the differences between them. They spoke differently. Rabin spoke to Israelis with the language they understood and liked: simple, straightforward, unadorned, sometimes not entirely fluent. It seemed right to them. "Israelis are a work in progress," Amos Elon said once, and that was Rabin's speech and manner. Peres was different. He aspired to be a statesman like those in Europe. He had an excellent command of the language and knew when to make literary references. When he gave speeches he often liked to talk about philosophy and intellectualism. That seemed extreme to many Israelis, too high a linguistic register.

He didn't relate to what it meant to be an Israeli in real time. Not everyone understood what he was talking about. Not everyone understood what he wanted. Not everyone understood what direction he was taking. He had a reputation for waffling because he always talked about dilemmas and both sides of an issue, since he could see the positive and negative in everything. Paraphrasing Mao, he once said that "If you want to understand a political problem, look at its internal contradiction."

Was that the explanation for the political behavior of the *mizrahis* in the peripheral areas who voted as a solid block for the Right? Were they putting their Jewish identity before the Israeli? Was there a clash between the two? Had they exposed the real lines dividing Right and Left? Did they vote for the Right because they felt it was closer to their Jewish identity? Did only secular Jews vote Left?

I went looking for answers in the development towns in Israel's north and south. From the beginning I felt at home. The residents, who were used to meeting Ashkenazi journalists, treated me like a member of the family. They considered the journalists who dropped in to write about them as just another octopus-like tentacle of the ruling Ashkenazi establishment. They spoke differently, they looked different, their questions alienated them. This was my first meeting with old-time immigrants from North Africa, who looked as if they had arrived only yesterday.

To them I was one of them, even though I represented a newspaper they hated. The Israel they saw in the paper was both hateful and suspect. Everyone I spoke to harked back to the nineteen fifties, when they had received the mark of Cain as primitive, violent, uncultured and without honor. Not for an instant did they hesitate when circumstances demanded they defend themselves. They were convinced everything was because of their origins, it was all because they were Moroccans. The more they were vilified, the stronger their bonds to Morocco became. That same Morocco they had left en masse was remembered with longing. Suddenly everything in Morocco was wonderful, the land of milk and honey.

The first generation, the generation of actual immigrants, had softened, and even perhaps forgotten some of the trials of absorption. The second generation, those who had been born in Israel, were louder and more aggressive. They had inherited from their parents a strong sense of having been insulted and disrespected, and it refused to pass, they refused to let it pass. They felt they were Israelis, but at the same time found it hard to hide their rage. They turned their anger on Ashkenazi culture as represented by the rich and bourgeoisie and Tel Aviv and the kibbutzim and the moshavim and the cultural elite and the culture of cronyism and arrogance and racism. And above it all hovered the founding clique affiliated with the secular Left, topped with Mapai, Ben-Gurion's party. And the deeper you went, the greater the hatred was for the overall political Left. Looking at their failed lives, they accused the state. It had brought them here and then neglected them, tossing them away to the most outlying, invisible places it could find.

Everyone claimed they had been exiled to keep them isolated, that the development towns had been built to provide cheap labor for the kibbutzim and moshavim. Young and old, man and woman, no one had any doubt. They were brought to be hewers of wood and drawers of water for a soulless Israel that had taken their self-respect and settled them on the country's borders.

Thus the rift between the political Left and the *Mizrahi* deepened and widened, handed down uninterrupted from father to son. Admiration for David Ben-Gurion, the founder of the State of Israel, turned into genuine disgust with him and his heirs. When they immigrated to Israeli they were called on to vote in the Knesset elections, and most of them voted "correctly," that is, for the ruling party, Mapai,[11] strengthening the party until it had almost an absolute majority of seats. That was their

---
11. Hebrew acronym for "Party of the Workers of Eretz Israel."

way of identifying with the government that brought them to Israel, but at the same time they hoped to benefit in return. An undisguised war was waged in the early days of the state for the votes of new immigrants, who barely knew Hebrew and could barely distinguish between the parties or know what the differences between them were.

In a study sociologist Dvora Bernstein published in Hebrew, she wrote that the North African immigrants were regarded by the parties, and Mapai most of all, as "a faceless mass, as a reservoir of raw material that had to be fought for and snatched from rivals and competitors. They were a generality, a commodity of political support that could be divided and distributed. All the party functionaries regarded them as a new source of votes, homing in on their political ignorance, lack of orientation and total dependence of the establishment absorbing them..."

Less than two decades later the political drama was played out, and for the first time those very immigrants put Mapai's rivals in power. In May 1977 one of my first missions for Haaretz dealt with the ascent of the Likud and the descent of the Labor Party. I was sent to the southern development town of Netivot to cover the reception held for Ehud Barak, head of the Labor Party. Decorations were put up for his visit, which would be widely covered by the media. He was about to do the unbelievable and ask the forgiveness of the *mizrahis* in the hopes they would return to voting Labor. A few months earlier Barak, a much-admired, much-decorated general, had inherited Shimon Peres' seat as party leader. He knew that victory in the 1999 elections depended on the residents of the development towns voting Labor. He knew he had to get them out of the clutches of the Likud, but how? That was his mission as new party leader.

THE IMMIGRANT

Barak entered political life like a comet. He would be the savior of the First Israel that Rabin had orphaned. Even as a young army officer a seat was waiting for him in the Labor Party, all he had to do was come and fill it. Like Rabin before him, legends and myths were spun, stories of his heroism. For many he was the incarnation of the ultimate Israeli, the mythological Sabra, the glory of those born in Israel. Even when he was in his twenties and thirties people predicted that some day he would be Israel's prime minister, right after he finished his term as chief of staff.

Still in uniform, he was head and shoulders above many other officers because of his quick intelligence and rapid-fire assessment of situations. He had the resourcefulness of a commando fighter coupled with burning ambition. That he would enter political life was no surprise and considered completely natural. Prime Minister Rabin and Foreign Minister Peres invited him to join the government as a player in preparation for the day he would become team captain. His first appearance before the Labor Party's Central Committee in July 1995 was unforgettable. All he had to do was enter the room. Thousands of electrified party members stared at him as though he were the Second Coming. He walked through the crowded aisles to the stage, crowded because people had left their seats to get a better look at him. He was wearing civilian clothing but he walked with military bearing and people couldn't stop staring.

When the time came to vote him in as a member of the party all hands were raised so high they practically touched the ceiling. His military past and decorations outshone any questions there might have been about where exactly he stood on political issues. The main thing, everyone thought, was that he had returned to his natural habitat, the familial intimacy of the Labor

Movement. "I feel like I have come home," he told the thousands of people in the audience. The admiration for him was obvious. They loved the way he spoke, his fluency, his military expressions and the nobility he radiated. "There is someone in the audience who led me to the one of the most elite units in the army," he said, looking with a bit of embarrassment at Yitzhak Rabin, who had a front-row seat. "I feel I can lead Labor to victory in the 1996 elections," he said. Foreign Minister Peres was sitting next to him, and wagged his head from side to side, sensing, perhaps, a personality cult developing. Once Barak had inherited the party he assembled all his forces to assault the government. To realize his ambition he had to defeat the undisputed king of the Other Israel, Israeli Prime Minister Benyamin Netanyahu.

A few days before Barak went to Netivot to ask for forgiveness I went to take the pulse of the locals. The Labor party was going to hold a festive meeting in the town's community center, during which Barak was expected to make his plea. People, both in Netivot and beyond, were intensely emotional when they heard he was coming to try to make amends and assuage the *mizrahi* hatred for the Labor Movement. Even to the most innocent it was clear that the man whose impassivity was famous was moved more by their potential votes than by insults that were all past history. Since 1977 the *mizrahis* had been only too willing to leave their original party powerless, stuck in the desert of "loyal opposition." There was strong public disagreement about the event, with extreme positive and negative opinions on both sides. Personally, I knew exactly how I felt about it. I didn't need anyone to say they were sorry, nor did any of my family from Morocco. But over time I had become exposed to the depth of the insult and offense felt by many Moroccan immigrants. There were many who felt that only a forthright, sincere apology could soothe their hurt feelings.

Suddenly I discovered I had a part to play in the political drama about to unfold in Netivot. A few weeks earlier Barak had called to tell me he had "greatly enjoyed" my book, *The Other Israel*. It had been published at the beginning of 1997 and recounted the rise of the Right to power in 1996. He called me because of a specific passage, where I had written that "Shimon Peres once asked Ariyeh Deri, the leader of Shass, why North African voters were against him and his party. Deri had immigrated from Morocco when he was nine. He had always admired Peres. 'The Moroccans don't like you,' he admitted. 'They still haven't forgiven the Labor Party for the way they were treated in the nineteen fifties.' '"What should I do?' asked Peres.

" 'Very simple,' answered Deri. 'You and your party have to go to those who came from Morocco and the rest of North Africa and beg their forgiveness for what was done to them. You cut them off from their religion, destroyed their Jewish values and humiliated them emotionally and physically. You should know they are not all in the Likud's pocket, not at all. They are moderate and tolerant. The reason they vote Likud is because of all those years of deprivation in the *ma'abarot*.' "

The sorrow and gloom of the *ma'abarot* began a process which ended with the Mizrahi supporters leaving the Labor Movement, regarding it as responsible for sending them there. Every *ma'abara* had its own painful memories which the passing years did nothing to dispel. There were 132 *ma'abarot* throughout Israel, and the conditions in all were nearly inhuman. In 1954, on the average, there were between three and four people in every dwelling unit and one shower for about every 16 individuals. The lack of hygiene was much worse in some. In the Kordani B *ma'abara* in Kiryat Motzkin, north of Haifa, there was one shower for 336 people. In the Karkur *ma'abara* there were 53 people for every toilet and in the Kastina *ma'abara*, 48. In the Zikhron Ya'akov *ma'abara* 23 families used the same water source. In the Rishon Letzion *ma'abara* there was one garbage receptacle for 30 families. In the Talpiot *ma'abara* in Jerusalem there was one shower for 100 people.

Despite, their names, "transit centers," and contrary to what might be expected, the *ma'abarot* were not transit camps. Most of the people lived there for ten and even twenty years in unimaginable poverty and degradation without being able to leave. In 1979, thirty years after the construction of the *ma'abara* in Holon, 120 families wrote to the Moroccan ambassador to Paris, saying "We are 120 families from Morocco...We live in terrible conditions and are sorry we decided to immigrate to Israel, leaving our beautiful homeland, Morocco. When we came to Israel they put us into shacks made of cardboard, like in refugee camps, and we have suffered under terrible conditions in summer and winter. It is because we are Moroccans and considered like the blacks of Africa... Therefore we appeal to you, Your Excellency the Ambassador, and ask you please to help us receive visas to return to Morocco as citizens..."[12]

What worsened the sense of discrimination in the *ma'abarot* was the fact that most of the residents were *mizrahis*. Almost a quarter of a million new immigrants lived in them during the first years. More than 80% came from North Africa. For the immigrants from Europe things were easier. Most of them had relatives who took them in. The Jewish Agency even found them permanent housing in the center of the country. The minutes of a

---

12. Dalia Gavrieli Nouri, "Ma'abarot is not just the name of a kibbutz," (Hebrew), 1979.

Jewish Agency meeting held on December 10, 1956 with the participation of Prime Minister David Ben-Gurion, refer to the distribution of immigrants to the end of the year: "In the past 27 months 85 thousand immigrants came to Israel and 85% of them were sent to develop areas outside the Gadera-Naharia strip. They were sent to places like Beersheba, Qiryat Gat, Qiryat Shemona, Betzet and Tzur. The immigrants from Poland are a different story. During the past two months more than two thousand Poles have immigrated. Some of them were sent to empty locations in the [Gadera-Nahariya] strip because there were empty apartments we could use. We will also send the Poles to Zikhron Ya'akov and Binyamina because we can't send them to tent cities and shacks, we have to put them in acceptable places."

By speaking in Netivot, Barak wanted to put the traumatic memory of those days to rest. He was convinced that if he could ask forgiveness the situation would change. "I am planning to do that," he told me on the phone.

"Do what?" I asked.

"Ask the *mizrahis* for forgiveness." He asked what I thought. I said I thought it was a good idea. I added that if his request seemed honest and genuine, it could be received favorably. "But if it seems phony," I warned, "it is liable to boomerang."

"I have thought about it a lot," he said, weighing his words carefully. "I have thought about it for a long time, and decided to talk to them straight from my heart..."

The conversation ended. Barak had called at around two in the morning. "Why in the middle of the night?" I asked. "It's the safest time," he said, "at this hour no one will listen in." I wished him luck. I thought about what he had said. I couldn't help smiling at his saying he would speak from his heart. That was the essence of the man I had known during the time we both served in the Knesset. Only on rare occasions would he speak without thinking and he always knew how to make his emotions subservient to his intellect. That was what he intended to do when asking for forgiveness, to speak with determination and calm. As if he were about to assault an enemy fortress.

It is unclear when Netivot turned into a religious town. Of the many settlements in the south that had become religious at the beginning of the nineteen eighties, Netivot had an undisputed status. Almost daily, thousands of despairing observant Jews streamed in to pray at the graves of famous rabbis and ask for help. With the exception of ultra-Orthodox Bnei Brak, there is no city in Israel with so many God-fearing people.

When the French entered Morocco they modernized it, threatening the spiritual links of the masses to the rabbis and sages of the Torah. As it turned out, there was no real threat. While many Jews were attracted to the charms of the French cultural emancipation, many more huddled in the collective rabbinical bosom. They were afraid that the new world heralded the end of their way of life. Even the Jews who had successfully assimilated into French culture preserved the Jewish traditions. The fanatic secularism of Europe didn't particularly influence the Jews who emigrated there. Israeli secularism was equally unsuccessful. There is almost no ex-Moroccan Jew who will say he is completely secular. Whenever I visited France I came face to face with Moroccan Jews who had attained the highest positions in French society but who had not abandoned or changed the traditions they had brought with them. They blended into their new secular society but never missed Saturday or High Holiday prayers in the synagogue and their kitchens were kosher. They said the blessings before and after meals, and there was always a *kippah* within reach, which they put on or took off depending on the circumstances.

I live with the same duality. While in Israel I lead a secular life, but when I am in Jewish communities in France, Canada or Morocco, I accommodate myself to the local customs. I never refuse to pray in the neighborhood synagogue on Saturday because I am secular in Israel. Secularity in Israel demands the same adherence of its followers as religion demands of the practicing observant. Among the Jews of Morocco, secularity loses its value as soon as it negates the existence of religious faith, as religious Judaism loses its value as soon as it negates the secular. That is the harmony Moroccans grew up with and are careful to preserve.

I met Andre Azoulay, economic advisor to the king of Morocco, at his office in the royal palace in Rabat. He told me about an incident with the king. A meeting of the king's advisors had been set for Yom Kippur eve. Azoulay couldn't decide whether to go or not. When King Hassan was informed, he ordered Azoulay to go to the synagogue to pray on Yom Kippur like any other Jew in Morocco. "As a faithful Muslim I would not consider preventing a Jew from fulfilling the commandments of his faith," he said.

Netivot took over most of the Jewish mysticism of Israel and left a few crumbs for the other development towns. It is crammed full of the yeshivas of famous Kabbalists, but two of them dominate the town and compete with one another: the yeshiva of the descendants of the Baba Salee, and the yeshiva of the "X-Ray rabbi," Ya'akov Ifargan. In the middle of the nineteen seventies the Baba Salee became known as a miracle worker. The rumors of his rare abilities and power to save souls spread throughout the country and rabbis began coming to Netivot to receive his blessing. They came from the development towns, the slums, the moshavim of *mizrahi* immigrants, and waited outside his house for hours in hopes of having some of his holiness rub off on them. Legends about his deeds and the miracles he had worked were spread by the synagogues and yeshivas and increased belief in his magical power. The media with a vested interest were overjoyed about what had been discovered in Netivot and reported stories about miracles he had worked and about people whose worlds had been changed by the Baba Salee's spiritual intervention. He could barely see or speak, he could barely stand up, but even his limitations became advantages. His fragile and ascetic aspect only increased his reputation and power.

Arriving in Netivot, I went to the local cemetery. There is no other city where the dead have so much power over the living. The great mystics who died, like the Baba Salee and the "X-Ray" rabbi's father, have graves that are practically mausoleums. Others have to make do with graves where their rare powers are written in letters large enough to be read by moonlight. In a few days thousands of Labor Movement activists would invade Netivot to try to change the town's traditional Right-wing voting pattern. Many of the people living in Netivot were aware of the plot. Here, as in many development towns, the residents continued calling the Labor Party by its former name, the *Ma'arakh* ["Alignment"]. Every time someone said *Ma'arakh*, it was said with a sneer. Michel Alkarat, a local resident, sat at the entrance to the cemetery. "Come here," he said, "and I'll tell you once and for all why the Moroccans vote Likud. That's why you came, isn't it? That's why all you reporters came. Because you want us to vote for the *Ma'arakh*. Listen to me, and then go tell those who sent you, the Ma'arakh, never went anywhere in a straight line, everything they did was always twisty. Even Ehud Barak is twisty. No one ever knows what he really wants. I used to vote Ma'arakh, but I got over it."

As Michel was speaking, Yehiel Zohar, head of the Netivot municipality, entered the cemetery. He offered to show me around so that I would understand the importance of the rabbis – alive or dead – as perceived by the immigrants from Morocco. He honestly believed that if the *Yishuv*, the Israeli – although he wanted to say "Ashkenazi" – pre-state settlement had opened its doors to the immigrants, they would not have turned to religion. "Sometimes it's more an act of desperation than faith," he said in a low voice.

Ever since religious fanaticism attacked Netivot, Yehiel Zohar found himself wearing a *kippah* more often than not. He did the math and came up with the answer that not one single day passed without his being invited to a religious event. Not a day went by without a meeting with one of Netivot's rabbis. When he was younger he never imagined the day would come when he found himself up to his neck in religion and rabbis. After immigrating he dreamed of the day he would be an Israeli and feel like an Israeli. He was born in Morocco and when he and his parents arrived they were sent to Netivot. Even as a young man he was attracted to politics, and especially to the Labor Party. He admired its leaders and dreamed of the day he could join the party.

However, life in Israel tricked him and sent him down another path. He planned to join the Labor Party and wound up joining the Likud. Despite his difficult childhood, he bore no resentment for the Labor Movement. "I grew up in a large family," he said, "and I also felt the humiliation of my parents. My father did low-paid unskilled labor."

I met him for the first time after Benyamin Netanyahu was elected prime minister. He was standing in a corner in the auditorium in Jerusalem and smoking a cigarette. There was a giant party in progress to celebrate Netanyahu's victory. The Israeli who came from America and conquered Israel was welcomed like a hero by thousands of party members. They cheered and gave him a long standing ovation. Yehiel Zohar found it hard to join the wave of enthusiasm. Even though he was a member of the Likud, he still had a lot of respect for the Labor Movement, despite its perceived injustices. "Take all the people you see here," he said, pointing, "and ask them about peace. They will tell you that they are willing to give up most of the Palestinian territories for peace. Take me, for instance. I am closer to Labor's policies than the Likud's. But I am a member of the Likud. Why? Because many years ago I returned to Netivot from the kibbutz where I grew up. I wanted to be a political activist and I went to the Ma'arakh office. I went in and found about ten old Mapai activists who looked at me as if I had just dropped from the moon. They said, 'Young man, go away. There is nothing for you here.' Every day they went to the Ma'arakh office, read Davar and went home. But first they locked the doors to make sure people like me wouldn't walk in.

"So what did I do? I went to the Likud office. I found young people who looked like me and spoke my language. The Ma'arakh slammed the door in my face. The Likud welcomed me and made me feel I was a person. My story is like the story of a lot of Likud members here tonight, they became members because it was the only political party that opened its doors to them."

We went back to talking about Barak and forgiveness. Zohar had already made preparations for the arrival of thousands of guests, headed by Ehud Barak. The visit and its media coverage were hard for the people sitting with us. They all looked deeply disgusted. One man said, "They'll come on Sunday, talk nonsense for a couple of hours, and then go back to their fancy houses in Tel Aviv. But *habibi,* we live in this hole all year long."

Someone else added, "You know why we vote Likud? Not because they are *mizrahis*. Because they are Jews. I won't forget how the Labor members humiliated us. All of them, from Ben-Gurion to Peres. They're all the same. They hate us." And Moshe Vaknin, wearing a crocheted rather than a black *kippah*,[13] said, "And what has the Likud done for us? We vote for them every time and every time they screw us. What have we ever gotten from them? What have we ever gotten from Shass? Yeshivas and *mikvehs.*"[14]

People were getting angry. The first man insisted the Labor Party had cut their ties with Judaism, turned to me and said, "You see, I'm not wearing a *kippah* but I keep the Jewish traditions. All the Moroccans keep the Jewish traditions. As long as they make fun of Moroccans and our traditions, there is no way we will vote Ma'arakh."

After the anger died down and we were drinking mint tea, and a Moroccan song came through the window of one of the nearby houses. Immediately the atmosphere changed and people sang along and clapped their hands. I looked at them as from afar. I didn't know what to do. I saw myself, the journalist who had come to write about Netivot and its residents, but at the same time I was one of them. Was I supposed to show my understanding for them? Again, the same dilemma I had been grappling with throughout my professional life. Was it my job to

---

13. That is, observant but not ultra-Orthodox.
14. Jewish ritual bathing houses.

be understanding or report what I had seen and heard? Did being Moroccan oblige me to show sympathy for the motives, loves and hatreds of the Moroccans I met in Netivot? While I was still taking notes, one of them raised his voice.

"And you, Mister Ben Simon! And you, yes, you, Mister Ben Simon! Are you with them or with us?" If only the earth had opened up and swallowed me! I was embarrassed. I couldn't answer. I knew exactly what he meant. He was also asking me to choose sides. Like my first day at the Religious Youth Village so long ago, I had to choose a side, although both sides were inimical.

Being forced to adopt and practice religion had made me distance myself from it as I grew older. In Morocco we were far from the Israel's uncompromising black and white, with us-or-against-us world view. Whatever we did, it was a question of compromise. From the price of shoes, which was always determined by negotiation and bargaining, to deeply difficult issues, everything was always settled with a compromise. If there is any trait that is ultimately Moroccan, it is the willingness to compromise. So it was absurd for them to have taken such a fanatical and utterly alien view of their heritage. Over time they turned into "haters of Arabs," "opponents of peace," "the extreme Right."

"Tell me the truth," he wouldn't let it go, "are you with the Ashkenazis or are you with us? What are you ashamed of? You are a Moroccan like us. My last name is also Ben Simon, maybe we are related. How can you not see what they have done to us? I see you on TV sometimes and you talk like an Ashkenazi. What's that supposed to mean? Didn't you speak Moroccan Arabic? And why do you work for Haaretz? There aren't any other newspapers? Don't you know Haaretz hates us? It has hated us from the day we came. How can you work for a paper that hates Moroccans? You never read what they wrote about us in the fifties? You must have read they were in favor of 'selecting' the Jews who came from Morocco. They didn't want us to come to Israel. Or have you forgotten?"

So, where am I? Who am I? Am I an Israeli who lives with his Moroccan roots in peace? Or a Moroccan who turned into an Ashkenazi, as I have been accused of many times. All the years I wrote about the periphery I was always faced with my identity, and sometimes in conflict with it. Other journalists were sent to write articles. It was as though I was being sent for psychological counseling.

Chapter Seven
Old Wounds

Relatives who emigrated from Morocco to France didn't have to pass the same tests as those of us who immigrated to Israel. There was an incident at the beginning of my military service, on the first Yom Kippur during basic training. I was at a Golani infantry camp near Kibbutz Lohamei Hagettaot, in the northern part of the country. I wasn't particularly observant when it came to religion but I did fast on Yom Kippur. There was no Jew from Morocco who dared, at least not openly, not to fast on Yom Kippur. In the afternoon, before the last meal before the fast, one of the commanders told us to divide ourselves into fasters and non-fasters. Almost all the soldiers in the company went to the fasting tent. Some of them, most of them kibbutzniks who had joined Golani with an eye to later joining its special forces reconnaissance unit, went to the non-fasting tent.

The army was my first meeting with kibbutzniks. They were so physically impressive, and their Hebrew so natural and faultless, completely different from what I heard in the Youth Village. I immediately felt close to them, maybe because they looked like the Israelis I had imagined, like the ones I had seen in the pictures of the *aliyah* representative. As I walked towards the fasting tent one of them called out, "Hey, Ben Simon, where are you going?" I told him I fasted on Yom Kippur. The kibbutzniks looked at me somewhat skeptically. They had expected me to spend the day with them. Other soldiers in the platoon, many of them with *mizrahi* backgrounds, had expected me to join them.

I doubt there is another country that puts its citizens in such a position. The rivalry between the camps within society is so fierce that siding with one seems like a threat to the other. That's what I felt at that moment. The relentless dilemma between the secular tent and the religious tent. Which one to choose? I felt pulled to the kibbutzniks' secular tent but felt the same pull towards the tent where soldiers prayed, because they both reflected the Jewish tradition I had grown up with.

Actually, why did I have to choose? Why would going to prayers in a military camp on the eve of Yom Kippur undermine my secular identity? Why were I and others like me always being tested? In Morocco we didn't have the same kind of secular Jews they had in Europe. We believed in an omnipresent, omniscient God. We were brought up to believe God watched over everything we did, even when we tried to hide. During the Yom Kippur prayer in the synagogue in Casablanca we used to sneak out, planning to steal a sip of tea at one of the coffee houses to make the fast easier. And we always found something inside us warning us that the omnipotent omnipresent God was watching us, and better not to do it.

In Israel it was different. Its overt secularity allowed

me to understand that God was not actually in every place at all times and was not interested it everything I did. Even in the Youth Village in Kfar Hassidim I allowed myself to drink milk on Yom Kippur, fresh from the udders of the cows, before I went to the synagogue. The cows had to be milked on Yom Kippur and the workers didn't join the prayers until they had finished milking. The first time I broke the fast on Yom Kippur I waited, tense and fearful, for retribution from the hand of God. When nothing happened, I realized I could sin even with God watching and not be struck down by lightning.

The search for the right identity from among the many available gave me no peace. I never denied I was Moroccan, despite the caricature image. There was no ethnic group in Israel so despised as the Moroccans, no cultural heritage so sneered at. As a journalist I was careful because I knew how sensitive the subject was. My greatest professional test would be writing an article for Haaretz that would include statements strongly insulting to the Moroccans in Israel.

No Israeli public figure had ever described the *mizrahis*, especially the Moroccans, the way Knesset Member Army General Ori Orr did. The irony was that what came to be known as the "Ori Orr affair" occurred exactly a year after Ehud Barak's speech in Netivot. Barak had hoped his speech would renew the relations between the Labor Movement and the *mizrahi* voters. One year later Orr was becoming increasingly frustrated, because the *mizrahis* had not ended their long love affair with the Likud and returned to him and his Labor Party comrades.

My visit to Netivot led me to believe that a reconciliation between the Moroccans and the Labor Movement would take a great deal more than a plea for forgiveness. It was obvious that the rage of the parents had been distilled into the lives of the children, who felt as though they personally had been insulted and humiliated. It is hard to describe how deep the feeling went and how hard it would be to heal the wounds, even two generations later.

I went to Netivot as I went to every other development town, as a journalist observing the lives of the residents, perhaps more anthropologist than journalist. I looked at the lifestyles of people who had no goals in life, no expectations, as though they had lost hope in anything beyond the horizon. I sat in their living rooms, ate with them and felt at home. They expected me to identify with them. They expected me to make their voices heard. They expected me to link their haplessness to Israel's dislike and rejection of them. They were completely convinced that if they had been treated differently their lives would have been different. They honestly believed that every failure they experienced was the result of being not wanted and rejected from the minute they set foot in Israel. If they had been received with acceptance, they told me repeatedly, they would be different people.

I did identify with them. Their hardships and distress touched my heart and their pain was my pain. Every time they opened their homes to me I felt I had returned to the Morocco of my childhood. The aromas from the kitchen reminded me of my parents' home in Casablanca. I wrote about fathers and sons who got up before dawn to work the first shift at a textile factory, and when they came home in the afternoon the mothers went to work the night shift. Twenty-four hours of work at noisy machines that had turned into an alternative family. In the space between home and factory lives had no meaning, no hope. Nevertheless, everyone was pleased to have work, because it not only supported the family, working in the factories created social circles. Everyone told me there was an atmosphere of togetherness and solidarity at work which made life easier.

I was received as a member of the family wherever I went. At the entrance to the community, as soon as I was identified, every door, every heart opened to me. The transition from the center of the country to the development towns in the south was like crossing a border. I could go from a developed country to a third world country in less than an hour. From the hi-tech industries in the center to the crowded coffee houses in the south, where many residents spent the day doing nothing. They seemed to be waiting for the establishment to save them, but the establishment had other ideas. Help yourselves, said the establishment, again and again, take responsibility for yourselves, take responsibility for your lives. However, they still waited for a sign of life from government institutions. Over time they developed a destructive dependence on the establishment. Many brought with them from Morocco dependence on an establishment so centralized and strong it seemed to hold life and death in its hands, and nothing could be done without it. In Morocco the state made sure everyone had cheap housing and enough money to subsist, and decided who would flourish and who would live in poverty. The Jews belonged to the middle class thanks to their initiative and ability to survive, but none of them fooled himself into thinking they could ignore the establishment, the *makhzen*. Its representatives were deployed in every city and every village and every neighborhood and every street. Any strange occurrence, any change, was reported to the authorities. The Jews, and Muslims as well, knew that the eye of the *makhzen* was open and watching at all times, and could make things better and make them worse.

Even after they immigrated to Israel, many Moroccans

found it hard to get used to the relative absence of the establishment. In Israel it was conventional wisdom that everyone took responsibility for himself, leaving a lot of immigrants feeling lost. As long as they were unemployed, or had economic problems, they expected the establishment to come to their rescue. Yigal Ben Nun, who studied the Jews of Morocco, thought differently. He said the problem was that they had unjustly been given the reputation of waiting for the government to supply their needs. The truth, he admitted, was that in Morocco they were dependent on the establishment, but only in the outlying Jewish communities in the Atlas Mountains. He claimed that if the lives of the Moroccans in Israel were so terrible and they made no effort to improve the situation, what else was there for them to do but sit in the coffee houses rolling cigarettes? It had nothing to do with Moroccan culture, he said, but it was a consequence of the having been pushed to the lowest stratum of society. It was desperation born of their situation in Israel, and ruined it the Moroccans' image.

The people I met during my journalistic encounters expected sympathy, empathy and understanding from me because I came from a similar background. From the start I felt sorry for them, and felt the need to stand up for the weak against the powerful. That has been my worldview for my entire adult life, and it was born here in Israel. It wasn't something I learned at home. I also learned justice and equality by following the lead of the pioneering Israelis.

For years I had become more and more admiring of the pioneers who built the country and the kibbutzim and moshavim, leaving everything behind, families and lifestyles. I identified with their sacrifices and saw them as the equals of the young people who left an old world in Europe to settle in a new one in the Middle East. I never accused the founders of the Labor Movement of being deliberately evil towards immigrants. They absorbed massive waves of immigration on the principle that the ends justify the means, and when the ends are a supreme goal, the price of the means in social or human terms is irrelevant. They also paid a price to build their homes here. They also abandoned the heritage of their fathers to create the New Jew. There was no reason, they thought, for the new immigrants not to undergo a similar process. According to a book by Ze'ev Sternhell,[15] everyone who immigrated felt inferior towards any New Jew who had grown up between the sands of Tel Aviv and the fields of the Jezreel Valley. Everyone became addicted to the Zionist dream of starting over and fixing everything.

As it turned out, the price was too high. The founders' demand that immigrants completely abandon the past was understood differently by the *mizrahis*. They regarded it as an attempt to dismiss and eradicate their culture and as an intolerable sign of arrogance from people who had been born in Europe towards people who had come from "backward" countries. The new immigrants didn't always know that before the founders came to destroy the culture and identity of the North Africans in the *ma'abarot*, they had done the same to their own. The Cultural Revolution was considered a necessary precondition for the national revolution. Sternhell wrote that those needs also determined the policy of settling the land and distributing the population to development towns far from the centers of culture, economic activity and developing technologies. It was one of the main reasons the *mizrahis* sank into

---

15. Ze'ev Sternhell, Building a Nation or Changing Society? Nationalism and Socialism in the Labor Movement in Israel, 1904-1940, (Hebrew), Am Oved Publishers, 1988.

backwardness and degeneration, he wrote.

The high price, alongside the anger felt towards the Labor Movement, were what caused many of the development town residents to fall into the arms of Israel's Right wing. They cared less about its politics and more about feeling close to the Jewish worldview and culture offered by Menachem Begin and his party. While they regarded the Labor Party as fostering the middle and upper classes, they felt the Likud was the home of the weaker classes, most of whom were *mizrahis*.

Asking the *mizrahis* for forgiveness didn't bring the hoped-for political capital. Visiting the communities of the south after Ehud Barak's speech, it quickly became obvious that they simply hadn't believed him. For some reason the speech was regarded as a cynical, virtually effortless and fairly superficial attempt to retrieve lost votes. The Labor Party was frustrated and began to be concerned lest its defeat in the 1996 elections repeat itself.

Knesset Member and former IDF General Ori Orr took that concern further than other Labor Party members. He was repelled by the Right and made even more anxious by the possibility that the *mizrahi* voters would return it to power. I could sense his unease every time I came across him in the corridors of the Knesset when I was covering it for Haaretz. One time he stopped me and said, "We have to talk." After a long army career, General Orr joined the Labor Party. Shimon Peres took him under his wing and even appointed him as deputy defense minister after he became prime minister when Rabin was assassinated. When Barak replaced Peres in 1997, Orr became a party soldier loyal to him.

The Knesset's summer recess would begin on Wednesday, July 29, 1998. On July 27 I was still looking for a topic for my weekly Friday column. I wanted a special angle for the end of Netanyahu's first term in office. He was about to end two frustrating years in an atmosphere of impending political change. Barak was charging full speed ahead, crisscrossing the country, drumming up support to challenge Netanyahu.

For the first time it was two Sabras facing off, both representing the second generation of the country's founders. Hebrew was their mother tongue and both their characters had been forged together with the state. Both had served in the Chief of Staff's elite reconnaissance unit, and they symbolized a new era, the conquest of Israeli politics by the unit's commander and one of its soldiers. Expert political analysts were of the opinion that Netanyahu was worried about entering the arena with his former commander. Now they had exchanged roles. As Netanyahu had convinced anyone willing to listen that he would defeat Peres in the 1996 elections, Barak convinced anyone willing to listen that he would defeat Netanyahu in the 1999 elections.

So on that pre-recess Wednesday a vote was going to be taken to disband the Knesset and hold early elections. A majority for the vote had been assured beforehand, and most of the parties were planning to use the recess to prepare for the election campaigns. On Monday evening, as I was sitting in the Knesset cafeteria, Ori Orr walked by. He again said he wanted to meet with me to discuss "something that was bothering" him. I was still worried about my column, and no scenario suggested itself in which a conversation with Orr could contribute anything. He was a fairly popular politician but not considered especially newsworthy.

I wanted to avoid the meeting, but a short time later one of aides came down to the cafeteria to remind me Orr was waiting for me. Journalists sitting with me couldn't understand why I was meeting with him. "It won't take more than ten minutes," I promised. I felt it was something I had to do for someone I considered honest and serious. It turned out he had read my book, *The Other Israel*, where I had written about the 1996 elections, and he was determined to discuss it with me.

Two weeks previously he had met with some of his comrades-in-arms at a small party in Motza, near Jerusalem. It was held for General Matan Vilnai, who was leaving active duty. His retirement had caused many sensational headlines. He was considered the natural next Chief of Staff and had been waiting for the call, but Defense Minister Yitzhak Mordechai appointed General Shaul Mofaz instead. Vilnai's father was Ze'ev Vilnay, an author and geographer, famous for his love of hiking through Israel. For many, his son's not being chosen as Chief of Staff was an attack on the holy of holies. A fluent Hebrew-speaking Sabra had been pushed aside by an immigrant from Iran who did not belong to the military elite.

Dozens but not hundreds of guests had been invited to the consolation party, and I was among them. Most of them were retired military brass who regarded Vilnai as one of their own. Orr moved among them, an embrace or a handshake here and there. He caught my eye and came over. "Danny," he whispered, "you see all these people? Each and every one of them belongs to the dying species of the Good Israeli. Look at their eyes and you will understand where they are coming from. They are generals and pilots and brave warriors. You won't see the Other Israel here, all those who keep yelling they are being deprived. This is the real Israel." Incoming Chief of Staff Mofaz had not been invited. Neither had Defense Minister Mordechai, both born in Middle Eastern countries.

I went into Orr's office. He greeted me with a broad

smile. In a few minutes a conversation would begin that would change the life of the man who was supposed to be tapped as defense minister in Ehud Barak's future government. His support for Barak was blind and unreserved. He was an army man, regarded the military as the fount of all values, and found it hard to accept criticism of someone he regarded as the all-time epitome of IDF warriors. He was upset as we began talking and unthinking in his choice of words to describe the ingratitude of the *mizrahi* voters towards Barak and the Labor Party. There was, however, nothing wrong with Ashkenazis voting against Barak.

During our conversation Barak was sitting in his office nearby, worrying about his upcoming visit to the United States where he would be introduced to the American leadership. He had asked Orr to meet with him because he wanted him as a traveling companion. Orr said he would come as soon as he finished talking to the journalist.

Orr talked and talked. He was obviously upset. He lectured me on the ingratitude of the *mizrahi* voters. He didn't understand why they had chosen Netanyahu over Peres in the last elections. Or why they didn't appreciate the enormous contributions the Rabin government had made to their towns and cities. As the minutes passed, he became more and more agitated. He had read my book carefully and even understood the complaints against the Labor Movement, but what was too much for him was Barak's request for forgiveness in Netivot. An entire year had passed and apparently it hadn't made the *mizrahi* voters question their loyalty to the Likud.

Orr had been in the audience during Barak's speech. He was impressed and his admiration for Barak grew. He left Netivot with the feeling that the speech was a success and would break the tie between the Likud and the Labor Party. A year had passed and he now felt nothing had come of it, and was bitter.

"I want to tell you something about Ehud's plea for forgiveness," he said, raising his voice. "I'm sorry it didn't help...I hope that's clear. I don't blame him, I blame the *mizrahis*."

I had come empty-handed because I wasn't planning to take notes. At a certain point, as he developed his theories about the *mizrahi* voter, I asked if I could document our conversation. He not only agreed, he gave me his pen. As he continued, his complaints snowballed into an avalanche. Orr took no prisoners. He went straight for the jugular, not choosing his words particularly carefully in describing the *mizrahis'* ingratitude.

I remembered our meeting at Vilnai's condolence party and I could see the direct connection between his frustration then and our conversation now. Of all the journalists, he had chosen me because I had seemed like an "intelligent Moroccan".

Orr hoped with all his heart that Barak's speech would improve relations between the old-timers and the newcomers both in and outside the Labor Party. "I have a feeling that the *mizrahis* want to drag out their frustrations for as long as possible and exploit them for political reasons," he said. "It makes me really sad, because I believed it would take less time to get over the fifties. However, I can see we still have a long way to go. I had hoped there would be a new generation of *mizrahi* leadership sufficiently open-minded and non-neurotic to talk to people like me. Unfortunately, I can see it didn't happen. They have no one of any stature."

He told me how sad he had been after his visits to immigrant *moshavim* and development towns. "The Right's only objective is to perpetuate their hatred for the

Labor Party and make political capital at the expense of the weaker classes. In addition, how can anyone form political opinions based on slaps on the back? I don't slap backs. But for the people in the slums they are more important than respect, so, slap their backs and they will vote for you. That's why they don't vote for us, very simple. I am sad because we did so much for them. We raised their level of education and lowered the rate of poverty and created a wave of development and did everything we could to help them get ahead, and it did no good. It meant nothing to them. You want proof? They voted for Netanyahu in the last election."

I sat there, writing down every word, except when he said something was off the record. Here and there he toned down something he had said before. He seemed out of control, releasing pent-up anger. While he continued his diatribe against the *mizrahis*, Ehud Barak was sitting next door in his office preparing the speech he was planning to give two days later to disband the Knesset. The longer Orr spoke, the more I felt he might be putting a noose around his own neck. No one had ever openly dared to speak that way about *mizrahi* politicians. Previously it had always been said behind closed doors, far from hostile ears.

When what he said was made public and a public scandal ensued, politicians and journalists asked Orr why he had been so foolish as to talk that way to a "Moroccan" journalist? They weren't surprised at what he had said, only that he had poured his heart out to one of "them." As long as he had grumbled and complained to journalists close to him, he had been met with understanding and even empathy. In his defense he said he honestly believed that a journalist with ties to Davar and Haaretz would not be suspect. It later became clear that he told me what he had told others, but no one else ever printed it.

Towards the end of our conversation he brought his face close to mine. "I know you are Moroccan," he said, "but I also know you are different from the rest of them, so what I am going to say now doesn't include you. When I talk about *mizrahis*, I especially mean the Moroccans. They are the largest and most problematic ethnic group. They have no interest in what is happening around them, or why it is happening. When I appear before them I see a total lack of interest in hearing about, understanding or knowing about life, about what is good and what isn't. That worries me, because it doesn't only harm them, it harms all of Israeli society."

I shook hands with him and went back to the Knesset cafeteria. I had a premonition it would not turn out well. No one sitting around the press table was interested in what Orr had to say to me. None of them expected it to make headlines.

When Aluf Ben, head of the news desk, read the article he was thunderstruck. He was the first person to understand how explosive the material was. He asked me for comments from all the people Orr had attacked. He meant all the *mizrahi* politicians Orr regarded as having an "ethnic complex." "The problem is that I can't talk to them the way I talk to other people," Orr had said. "Every time you say something they react emotionally and are insulted and offended and go nuts. They are too sensitive and have problems with feeling disrespected, and that makes it impossible to have a normal conversation with them."

Orr was particularly hard on two people, Professor Shlomo Ben-Ami and Defense Minister Yitzhak Mordechai. "I don't understand Ben-Ami," he said, "he was number 34 on the Labor Party's Knesset list, the last place on the list, we welcomed him and by his own efforts he climbed to party leadership and became a minister. But he can't stop complaining...The problem with people like him is that they interpret legitimate criticism as ethnic slurs. You can't run a political party like that. You can't say anything to those people without its being interpreted as an ethnic slur or part of a plot against them. You tell me, is that normal?"

He saved the best for last, for Defense Minister Yitzhak Mordechai. "Yitzhak Mordechai is the world champion of complexes... When he was in the army he was always playing games, testing to see if he was respected. Take Matan Vilnai, for example. Mordechai kept him from being appointed Chief of Staff because he was determined to command respect. Mordechai never forgave Vilnai for being promoted before him. I remember when Mordechai replaced him as commander of the 35th Paratrooper Brigade. Everyone knew, and even the soldiers made no secret of it, that he could never fill Vilnai's shoes. And Vilnai paid for it with the position of Chief of Staff, only because Mordechai thought he was being deliberately disrespected."

That evening the Labor Party corridors were a circus. The rumors about the article that would be printed the following day spoiled the joy of the upcoming elections. All of Orr's "victims" who had been asked to comment rushed to plant the explosives they would detonate the following day. They broke into Barak's office to inform him. Barak was stunned. He already saw himself in the prime minister's seat, and a hand grenade had been tossed that could ruin his plans. He couldn't believe what he heard. I got a phone call from Aliza Goren, his spokeswoman. She passed him the phone and after hearing what would be in the article, he said a weak "thank you" and hung up. She later said he looked as though the rug had been pulled out from under him. He covered his face with his hands and ordered her to get Ori Orr into his office.

Barak came into politics with a clean record. He was born on a kibbutz and spent most of his adult life in the army. He spent a long time learning about Israeli society first hand, and was genuinely anguished by the rift between *mizrahis* and Ashkenazis. When he entered political life he was determined to do what it took to defuse the relations between the Labor Party and the *mizrahi* population. He visited the peripheral settlements, went to the homes of the residents, ate with them, had his picture taken with them, whispered in their ears about changes in the world order. His one-on-one friendliness, treating them like equals, took down barriers and won him friends in places where Labor Party activists had never set foot. His impressive military record also helped. Who would oppose the most decorated soldier in the history of the IDF?

All that was in the background as he gave his speech asking for forgiveness. All the criticism of him notwithstanding, he believed that if the Labor Party took responsibility and bore the blame it might ease the pain of the *mizrahi* voters. Now Ori Orr had come along to end Barak's new romance with the weaker strata of Israeli society.

The day the interview was published a political earthquake shook Israel. Orr's comments were printed in large-point type not only on the front page but on the inside pages as well. There is nothing like Ashkenazi-*mizrahi* relations to ignite emotions in Israeli society. From the first, the arrival of immigrants from the Arab countries was a wound that refused to heal. Every time one side or the other was blamed there was a storm in the media. The Labor Party was convinced certain victory in the 1981 elections had been snatched by a comment by the late Dudu Topaz, a comedian who used an ethnic slur[16] to describe *mizrahi* Likud voters. A few days before the election he had performed stand-up comedy in Kings of Israel Square, later renamed Rabin Square, before hundreds of thousands of Labor supporters who cheered when they heard the description. The next day Prime Minister Menachem Begin appeared before hundreds of thousands of his own supporters, calling racism endemic to the Labor Movement.

The same thing was happening again. The country was a seething cauldron, with everyone talking about the Ori Orr interview. Israeli radio and TV changed their programming schedules and broadcast reactions from politicians and the man in the street. The Knesset, which was supposed to discuss disbanding, discussed instead what Orr had said as printed in Haaretz. The Knesset deliberations were broadcast live on both radio and TV. No matter where you turned there was no escape. One after another, Knesset members spoke, mourning the fate of the country and the way it treated the *mizrahis*.

Ehud Barak drove to the Knesset for what was supposed to be a happy day with the radio turned on. Every station reported the same story. During the day the telephone didn't stop ringing. Everyone expected him to step up as a leader and deal with the crisis. Orr related the story of that day in his book, *These Are My Brothers*, saying,

"Ehud still didn't realize what had happened...I went into his office and looked him in the eye and told him how the events had played out, starting with my conversation

---

16. He said chach-chach, a vicious ethnic slur with no real meaning, used to describe North African Jews and incorporating all the negative qualities ascribed to Moroccans. It is probably an unflattering imitation of the way Moroccans pronounce certain Hebrew consonants.

with Daniel Ben Simon. Ehud and I have known each other for years and I could tell by looking at him what he was thinking.

"Before noon political columnists, inspired by Knesset members from the Labor Party who opposed Ehud Barak, asked what Barak would do. They more or less agreed he had to force me to resign from the Knesset, otherwise their chances of winning the election would be seriously endangered... Ehud began to see the whole picture. His aides kept sending him messages. Aliza Goren kept updating him on the media frenzy, on all the Knesset members who claimed Ehud wasn't dealing with it, licking their chops and rubbing their hands in glee.

"Ehud listened to me and said, 'Ori, I have known you for years and I believe you. The problem now is this is a war more against me than you. You are a wonderful way for them to test me...' He talked and I watched his face and body language and I saw embarrassment and indecisiveness. He tried to gain time. Before I left I told him that this time I wasn't going to help him. I told him I had no intention of resigning from the Knesset because I hadn't done anything wrong except be too naive. 'I fell into a trap,' I said, 'and I am sorry to say I harmed you, but it can be fixed.' "

Prime Minister Benyamin Netanyahu, who was about to hold the vote to disband the Knesset, ran to his seat, incapable of hiding his satisfaction. Not far from him sat Barak, his face a mask of mourning, listening to the speakers. Why was this happening on his watch, he wondered, and shared that thought with others.

It was a day of mutual catharsis. Knesset members stepped to the podium and talked about their first days in Israel. One personal story after another. Even those upon whom fate had smiled remembered how hard their acclimatization had been. Sometimes it seemed like a parliamentary Yom Kippur, with Knesset members voicing their regrets, beating their breasts, atoning and demanding the country ask for forgiveness for everything it had done. Some were teary, some voices broke with emotion. It was a field day for members of Shass, who specialized in describing what they called Israel's "contemporary racism." They used Orr's comments to justify their political existence and their barricading themselves inside the *mizrahi* ghetto.

And then Netanyahu stepped up to the podium. A golden straw he could use to avert the crisis seemed to have fallen into his lap, and he clutched it with both hands. Initially he had made sure to disarm Ori Orr, telling him that he had no intention of using the issue in his speech. "Before I got out of the car the phone rang. It was Shai Bazak, Netanyahu's media advisor," wrote Orr. "He wanted to know if the article was true. Bibi and I admired each other, going back to the time his brother, Yoni, who was killed in Entebbe, transferred to the Seventh Armored Brigade under my command... Shai Bazak heard what I had to say. A few minutes later he called back and said the prime minister would try to keep the article out of his speech in the Knesset. I thanked him, but sadly, later on he called again and said that in light of the media and remarks from senior Labor Party members, Netanyahu had no choice but to relate to it. Especially today, when the Labor Party was going to propose a vote to hold early elections."

Netanyahu looked out over the Knesset. "I opened the paper this morning and what I saw made me very sad," he said theatrically. His obviously staged sad expression fooled no one. Knesset members jeered at him, booing and calling out insults, interrupting him and keeping him from speaking for a long time. He stood there, watching them with a little smile. He had not originally been on the agenda to speak.

He said: "I never imagined that after fifty years, after the ingathering of the exiles, after the assimilation of the immigrants, I would again hear those awful things that divide the nation, drive us apart, such arrogance, such alienation. No one is permitted to do that. Our existence depends on our ability to unite as a people...Israelis form a wonderful mosaic of ethnic groups. No one group is better than another. No one group is superior or inferior. We all belong to the same nation...On this sad day, Tisha B'Av,[17] the day that reminds us of the terrible price we have paid throughout our history for the unreasoning hatred directed against us, I want to appeal to the *mizrahis* in general and the Moroccans in particular. I want to tell you, in the name of the State of Israel and the people of Israel, that we are you and you are us. No one will send us fifty years back into the past.

"I heard Ehud Barak say that in the name of the generations of the Labor Party he asked the forgiveness of the people who came from North Africa. That's what you said, Barak. The arrogance and disconnect of the Labor Party have resurfaced. Ori Orr didn't invent them. Someone asked after the last elections who lost. All of us lost. That is the worldview of the Labor Party. Not of Ori Orr.

"You are the Israelis! Defense Minister Yitzhak Mordechai isn't an Israeli? Chief of Staff Shaul Mofaz isn't an Israeli? Avigdor Kahalani, a decorated hero, isn't an Israeli?[18] Where did he come from, Thailand? What are you? Who guards us in Lebanon? Who goes into

---

17. The ninth day of the Hebrew month of Av, a day of mourning which marks the anniversary of the destruction of the First and Second Temples.
18. Note: None of them is North African. Mordechai was born in Iraq, Mofaz in Iran, and Kahalani in Ness Ziona, a city in central Israel.

the elite units? Israelis from all over, from Morocco and not from Morocco...Disband the Knesset if you have the courage, but who will support you in the elections? You have already lost of the religious voters, you loathe the ultra-Orthodox, the Sephardic Jews aren't Israelis as far as you're concerned, and the Moroccans cannot tell the difference between good and evil. So who've you got let? Tel Aviv? You're going to get elected by rich neighborhoods and bohemians in Tel Aviv?"

Haim Ramon, one of Orr's colleagues, was chosen to respond for the party. He was considered a political phenomenon. He had climbed the ladder of the Labor Party but hadn't quite made it to the top. He was young and talented, a rebel at heart and considered by the old-time Labor Party members as a revolutionary who couldn't sit still. Many of them regarded him as an upstart and a street urchin, and others found it hard to follow his train of thought, thinking him slightly unbalanced. A few years earlier he had been elected chairman of the Histadrut, leading one of the most impressive political upsets Israel had known since its founding. The Labor Movement and the Histadrut had ruled Israel for seventy years with limitless power. And then in 1994 in one stroke of virtuosity, Haim Ramon had challenged the power of the old guard and been elected chairman.

Now he stood at the podium, finding it hard to believe that his bid for early elections had been intercepted and shot down by a member of his own faction. Of the anger and insult felt by the Labor Party, about 90% was his. For years he had been building bridges between the *mizrahi* Shass and the Labor Party, regarding Shass as a possible moderating influence on the disagreements between Left and Right. Standing there he was patently upset, watching his life's work disintegrate.

"There is racism hiding in every one of us," he began

emotionally, "no one is without it and everyone fights a daily battle against it. It used to be called 'a little Kahane'[19] inside each of us, and most of us, I hope, can control it... The prime minister's speech began well. He talked about Moroccans. Fine, I thought, maybe something changed, maybe this isn't the Bibi[20] we know. But his urge to drive wedges between us hasn't changed for a second.

"What did he say? That half of the country is racist? That all of us here today, we are all Ori Orr? Why? To save himself after losing the Knesset majority? Because you, each and every one of you, don't believe a word of what he says? I'm not going to repeat what you say to each other in the cafeteria...The prime minister said he was 'sad' this morning? Sad? He is dancing on the table..."

That morning I was on my way to research an article about Beit Shemesh. I had already arranged with Alex Levac, the prize-winning Haaretz photographer, to pick him up at his home in Jerusalem. I didn't think the article on Orr was particularly important and I planned a normal workday. I thought there might be some political repercussions, but nothing like what happened. A little noise, yes. But not an earthquake. As it turned out, everyone was looking for me. The telephone at home kept ringing. I didn't answer it. The radio stations were chasing me. There were photographers waiting in front of the house. At noon I got into my car and drove to my parents house, near Haifa, to get away from the commotion. When I arrived I found that reporters and cameramen were waiting for me and were engaged in a lively conversation with my mother.

---

19. Meir Kahane, born in America, a militant ultra-nationalist Orthodox rabbi, assassinated in New York in 1990.
20. Netanyahu's nickname.

I have always disliked personal journalism. I kept my distance from the articles I wrote. I didn't like articles that involved the author. The so-called "new journalism" had cut a very successful path through the Israeli media. Journalists wrote in the first person singular and described what they felt about the subjects of their articles. I didn't. While the interview with Ori Orr had been personal and dealt with Moroccans like me, I hadn't expressed an opinion in it. I believe in separating facts and commentary. Let the reader decide for himself.

I didn't look for scoops or run after exclusive stories. That was before the Internet revolution, and every day journalists hunted for exclusive stories that would put their names in front of the public. The main headline could always be replaced by an exclusive story, and there was a lot of competition for them. There were almost no limits or caveats. Getting an exclusive story was supremely important.

The media frenzy around Ori Orr put me in the spotlight. Everyone wanted to read the interview, and people besieged the Haaretz building in the hope of getting a copy as a souvenir. The day the article appeared the paper sold out.

Without intending to, I had let the sleeping genie of Ashkenazi-*mizrahi* relations out of the bottle. Open-mic radio shows couldn't answer the phone fast enough for people who had an opinion to share. Two camps faced one another: the *mizrahis* who protested the insult, and the Ashkenazis who understood the seriousness of the insult but did their best to minimize its importance. Orr was representing only himself, they said. Everyone was concerned lest what was known as the "ethnic genie" run amok through the country again.

And where was I in the midst of all this? How did I get into this ethnic maelstrom? I, who from the first day sought only to assimilate and blend in, found myself in the center of a wave of ethnic debate that threatened to drown me. Some critics said that because I was Moroccan I couldn't be objective, others said I had deliberately set a trap for a general who was an Israeli hero, others said all Moroccans had complexes and I was one of them. I was suspected of having an ulterior motive, that I had planned to sacrifice Orr on the altar of my inferiority complex. Even people who worked with me at the paper looked at me askance and wondered about my motives. A few days later Haaretz held an evening party at the American Colony hotel in Jerusalem. Holding a glass of wine I went to sit at the edge of the pool. I didn't know how to interpret the looks I was getting. Did my colleagues appreciate my journalistic achievement, or were they concerned it would harm the Israeli Left, which would now be considered racist?

Uzi Benzamin, the editor who had originally questioned my ability to write in Haaretz' Saturday supplement because I was too new to the country, walked over. "Tell me," he said, looking displeased, "I want to ask you something. Why did you find it necessary to interview Ori Orr? Was it your idea? His? Tell me, did he really say the things you wrote?" Wherever I went there were questions about my "real" motives. To say nothing of my veracity vs. the veracity of Knesset members. It was represented as so unlikely as to be scandalous, it was considered impossible that a man who had grown up in Israel, a military hero, possibly the next defense minister, could say such things "of his own volition." Perhaps I had pushed him, goaded him, maybe he wasn't concentrating, maybe he mistook my ethnic origins, maybe he thought I was an Ashkenazi, maybe he forgot I was a Moroccan. Otherwise, why would he commit political hara-kiri?

The affair put me on the side of those who had ceased to believe the country had good intentions towards the *mizrahis*. I found myself invited to meetings of *mizrahi* fringe groups tired of coexisting with Ashkenazis. How had this happened to me? I, who for most of my life had been accused of crossing the line and living harmoniously with Ashkenazis, was now at the center of an ethnic discourse that had nothing to do with me or my worldview. It was my second year of working for Haaretz, and according to rumors I was a fifth column. My "Ashkenazi friends" were disappointed because the affair had uncorked the ethnic-genie bottle. They had never expected someone who had paved the way to Ashkenazi-land to drop a bomb on those who had accepted him. Other journalists claimed I had a persecution complex that I hadn't gotten over the events of my absorption into the country. Worst of all was the fear that the interview would harm the chances of the Left, led by Ehud Barak, to regain power.

A few days later Etan Haber, a journalist and office manager for Prime Minister Yitzhak Rabin, wrote in the daily newspaper Yedioth Ahronoth that Ori Orr had to be warned. "Let there be no mistake," he wrote, "all the politicians who attacked him, Left and Right, in demagogic propaganda speeches, 'for the sake of Moroccans,' couldn't care less about them. Their happy or sad faces have one purpose and one purpose only: to get their votes. That is the only currency that exists in today's political market. If the Moroccans had only 5,000 votes, no politician would give them a second thought. But half a million…"

I hoped my fellow journalists, more than others, would see the journalistic value behind the insults of a man considered a living symbol of what it meant to be an Israeli. Instead of asking how and where he got his ideas about *mizrahis*, they were afraid to invade his conceptual territory, possibly identifying with him. Hundreds of letters were sent to Haaretz' editorial office, hand written and typed. Most of them weren't printed in the paper. The editors were concerned lest printing such overt support for what Orr had said would harm the paper's liberal-progressive image. Many readers were furious with Haaretz for printing such an "inferior" article. Others cancelled their subscriptions because they felt they had been humiliated. All of them supported Orr. The writers, most of them Ashkenazi, didn't understand what the fuss was about. They were especially sorry that he had suspended himself from the Knesset. I received hate mail from people who were long-time readers of Haaretz, who said they were ashamed that a "tabloid" had caused the fall of "an Israeli hero." "We were wrong about you," wrote an anonymous reader, "but I had the misfortune to discover that you are a Moroccan first and a journalist second."

I was torn. Never had my Moroccan background come to the fore as strongly as it did now. I felt caught in a vise that was crushing me. What was I supposed to do now? Haaretz symbolized the liberal-Ashkenazi-ism that was trying to preserve the remains of a deteriorating European outlook in the Middle East. For many, it was as if what Ori Orr said had exposed what the paper's editorial policy had been when the State of Israel was founded. Almost fifty years previously the paper's writers and editors had tried to stem the tide of immigration from North Africa. The difficulties involved in immigration had been immense. Israel was on the verge of complete bankruptcy. Massive immigration would solve one problem and cause another: it relieved the demographic anxiety of a Jewish minority in the Land of Israeli, but caused the demographic anxiety of the loss of a European majority and a change in the character of the Jewish state. One year after the establishment of the State of Israel Haaretz published a series of articles by Arieh Gelblum dealing with mass immigration. The article about immigration from North Africa was considered the most important and led to a storm of reactions inside Israel and abroad.

He described the North Africans as ..."a people who are the epitome of the primitive. When it comes to education they are almost completely ignorant, and worse still is their lack of ability to learn anything theoretical...They operate on primitive, feral instincts..." The article was in no way considered exceptional. It expressed what many people thought about the image of the young country. Three years later selective immigration was begun.

Chapter Eight
People Without a Future

"The page of the disgrace
of a father whom the great Return to Zion
commanded to jump, and he,
in his little circle,
ran, ran, and in his heart
a prayer to God Almighty,
to help him not to feel
the aching in his leg..."
Nathan Alterman,

"The run of the immigrant Danino," The Seventh Column, December 1955.

The Other Israel became the main arena for my writing, a place I routinely entered and exited. I was loyal to it all through the years I worked for Haaretz and returned every chance I got, like an persistent suitor.

People Without a Future

I was drawn to the settlements of the south as by a magnet, returning again and again to people and places the First Israel regarded as the country's garbage dump. I focused on the south, where there was a combination of ills, hardships, relative poverty and absolute, wretched poverty, desperation, despair, and a black future. It was the part of the country settled by new immigrants and more new immigrants, who kept coming and kept being sent to live next to immigrants who had only arrived the day before. A whirlpool of languages and cultures, a mosaic unique to Israel.

In most of my visits I couldn't hide my personal interest. I felt like an immigrant writing about other immigrants. The more I dealt with them the more I was reminded of my own first days in the country, to the point where I identified with their hardships. It was ironic and depressing that during all those years I hadn't shaken off the feeling of being Other. That is apparently the fate of anyone who moves to another country without being able to free himself from being from someplace else. The deeper I felt my roots going into Israel and the more I felt at home, the more memories of the past came flooding back to haunt me.

A foreign accent will always contain traces of the language previously spoken and expose one's other identity. And not just an accent. In Israel, where immigrants from so many countries live, every immigrant brings with him souvenirs of his previous life. Some aspire to rid themselves of it and others to perpetuate it. But none of them can ignore it. They migrants all live with nostalgia. Those who have good lives in the new country and those who had better lives in the old. Nostalgia is always at the side of the emigrant. That is what Svetlana Boym says in her book *The Future of Nostalgia*. Boym, a Jewish woman who emigrated from Russia to the United

States after she finished studying in Leningrad, followed the lives of her friends who had left the countries of their birth and found they possessed a certain disquietude that never left them. She herself often suffered pangs of nostalgia for her previous life in Russia despite the fact that her parents had already left the Soviet Union and a red carpet had been laid out for her in Boston. As an emigrant she was bothered by two questions: could a lost past be compensated for by nostalgia, and should it be?

My meeting with the residents of the development towns reawakened my sense of belonging to the world I had left behind. But something was different. I hadn't been aware of such striking differences within the Jewish community from which I had come. Everyone lived in neighborhoods close to or in the Jewish quarter, in both Meknes, the city of my birth, and Casablanca. We studied in the same educational frameworks, led the same kind of community life and saw our futures in a similar light. I met Moroccans again, this time as immigrants in Israel. Here I discovered that most of them had sunk to the bottom of the socio-economic pool. Most, if not all of them, were openly and deeply angry about the respect they had lost and their empty lives. They could not stop comparing their lives before and after immigration, and the real or imagined result of the comparison was always that their lives had been better in Morocco. Even if in reality, they hadn't really lived the *dolce vita in Morocco*, nostalgia provided them with rose-tinted glasses. Only someone who has never left something behind can feel nostalgia. Anyone who has finds himself hanging onto memories and dreams.

The worse the economic situation of the development towns became, and the more the residents felt humiliated, the more they saw their new lives through an ethnic prism. Whenever I met them they kept recalling the glory of their old world while bewailing their new lives. I found myself listening to endless complaints about injustice and discrimination and racism and hatred and sneers and slurs. What was I supposed to do with all that baggage? They kept asking me what I thought. I came to ask questions and found myself having to answer them. It happened all the time. How could I agree with them when my life had taken a completely different turn? How could I identity with them when it seemed to me that most doors had been courteously and generously opened before me. If they were right, I was the exception. If I wasn't the exception, then they were almost certainly wrong. What was the truth? Every visit was loaded with dilemmas and questions marks.

More than once I thought that in other circumstances I could have found myself in one of the same remote places they had landed. I could have been sent to some God-forsaken development town and eventually found work in a falafel stand in the town center. I couldn't stop tormenting myself, thinking about the power of blind fate. It is good to some and cruel to others. Was I just lucky? Had I made more of an effort? Had they made less of an effort? Did they lack the will to succeed? Had obstacles been placed in their path? Had they been the victims of discrimination? Those were some of the questions I kept asking myself. The residents of the development towns kept busy by looking for someone to blame. In most instances they came to the conclusion that they themselves were not at fault but rather the state. I met immigrants who had come to Israel the same year as I, who had gone to the same kind of school, who came from supportive families and still lived marginal lives in remote development towns which had not been kind to them.

Life in Israel had made us antagonists. I wrote for

Davar. They despised Davar because it symbolized the Labor establishment. I wrote for Haaretz. They despised Haaretz because it symbolized the elite Ashkenazi establishment. I was identified with leftist politicians. They despised the Left and everything it symbolized. I had run for a Knesset seat on the Labor Party ticket. They despised the Labor Party, or as they called it, the Ma'arakh. I considered myself secular and a little bit traditional. They recoiled from the secular life style. They had absorbed the Jewish tradition of Morocco with their mothers' milk and regarded Judaism as the anchor of the Jewish people's existence. As a graduate of the Alliance school network I considered myself the legitimate scion of Western culture. They considered Western culture a bastard son, and kept their distance. I saw Zionism as a historic effort to unite the Jews into a single international community. Many of them equated Zionism with Israeli patriotism. I regarded the world as a full partner in the fate of the State of Israel. They were suspicious of the world's motives towards Israel, regarding it as hostile and alienated.

It was obvious to one and all that my personal and professional abnormality could only have one explanation: my attempt to integrate into the dominant Ashkenazi culture had made me lose my mind and caused me to betray my Moroccan heritage. The choices I had made, after careful consideration, were suspected as having been mistakes made to rip out my roots and bring me closer to the Ashkenazis. Their hatred for the Left and the Ashkenazis and everything they stood for was so strong that sometimes I felt guilty for the choices I had made. Had I been mistaken? Were they right? Had I strayed from the path I should have taken? Maybe I had some kind of neurosis. Maybe I had fallen victim to a false view of reality.

I was being watched all the time by both Ashkenazis and *mizrahis*. Both sides examined what I said and what I wrote to see where I was in the salad bowl of Ashkenazi-*mizrahi* relations. I often wrote about poverty and hardship and their close connection to the *mizrahi* population. Nearly everything I wrote raised questions. Was I blaming them for their poverty? Had they been deliberately made marginal? Had they made enough of an effort to succeed? Had they or had they not sunk into a culture of helplessness which had dragged them down? In my articles and books I made an effort to understand the reasons behind the conditions of those ill-fated immigrant settlements. I was not in an easy situation. Often my articles were interpreted as attempting to appease the paper's owners and readers. It became so extreme I was publicly accused of writing through Ashkenazi eyes. An academic study was devoted to my articles, books and interviews about life in the periphery. The author, Dr. Yitzhak Dahan, concluded that I had betrayed my professional calling and *mizrahi* roots, doing a terrible injustice to an entire population which had already been cruelly treated by fate.

His indictment came as a surprise. In May 2003 the Institute for the Study of Zionism held a seminar at Beit Hatfutsot in Tel Aviv. Its title was "Haaretz – Portrait of a Newspaper." The audience numbered in the hundreds. Young researchers mounted the stage one after another to talk about the paper in the various epochs of the State of Israel. The two lectures that captured the interest of the audience were about Haaretz vs. the *mizrahis* and the paper's coverage of the periphery compared to its coverage of the center of the country. Almost all the members of the Shoken family, the paper's owners, were in the audience, sitting with employees. I had been asked to cover the event for the weekend supplement.

THE IMMIGRANT

I had no idea of what was about to happen. Shortly before noon a young man mounted the stage wearing a *kippah* and dressed in typical academic fashion. He told the audience he was going to speak about a certain journalist and how he covered the periphery for the paper. "I am of course talking about Daniel Ben Simon," said Yitzhak Dahan, and all eyes were turned on me.

From his tone of voice it was obvious he had nothing good to say. For an entire hour he revealed my "crimes" towards the residents of the development towns. He said that for seven years he had been following the articles I wrote about them. Following closely, he said, making it sound like a police stakeout, every word I had written and every word I had spoken. He accused me of betraying my journalistic duty because the world view I had adopted was divorced from the country of my birth. He also accused me of doing untold and infinite damage to those I had written about. He claimed I wrote about them from an angle that was too universal, too secular, too divorced from the *mizrahi* heritage and too alienated from the culture of the local residents. He claimed they had chosen to lead religious lives of their own free will. He claimed they had chosen to embrace the Shass party on their own, and not because of economic hardship. He claimed the wave of people turning to religion in the southern development towns and cities was the result of a genuine need to return to the roots of their Moroccan Judaism. He claimed their massive support in the polls for the Right-wing parties had nothing to do with the trauma of their immigration, but was rather the result of a clear-eyed view of the internal and regional political situation. He claimed that regarding all those existential issues, I had sinned against the *mizrahis*. He claimed I had examined their behavior according to Western-Ashkenazi standards and methods, divorced from their real existence. "The local lens the writer for Haaretz claims he has used to examine the development towns is in fact a universalistic lens," he said, reading from his study. "Haaretz does not interpret local events locally, it translates them into a language that sounds familiar to and is understood by the elite circles, Europeans, the economically comfortable, 'Israelis' and 'normal' people."

Dahan represented me as having betrayed my heritage and the heritage of my ancestors. Throughout the reading of the indictment he didn't look in my direction once. Before the lecture he seemed like just another face in the crowd. There was no way I could have known he had been stalking me for years and not sharing his "findings" with me. When he had finished a woman in the audience asked if he hadn't sinned against the writer. Dr. Dahan, true to himself, exploded a bombshell and "revealed" to the audience that I had been born in Morocco and not Europe, and that he expected me, as a Moroccan, to show more sensitivity and greater empathy and sympathy for the residents of the development towns. Instead, he claimed, I had adopted Haaretz' universalistic worldview, and had thereby sinned against myself, the residents of the periphery, and the calling of journalism.

For years I had found it hard to become reconciled to the sense of failure I found in the development towns. I found it hard to hide the anger that seeped into me at their failure, which I thought was the failure of the immigration from Morocco. Many of them were angry with the way I criticized them or the tone I used when I was interviewed on the radio or TV. They regarded my remarks as another blow to those who had been sentenced to live on the periphery.

Writing about victims gave birth to a journalistic dilemma. Was there a fair way to write about hardship without hurting the victims? Should I focus on failure or success? In Kiryat Malachi, a development town in the south that I wrote about extensively, I painted the absorption of the immigrants from Ethiopia in somber colors. I wanted to sound an alarm to alert the country's leadership to the drama of the Ethiopians: the suicides, the depression, the drug abuse, the drunkenness, the violence. All the signs of people whose lives had come to a dead end.

There were Ethiopians who were furious at what they called the "black" picture I had painted of their community. They had expected me to write about the officer in the elite IDF unit, the Air Force cadet learning to be a pilot and the students at the Technion, Israel's MIT. All of them were bright lights for the community, and whenever they returned to Kiryat Malachi they kindled local pride. How was I supposed to carry out my journalistic duty in such situations? To show the vast shadows or the points of light? In most instances I took the first alternative, because I viewed my calling as fighting injustice and showing the public what non-normative life was like. The immigrants from Ethiopia were furious. The elders accused me of libel and character assassination. "After what you wrote, who would want to live here?" an angry Motti Malka, Kiryat Malachi's mayor, asked me.

On one occasion I wrote about what veteran immigrants from Morocco thought about the new immigrants from Ethiopia. They were clearly racist. They accused the new immigrants of being unaesthetic, of throwing their garbage out of the window, of not knowing how to eat with knives and forks, of hitting their children, of being hundreds of years behind the times, of having lowered the quality of life and of having too many children, and claimed Israel had made a mistake by bringing them to the country.

People Without a Future

Publishing the article caused Kiryat Malachi's residents to accuse one another of racism. People involved in immigrant absorption accused the Moroccans of anti-Ethiopian racism of the same sort they had been victims of in the nineteen fifties at the hands of the establishment. On my next visit to the town I was accused of focusing on the negative aspects instead of the positive. I was accused of slandering the entire town. The dilemma of how to describe a situation plagues every journalist. To expose problems and try to fix them or ignore and whitewash them?

The Jews of Morocco were not all cut from the same cloth. Many of the Moroccans sent to the development towns in the south came from the Atlas Mountains. The Muslims in Morocco were very sorry when they learned the Jews had left. They loved the Jews and had given them jobs because of their economic resourcefulness and highly-developed commercial acumen. Today there is almost not one Moroccan who doesn't regret that the Jews left, leaving every city and town with a vacuum in its economy. Visiting Tinghir, a village of tens of thousands of residents in the southeastern part of the country at the foot of the High Atlas Mountains, wherever I turned I was met with a still-persistent longing for the Jews. Wherever I went I was asked about the Jews. At a coffee house where I joined patrons drinking from a never-emptying teapot, at the entrance to a restaurant where the heads of freshly-slaughtered sheep were hung, and in a souvenir shop, everyone asked about the Jews. The village was as it had been for years: little adobe cottages where Jews and Muslims lived side by side.

An old man told me that his Jewish neighbors used to share their Saturday meal with them, and actually, shared everything with them. They had lived that way for centuries, in the shadow of the Atlas Mountains, until one day all the Jews disappeared. Or more accurately, one night. It was awful, he said, to wake up the next morning and find that of the thousands of Jews who had lived in the village, only a few remained. Hundreds of families had been loaded onto trucks in the middle of the night and taken to the coast, where a ship was waiting for them. The crew spoke Arabic and French, and the ship was going to sail from the shores of Morocco to the shores of Europe. "We cried the whole day," he said, "we were dependent on them because they controlled our commercial life. We loved them like family. What hurt most was that they left without saying goodbye. They left their pots in the kitchen and the beds and they didn't even take the blankets. They left everything. They left and went there, to Israel. Inshallah, may Allah grant them good lives in their country. If you meet anyone from this village, tell them the people of Tinghir still miss them. A lot."

The old man led me by the hand to the village's commercial center. "You see that store?" he said, pointing. "It belonged to the Malka family. And that store over there to the Maluls, and that one to the Amars, and that one to the Abus." Then he took me to houses built into the living rock, reminiscent of the synagogues of days past, a memorial to the life of the community that had vanished. "Do you want to pray?" he asked me with a smile. I shook my head. "Don't be frightened, we can find a *minyan*[21] right now." He said *minyan* in Hebrew, a word he remembered from the distant past. He especially remembered the Sabbath and holiday prayers; the Jews prayed aloud and in chorus, and their singing could be heard throughout the streets of the village.

---

21. Ten Jewish men over the age of 13, necessary for public prayers.

The French occupation didn't reach the Jews of the Atlas Mountains. Those of us who lived in the cities called them "the ones who had been sent away," a euphemism for "primitive," because they hadn't clothed themselves in the glory of Europe and spoke only the Berber dialect. The French presence changed Morocco forever, bringing its language and a European lifestyle. But not to the Jews of the Atlas Mountains, who wore the local dress of long caftans and small tarbushes, while those who lived in the cities looked and behaved like every other Frenchman. We wore suits to school and spoke only French.

Most of the Jews of Morocco, before they immigrated to Israel, lived in the large French-influenced cities. Only about a third lived in the arid Atlas Mountain region. At school and in the streets we only rarely came across Jews from there. We studied in a school modeled on those in France and with the same curriculum, while the Jews from the Atlas Mountains sent their children to Talmud-Torah schools, which prepared them only for further religious studies.

An Israeli representative toured Casablanca in the winter of 1953 to establish a foothold for one of the pioneering youth movements. He wrote back to Israel describing the socio-economic division of the Jews in Morocco. He wrote, "When you talk about a city you have to know that it is in fact three cities: the European city, the *medina* [the Muslim city], and the Jewish *mellah*. When you talk about the Jews in a city, you divide them into two groups: the residents of the *mellah* and the residents of the European city. And you have to know that they have no contact with one another and that it is out of the question to bring them together in the same place. And there is more, because among the Jews there are actually three classes: the poorest, the middle class, and the wealthy, which views itself as the aristocracy...Thus in fact it is almost impossible to bring them together at all."[22]

The establishment of the State of Israel in 1948 created a kind of mystical fever that led to the immigration of many of the quarter of a million Jews living in Morocco. It was a mixture of Messianic hope and the desire to leave the materialistic hardship of their lives. After the first wave of immigration, the image of Moroccans as problematic began to form. Many of them had been brought from villages like Tinghir in the Atlas Mountains.

The new country of Israel, which hoped for young, modern reinforcements from Morocco, found itself with "natives" who looked like they had come from another century. From the minute they arrived they were met with hostility. Another Israeli representative, Ephraim Ben-Haim, divined the future when he wrote to his superiors in December 1948 that "There is discrimination today, blatant discrimination. It begins with North Africa... No one knows how to receive someone from North Africa, perhaps they are primitive or perhaps naive, but all they ask for is understanding and decent treatment, and instead they get Ashkenazi arrogance and a European sense of superiority. The problem is Israeli. Are there going to be two racial blocs here, or one people?"

The scars remain. Among the children who grew up in Israel there are those who refuse to remember the brief parting from their parents. Others still carry with them the repressed pain of leaving parents and relatives. Even the third generation born in Israel suffers from the original trauma, which to a great extent contributed to the formation of their ethnic identity.

---

22. From Yaron Tsur, The Torn Community, (Hebrew), Am Oved Publishers, Tel Aviv, 2001.

Strict medical and societal limitations were placed on Jews who wanted to immigrate from Morocco. Candidates had to present themselves for medical exams, and hanging over their heads was the threat that if they didn't come, or didn't behave well during the exam, they would be rejected. An Israeli doctor sent to Morocco wrote that at first glance he rejected those who looked "too fat or too thin, had crooked bones, mental impairment, white spots in the corners of their eyes, conjunctivitis or contagious skin infections."

Selective immigration was imposed in November 1951. The Jewish Agency devised a five-point policy sealing the fate of hundreds of thousands of Jews who wanted to return to Zion:

1. Eighty percent of the immigrants from [North African] countries were to be chosen from candidates for participation in the Youth Aliyah program, pioneers, core groups for founding settlements, professionals thirty-five years of age or younger and families where the breadwinner was thirty-five years of age or younger.

2. The candidates had to agree in writing to work in agriculture for two years.

3. Permission would be given only after a thorough medical examination performed by a doctor from Israel.

4. No more than 20% of the immigrants from [North African] countries could be older than thirty-five years of age.

5. Permission for immigrants of relatives in Israel would be given only based on a statement by the relatives that they were able to absorb the immigrants.[23]

The decision was confirmed by a government

---

23. From Dr. Avi Picard, Immigrants Drop by Drop, Israeli Policy on the Immigration of North African Jews, 1951-1956, (Hebrew, in press), Ben-Gurion University.

coordinating committee and became the official policy of the Israeli government. Overnight the "policy of return" became a political of emigration, in opposition to the central, founding concept of the State of Israel.

In the dilemma between rescuing the Jews and building the young state, more than once rescue was considered of secondary importance. Limited immigration was applied more to Jews from North Africa than from other groups. Giora Yoseftal, one of the authors of the decision to impose selection, claimed that before 1951 the Absorption Department believed the *Yishuv* could absorb a specific number of immigrants. "When did we say we had enough? With the last immigrants from Morocco and Tripoli in 1951... They were the *Lumpenproletariat*, people without a future," he said at a meeting of the Jewish Agency directors.

There is no lack of corroborating, if horrifying, evidence. For example, Alexander Ben-Nun, an educational worker, was asked to describe the prominent traits of what he called the "psyche of the Morocco child." He found three: primitiveness, brutality and an exaggerated sense of self-worth.

However, in reality, while the economic hardships in Israel influenced the decision to apply selection, there was also the annoying question that troubled the sleep of the heads of state: what would Israel's image become if the number of North Africans grew? During those years a great deal was invested in fashioning Israel's future international image. Hundreds of thousands of immigrants from Islamic countries had cast a giant shadow on the Israeli aspiration to establish a Western culture based on the values and ideology of the first pioneers.

The answer to that annoying question was to liberate the immigrants from the excess ethnic baggage they had accumulated in the countries of their birth. Academics soothed Ben-Gurion, telling him that the day was not far off when the second and third generations of immigrants would become legitimate sons of Israel and march to the drum of the culture and ideology of the country's European founders. "Once the generation that wandered in the wilderness for forty years is gone," they told him, "Israeli society will be free of the culture of the Levant."

Study after study, book after book proved the young country allowed itself – in the name of the supreme effort to found itself – to do anything it chose. It declared people null and void, worthless, it wiped away their identity with a wave of its hand, it humiliated the immigrants and mercilessly separated parents from their children. It is hard not to feel sorrow at the human price hundreds of thousands paid for wanting only to join their historical people in the Land of Israel. It was easier for the first Jews who came to build the country, their struggle and pioneering gave them haloes. Anyone who participated in establishing a kibbutz felt he had participated in founding the country. On the other hand, anyone who lived in a development town felt like a weak link in a chain of failures. They were always being compared to the members of the kibbutzim around them. While the sacrifice of the kibbutzniks and Sabras was praised, the residents of the development towns were scorned as parasites who never stopped complaining.

Perhaps the hasty immigration of the Moroccan Jews had not sufficiently prepared them for the ruling Zionist concept, that an individual is responsible for himself, his own life and his family. Israel received the new immigrants and provided for their basic needs, assuming they would work for the rest. It was a tragic clash between two world views, and many years, decades, were needed to bridge the gap. The immigrants' expectation that the country would step in, as they felt Morocco would have stepped in, ruined their reputation. Established Israelis regarded them as parasites, lazy, impatient, trying to squeeze everything they could out of the country and addicted to thinking they should have everything handed to them.

It was an unavoidable culture clash between European Zionism, which sought to fashion the New Jew who relied on himself, and the immigration from North Africa, which sought to preserve itself, its identity and its traditions. The dramatic changes taking place in the country were too rapid for the Moroccan immigrants to deal with. Life in Morocco moved slowly and the Moroccan outlook was fairly passive, the regime was considered the source of authority, while to a great extent life in Israel preached self-reliance without the intervention of the authorities.

In Morocco the Jewish community took up the slack. American Jewish organizations developed widespread support networks which began with providing meals for school children. Every morning, two hours after we arrived at the Talmud-Torah school in Meknes, we recessed for breakfast. We stood in a long line at the entrance to one of the storerooms where hundreds sacks of powdered milk were piled up, waiting our turn for a glass of milk. An employee would take a teaspoon of powdered milk, put it in cup and stir in hot water. We waited impatiently for our milk break every morning.

Maybe the Moroccans' original sin began when tens of thousands were herded into trucks and brought to the middle of the desert. They were expected to create new lives without proper economic resources, education or training. The development towns were established for them. Textile factories were built so they would have somewhere to work, as were other industries that required large work forces, most of which failed over the years. While the rest of the country moved forward, the residents of the development towns were treading water. When they tried to raise their standard of living they discovered the conditions were unsuitable. Again, they expected the state to come to their aid, and in fact, every government poured money into failing factories and increased welfare payments to needy families. Thus both sides won, or lost, depending on your point of view: the country kept the residents in the development towns quiet and the residents increased their dependence on handouts from the government.

I often found myself having to mediate between residents and the authorities. My connection with an influential newspaper looked as though it would open doors that would otherwise remain closed. After I finished gathering material for an article I would stay with the locals and listen to what they had to say. All of them complained of the poor quality of their children's education. They were particularly concerned that poverty and hardship would be perpetuated into the second and even third generations. They feared for their children's future. Their children, born in Israel, weren't meteorically successful. Many of them dropped out of school and others were shifted from academic programs to learning trades, to become auto mechanics and electricians. I used my journalistic visits to drop in on schools. I viewed the students and level of instruction they received as a barometer for the development town's future. If they had great dreams for the future now, that would certainly be reflected later on. In most cases I was disappointed. Many of them, when asked, said they wanted to stay in the town, despite its endemic hardships. They were afraid of the center of the country and the alienation of people living in big cities, yearning more for a familial atmosphere. In a town where everyone knew his neighbors, in many instances community intimacy was stronger than the desire to develop a career.

Whenever I went to the schools I was again struck by the students' strong sense of local patriotism. In the development towns I almost never had to find a house or street on my own. When I wanted an address I said the name of the person I was looking for and was given directions. Everyone knew everyone else. For better or for worse... Anyone looking for anonymity wasn't going to find it in a development town. Everyone knew everyone else's problems, celebrated their joys and mourned their losses. They called the crowding and familiarity "human warmth," and it was the alternative they preferred to life in the big city where no one knew his next-door neighbor.

"Pay close attention to what I am going to tell you, Ben Simon," said Barukh al-Makayis, who for many years was head of the Yeruham municipality. We were walking along the bank of the artificial lake he had had built at the entrance to the town as a tourist attraction. I had asked him about Yeruham's chronic problems, and he said, "If you are walking on a street in Tel Aviv and go into cardiac arrest and fall onto the pavement, let's say in one of the fancy neighborhoods, everyone will walk around you and no one will bother to wonder if you are alive or dead. If it happens in Yeruham, I can assure you that your funeral will be held the same day and thousands of people will come to the cemetery to pay their respects. Even if they didn't know you. Where else will you find something like that? That's the difference between Tel Aviv and Yeruham."

What he was talking about was the "human warmth" everyone praised, the great virtue of the peripheral development towns. Even if life didn't smile on you, you could always rely on finding a friend or neighbor who would help you with your pain or rescue you from loneliness. But once the "human warmth" had eased the existential Angst, there was always the exhausting, exasperating matter of education. Visiting classrooms, it was not hard to notice that the level of instruction was lower than in the center of the country. Even in the high schools, many of the students had difficulty reading, made spelling mistakes and couldn't use standard Hebrew diction. Their matriculation scores reflected the unhappy situation, and kept them from being accepted by the universities. Over all of them hovered a kind of marginality you could see on their faces, whether because of the level of their education or for some psychological reason. Eventually that marginality kept them from moving forward and leaving their hardships behind. They couldn't tell me what they wanted to be when they grew up. They had no burning desire for a profession. It was as if they didn't believe they could succeed at anything. In most cases they hoped their army service wouldn't be onerous, something that would enable them to learn a technical trade once they finished. The possibility of moving to one of the big cities in the center of the country terrified them.

Kiryat Malachi epitomized the hardships of the development towns. On one occasion I visited the high school, which is situated not far from the entrance to the city. Of the desperation and helplessness fate doled out to Israel's south, Kiryat Malachi got more than half. I came in the morning. The school opened at ten past eight. As soon as the bell rang hundreds of students pushed towards the staircase leading to the classrooms. A veritable tsunami of boys and girls aged twelve to eighteen shoved their way forward. Three floors and a few dozen stairs, but the assault was stunning. The pressure was terrible and there was a real possibility of accident. The younger students looked particularly unhappy, because the fight to climb up the narrow staircase wasn't meant for the weak. That was why they hung back and were the last to enter the school. It wasn't easy for the girls, either, they had to elbow their way in just like the boys.

Only one staircase, suitable, with difficulty, for an eight-unit apartment building. Every day 1,200 students pushed their way up, hoping to reach their classrooms in safety. There were only a few dozen stairs, but it took ten minutes for everyone to enter. The result was that most of the teachers had to start the lesson late. One of them told me that some of the students were out of breath when they reached class. "They get pushed on the stairs, so they push back," he said. "Sometimes there is violence and they hit each other. My students come into class virtually traumatized, huffing and puffing and sweating, and it is only eight in the morning."

Another teacher told me that starting class late made it difficult for him to teach and lowered the level of instruction. He needed more time to get the children settled and ready to concentrate. "It breaks my heart," he said. "You do your best to give them the chance they deserve. As it is, they don't come from the greatest homes in the world and they live in a city which is not exactly a paradise. You know that a good education is their only chance to better themselves. But when you see what those poor kids have to go through before they get to class, you understand why there is no chance of bridging the gap between them and the students in the center of the country."

The problem of the narrow staircase wasn't new. For years the ministry of education had been promising tens of thousands of shekels to widen it. But the ministry had run out of petty cash. New desks and chairs hadn't been bought in years. Some had cracks and some were simply broken. The classrooms were too small for forty students. In most cases, the first row of desks was about half a yard from the blackboard. The students unfortunate enough to sit in the front row had to tilt their heads back to see what was written on the board. In one twelfth grade class there was no room even for a desk for the teacher. "I don't have anywhere to teach from so I walk around the room for the entire lesson," he told me. "Sometimes, when I get tired I lean on the door so all the students can see me."

The school needed more than a couple of hundred thousand shekels to make like easier for 1,200 students and their teachers. The money was nowhere to be found. At that juncture exactly Benyamin Netanyahu, at the time minister of finance, decided to cut allowances for balancing the budgets in the development towns, and that included Kiryat Malachi. The allowances were a lifeline and enabled the development towns to make up for the property taxes they couldn't collect from indigent families. If more proof were needed of the hardship of Kiryat Malachi's residents, five soup kitchens had been opened not far from the school to feed the hungry. For the first time in years, not all the residents could afford to buy food. Nicole, a woman who operated one of the soup kitchens, told me that there were days when a hundred meals were served, and days when the number reached two hundred. After it while it became five hundred meals a day, because children joined the ranks of the hungry. To be able to continue feeding them, Nicole asked nearby military bases for the food the soldiers hadn't eaten.

It is unclear what the criteria were and what the policy was when most of the immigrants in the worst possible circumstances were sent to live in Kiryat Malachi. I could never understand why they had been concentrated there, in one of the poorest places in all of Israel. Every ethnic group had its own separate neighborhood to make sure they didn't intermingle. Next to the neighborhood of North African immigrants who had arrived in the nineteen fifties, a neighborhood was built for Romanian immigrants. Not far from there a neighborhood was built for immigrants who had fled the Soviet Union when it fell apart at the beginning of the nineteen nineties. After them came Bukharians and Georgians. And finally they brought thousands of Ethiopians from two great waves of immigration, Operation Moses and Operation Solomon.

Every wave of immigration was bitterly opposed to the previous wave and the immigrants were angry with and resented one another. The North Africans were afraid the Russians would rob them of the meager resources they had managed to accumulate over the years. The Russians were afraid the Bukharians and Georgians would get better conditions and it would come at their expense. All the immigrants, old and new, formed a united front against the immigrants from Ethiopia. Regardless of past conflicts, grievances, jealousies, fears and resentments, they joined hands to make sure the "black" immigrants from Ethiopia would never get a foothold in Kiryat Malachi. The old-time and not so old-time immigrants stormed the office of Moshe Shimon, the mayor of Kiryat Malachi, demanding he bar the entrance of Ethiopian immigrants. Having no choice, he surrendered to the rage of the locals and told Prime Minister Yitzhak Rabin not to send Ethiopians to Kiryat Malachi.

For the local residents, the arrival of the Ethiopians was a *casus belli*. They planned to fight to the death to keep them out. They were especially worried that the welfare department would exhaust its resources. If it supported thousands of immigrants from Ethiopia, where would it find money for others in need, those who had been here longer? It was a classic struggle of budget allotment. One set of unfortunates struggled against another set of unfortunates, fearing they wouldn't be able to feed their families. "It is clear to you, isn't is, that those Ethiopians will take our money," Avi Shitrit, one of the locals, explained to me. We were standing with one of his friends on the main street. The friend pointed his finger at the fresh immigrants who had taken over the public park at the entrance to the town. "It took our *mizrahi* parents four decades to assimilate into Israeli society," said Avi. "Just when they started raising their heads, they brought those immigrants in and pushed my parents back down."

The arrival of the first Ethiopian immigrants to Kiryat Malachi was traumatic, not to say tragic. They were brought in Operation Solomon, which came after Operation Moses. The entire world watched the drama unfold as Jews were clandestinely brought from Ethiopia by the Mossad in a heroic journey fraught with danger and unspeakable hardships. Only after they landed in Israel did it become evident that their trials had just begun. One Friday, not long before the Sabbath began, a minibus entered Kiryat Malachi bringing several families of immigrants who had landed only a few hours previously in Ben-Gurion International Airport. The leaders of the development town, who knew about what they called the "plot," were waiting for them. The immigrants stood on the sidewalk of the main street, helpless and not knowing where to turn. Mothers carried babies in white slings wrapped around their bodies. Some had one baby. Some had two. Some that three. The head of the local council, Shimon, accompanied by some council employees, told them to get back into the minibus and ordered the driver to let them out on the main road outside the town.

It was pitiful. Months of a painful, dangerous trek

to Israel hadn't prepared them for such a humiliating reception. The residents of Kiryat Malachi had no pangs of conscience. They were certain that their weak, narrow shoulders wouldn't be able to bear a new burden loaded upon them.

The authorities were informed of the Ethiopians' situation and rushed to Kiryat Malachi to convince the council head to take them in. They tried to bribe him, promising him practically anything, but he refused to budge. In the end Prime Minister Yitzhak Rabin had to intervene. Shimon sent him a letter demanding a complete and total end to the absorption of "Russian and Ethiopian" immigrants in Kiryat Malachi on the grounds that it couldn't bear more hardship, hardship piled on distress, distress piled on wretchedness.

We were sitting in his office, and he showed me the letter he had sent to Rabin. He read some of it out loud: "The employment situation is impossible and we cannot find work for those immigrants, and in any case their economic situation is getting worse...The immigrants tend to keep to themselves and that hampers their assimilation... I demand that an immediate stop be put to the harm done to the immigrants and to stop sending them to Kiryat Malachi."

As the years passed Kiryat Malachi's anger with the State of Israel only increased: Kiryat Malachi lacked the good education given to students in the center of the country; socio-economically weak immigrants were stacked up, one layer on top of another, and the town's economic capabilities collapsed under their weight; the local residents felt they weren't even being thrown scraps of the country's growing prosperity; even the third generation couldn't break out of the cycle of poverty; technologically advanced businesses were located elsewhere; they had to go to Beersheba or to the center of the country to get decent medical care; there were no places of entertainment – and perhaps worst of all, the feeling that in modern, progressive Israel, no one gave them a second thought, as though they belonged to a different people, a different country. They had the sense that there were two kinds of people living in Israel, both Jewish but different and disconnected. One was well-established, mostly Ashkenazi, settled in the opulent center of Israel, and the other poor, mostly *mizrahi*, sent to settle along the hostile borders. Time didn't heal the wounds, it only made them fester. Anger and rage were expressed in political terms every time elections were held. The anger built up, and people wanted revenge on the state and anyone who seemed to be oppressing them. During the past decades the leftist parties and their satellites were perceived as guilty of responsibility for their and their children's unhappy lot, especially because of what they viewed as alienation, discrimination and condescension.

There was a determined, unending struggle for the image of the state. Even after I left the world of journalism in 2008, I couldn't ignore it. Fascinated, I followed the outbreak of tribalism in Israel. The past three decades have witnessed the accelerating fall of statehood and its replacement with a society factionalized into tribes. It erupted in the elections of 1996 and has continued unabated.

In the 2015 elections a popular coalition emerged to challenge secular Zionism. The coalition was formed by *mizrahis*, traditional religious and ultra-Orthodox, lower-class immigrants, residents of the development towns and the underclasses of the periphery, all of whom felt alien and alienated from the mainstream Israeli experience, and were of the opinion that the gathering force of secularism was pushing them to the sidelines and threatening to destroy their spiritual and cultural worlds.

During my political life, as during my life in journalism, I was in the middle of the argument. The new Israelis rebelled, the old Israelis rose up against them, saying, "We also suffered when we came to the country, our parents were also sprayed with DDT, we also lived in sub-standard housing, we also had no money. How long can they drag out their resentment? Why don't they work? Why don't they invest in education instead of luxuries? Why aren't they ambitious the way we were? Who is insulting them? Why do they keep waiting for the state to help them? Why can't they shake off the culture they brought with them from Morocco? Why do they refuse to move forward?"

Several heads of development towns in both the north and south came to one of the Knesset financial committee meetings. They needed urgent financial aid for after-school activities. With tears in his eyes, Shimon Swissa, the mayor of Hatzor Haglilit, begged the committee for two million shekels to keep the community center in his town from being shuttered. He said that without the center's daily activities the children would have no social life, and would wander around the streets instead of attending enrichment programs. At that moment the unhappy history of Hatzor Haglilit flashed before my eyes. It had been founded in the nineteen fifties and had never succeeded in gaining an economic foothold. As if it were an illegitimate child they wanted to marry off, the town's leaders had looked around for a good financial match, something that would support the town and give it a decent standard of living. Joining forces with the flourishing town of Rosh Pina, a few minutes' walk away, looked like the natural choice. However, Rosh Pina's leaders barricaded themselves behind the claim that joining forces with the residents of Hatzor would weaken and obscure Rosh Pina's character as a bastion of the pioneering spirit. On one occasion I asked Yossi Alul, former head of the Hatzor local council, why Rosh Pina had refused. He smiled, perhaps out of embarrassment or perhaps because he simply accepted reality, and then taught me a lesson about the strained relations between settlements in the peripheral areas of the country. He said, "They simply didn't want us." Why, I asked.

He told me that one day he had gone to a meeting of the committee appointed by the ministry of the interior to discuss joining local regional councils. He told the committee that uniting Hatzor and Rosh Pina was a natural move that could save millions of shekels by merging the hundreds of functions which were the same in both places. He was told that Rosh Pina strongly objected. "Why don't we unite you with Safed?" suggested the committee. Alul couldn't believe it was a serious suggestion. Residents of Hatzor could walk to Rosh Pina in five minutes. Safed was a 25-minute drive away. "How can you suggest we unite with Safed, which is far away, when Rosh Pina is next door?"

At the time, Shimon Swissa ran the community center in Hatzor and I went to visit him. That was in 2004. Benyamin Netanyahu, minister of finance, had just finished a round of budget cuts so brutal the towns in the periphery collapsed like a house of cards. The community center, which was situated on the main street, was considered Hatzor's beating heart. It was the after-school home for hundreds of children and adolescents. The government budget cuts forced it to close.

Swissa stood in front of the building, helpless. "That's it," he said, "there is no more money and the center had to close. It's like a bus with the motor of a washing machine. And what happens now. The kids leave school and hang out in the street with nothing to do. Instead of activities in the community center, they sit on the railings and wait for time to pass. It hurts me."

As time passed the general distress was spiked by the economic distress of the repeated closures of Pri Hagalil, a fruit and vegetable canning plant that employed hundreds of residents from Hatzor and the surrounding area. Its frequent closures rocked the town. The factory was always in need of government help. Every time help was delayed, the owners threatened to close the factory. It was a chronicle of pain with a set scenario. The workers set fire to tires, the town went on strike, politicians rushed to Hatzor in a show of solidarity and to have their pictures taken with the demonstrators, the prime minister entered the picture, and *mirabile dictu*, or *visu*, the money was found to keep the factory alive a little longer, until the next (predictable) crisis.

Five years passed and Shimon Swissa, who is now mayor, continued explaining to the Knesset financial committee how critical the grant of two million shekels was (about $500,000). Representatives of the ministry of finance were invited to attend the meeting and listened as he and his friend Bouskila from Sderot begged for a small grant for cultural activities for the children of Sderot. Because of the budget cuts to grants for development towns there was nowhere to take the funding for the community centers. The committee chairman, ultra-Orthodox Knesset Member Moshe Gafni, prodded the ministry to authorize the grants. The ministry representatives said they were worried about going beyond budget restrictions. It would only have been a couple of million, but it could have destroyed a budget of more than 300 billion shekels...

During the deliberations Gafni and I were called way for a meeting of a different committee, the joint financial-security committee. There were four Knesset members and several high-ranking IDF officers in the room when we arrived. I was given a document relating to a demand for an unexpected increase in the army's budget. The bottom line was two billion shekels (at the time, give or take $500 million). Right-wing Knesset member Uri Ariel conditioned approval on the transfer of tens of millions of shekels to the settlements in Judea and Samaria. Gafni conditioned approval on the transfer of tens of millions of shekels to the ultra-Orthodox sector. Coalition chairman Ze'ev Elkin, from the Likud, said he saw no problem in transferring the funds. The IDF officers followed the short discussion calmly because the scenario was familiar. The army only got its money if the others got their palms greased.

Within minutes an additional two billion shekels had been authorized. The vote was taken, hands were raised, and the smiling officers rose from their seats. Within one hour I had learned to understand something more about Israel. It was the story of two clashing agendas, defense and society, both fighting for resources. That's how it was when the country was founded and nothing had changed, nothing has changed to this day. The battle always ends with the victory of the defense establishment and Orthodox over the needs of the development towns.

I returned to the meeting of the finance committee. The fight was still being waged over a couple of million shekels for community centers about to be closed in the peripheral development towns. The scenario repeated itself over and over. Representatives of the ministry of finance, who cowered and surrendered immediately to demands of the defense establishment, were now standing straight and tall and showing the beggars from the development towns how strong they were.

Chapter Nine
Infants Taken Captive

A few years before his death my father discovered and devoted himself to religion. As the years passed he found refuge on the benches in front of the synagogue, a few dozen yards from where the family lived. He never spoke to me about his suffering. He wasn't the sort of person who would expose his weaknesses. Sometimes, when I dropped by to visit, my mother would send me to the synagogue when I asked about him. He sat with friends from the neighborhood and they passed the time talking about the lives they had left in Morocco. They spoke about the past in French as though it were still the present.

He never suggested I go the synagogue or pray. People who had known him in Morocco were surprised by his devout observance, not expressed through prayer but rather by his constant presence in the synagogue.

He could barely say the prayers but he learned to follow the other worshippers. When they stood up, he stood up, when they sat down, he sat down. When they raised their voices, he raised his. When they mumbled, he mumbled. Sometimes someone standing next to him helped him find the right page. Sometimes I would ask him what he had learned from the portion of the Torah they had read that week, or something impressive the rabbi had said, and he always smiled, as if he knew what I was doing but wouldn't acknowledge it. Decades of having nothing to do with religion were an obstacle to his newly-found religious fervor. Regardless of how often I saw him with a *kippah* on his head, it never failed to amaze me. He had no years of habitual *kippah*-wearing to fall back on, so he slapped it on his head any-which-way. Sometimes it fell off and he didn't notice, sometimes he shoved it into his pocket, sometimes he forgot about it for days on end until the other men in the synagogue reminded him his head was bare.

In the early nineteen seventies, when the rest of my family immigrated, their new neighborhood looked just like the *mellah* in Morocco. When they came to the country they were sent to live in Kiryat Shmuel, one of the communities surrounding but not actually part of the city of Haifa, familiarly known as the "United Emirates of Haifa Bay." They rapidly discovered they were in good company. The four-story, tiny government-built apartment buildings were stuffed to bursting with immigrants from Morocco, most of them from Meknes and Casablanca. The entrance to the building was so low that some people had to bend over to keep from hitting their heads.

Now that the whole family was in Israel it was time to reforge family bonds. Three waves of immigration met under one roof for the first time. It was not an easy situation. How could we bridge the separation? My visits to my parents' home instantly transported me back to the Morocco I had left behind. My life between the two worlds deepened my sense of alienation. Suddenly my former life seemed so far away, such an anachronism, so different.

At home we spoke French. Here and there my mother spoke with her new neighbors in Moroccan Arabic. The first time I ate my mother's cooking again I was overcome with nostalgia. The government apartment my parents lived in was too small to hold the entire family. My brothers had to squeeze themselves, two or three into one room. During the holidays, when the entire family was home, it was even harder to find room for everyone. They slept in the living room, or on mattresses on the floor.

It was a pleasure to reacquaint myself with the religious tradition I had known in Morocco. Robert, Michel and Linda, who had immigrated to Israel before me, were sent, as I was, to religious boarding schools, but when they went home they reassumed their status of somewhere between religious and secular. *Kippah*, but only when strictly necessary. There was a pile of *kippot* on a sideboard in the living room, so whenever there was a blessing to be said or someone went to the synagogue, he took a *kippah* from the pile. That was religion as I remembered it from home, before we had been sent to religious boarding schools. On Saturday we prayed in the synagogue in Kiryat Shmuel, at lunch we ate the *defina* my mother had prepared on Friday, and in the afternoon we went for a walk on the beach. Since my parents had neither Arab neighbors nor a communal public oven in Haifa, the *defina* was cooked at home. Our neighbors did the same as we, prayers at the synagogue on Saturday morning and a walk along the beach after lunch. We did what we had done in Morocco, a combination of prayer and having fun at the beach, as though they had been created for each other. Parents and children sat on the beach, drank coffee and smoked cigarettes. Even those who kept the Sabbath down to the last *mitzvah* went to the beach with their families. They sat on the sand, their best Saturday clothes notwithstanding. Some of them wore their *kippot*. That was how I remembered Saturday in Morocco. The religious and secular didn't alienate themselves from one another.

As the years passed that long-standing tolerance and moderate approach came under existential attack from *mizrahis* from North Africa who had become Orthodox and from the Shass movement. Rabbi Massas, one of the great Moroccan rabbis, was asked by one of his congregation whether or not it was permitted to go to the public swimming pool on Saturday. The rabbi offered the following compromise: if you remain for the entire Saturday prayer and listen to the sermon afterwards, you can go to the swimming pool. Thus he ensured that the Jews would come to the synagogue and stay for the prayer, the price they paid for going to the pool afterwards.

In the early nineteen seventies, when my parents came to Israel, religious differences weren't as prominent as they are today. Religious and secular people lived in the same neighborhoods and respected each other's way of life. The Jews who came to Kiryat Shmuel from North Africa had been preceded by *kippah*-wearing Jews from Eastern Europe, who had immigrated in the nineteen fifties and even earlier. They lived in detached houses. The new immigrants lived in blocks of apartment houses. They lived in peace together and no one thought to limit anyone else's freedom of movement. In every Knesset election the National Religious Party, which represented the moderate Judaism the Moroccans were familiar with, won most of the neighborhood votes. Dr. Yosef Burg, who headed the party, was considered a hero by the traditional Moroccans. My father admired him. He waited eagerly for Independence Day to be able to watch TV and see Dr. Burg lead the panel of judges for the World Bible Quiz. Especially when he spoke fluent French with the contestant representing the Jews of France. Hearing French spoken at such an important national event filled my father with joy. I think Dr. Burg was responsible for several of the few moments of happiness my father had in Israel.

The synagogue of the immigrants from North Africa was built next to the synagogue of the Ashkenazis, and the spirit of religious tolerance served the Jewish tradition I had grown up with. During my first years in Israel I didn't perceive religious fanaticism among the Jews from Morocco. I became aware of it only in the early nineteen eighties, with the Orthodox revolution which erupted among the *mizrahis* like fire and brimstone from a volcano. Was it always simmering beneath the surface, even before they came to Israel, or was it born out of what they found here?

A few days after the 1984 Knesset elections I was assigned my first task as a journalist in Israel. For the first time there was a new player on the political field, a *mizrahi* religious party. Until 1984 the *mizrahis* has been assimilated into the world of the Ashkenazi Orthodox Jews, or if not assimilated, hidden. There were many journalists crowding in the Rehavia neighborhood of Jerusalem to cover the first meeting of the heads of the Labor Party and the founder of the new *mizrahi* movement, Rabbi Ovadia Yosef, which had just won four Knesset seats

The Labor Party leaders, Shimon Peres and Yitzhak

Rabin, climbed the steps to Rabbi Ovadia's little apartment to ask for his support in forming the new coalition government. The two big parties, Labor and Likud, had tied, and both were actively courting the small satellite parties. Shass, in its first political appearance, was wooed with unprecedented fervor in the hope of gaining its support. The home of Rabbi Yosef became a Mecca for pilgrimages by the heads of the political parties.

I was standing next to Rabin. Before he mounted the stairs he asked his aides about the rabbi. Apparently he didn't have the slightest idea who he was. Within a few minutes he received a quick review of *mizrahi* politics and where Shass was on the Orthodox Jewish palette. His aides told him about the schism that occurred in Orthodox Jewry when the *mizrahis* decided to take revenge on the Ashkenazi for what they felt were years of racism and discrimination by running for the Knesset on an independent ticket. Peres, who was standing next to Rabin, didn't seem particularly interested. He had already tacked a *kippah* onto his head and was standing next to the door. One of the aides extended a black satin *kippah* to Rabin, who asked, "What's this for?" He was told, "You have to respect the rabbi. He is a great Torah scholar."

The walls of the rabbi's living room were covered with bookshelves holding thousands of volumes. The seated Rabbi Ovadia, who was wearing an embroidered black robe and a hat, did not stand to receive his visitors. Peres and Rabin came forward and shook his hand. Peres bent over and I thought he was going to kiss Ovadia's hand. I was nonplussed. Doesn't a host always rise to greet his guests? In front of him were a former prime minister and a future prime minister. As the years passed he continued to sit, his way of deliberately showing political leaders where they stood in his eyes. The more political clout Ovadia Yosef amassed, the less respect he showed for those who visited his house.

He was surrounded by yeshiva students, some of them wearing black hats. I recognized one of them: he had been a neighbor in Meknes and came to visit my parents all the time. He was a smart-aleck kid who went to the same Talmud-Torah all the Jewish children in Meknes attended. He and his family immigrated to Israel at the end of the nineteen sixties and I hadn't seen him since. Was this bearded man with his large black *kippah* really Ariyeh Deri, my former neighbor? Was the kid with the big mouth, who looked like every other child in the neighborhood, the same Ariyeh Deri from Meknes? As far as I could recall, his family was like every other. They were traditional. The father went around bare-headed, like everyone else. Ariyeh himself went to a traditional school where secular and religious subjects were taught. The Deri family that lived in our neighborhood had never shown any signs of Orthodoxy.

Given the number of times he whispered into Rabbi Ovadia's ear, it was obvious that Deri's status was greater than that of the other young men in the room. I had missed the birth of Shass because I had been studying in the United States at the time. Shass surprised me. Jewish fanaticism, which perpetuated insulation and alienation from the rest of the world, didn't seem to me as something that could strike roots in *mizrahi* Judaism. There could be no such thing as *mizrahi* fanatics, I thought. I had returned to Israel from the United States at the beginning of the movement, yet it seemed to me that the Ashkenazi ultra-Orthodoxy had been imitated to perfection. The *mizrahis* wore the same black hats over the same black *kippot*, the same black suits, and grew the same beards. Some of them had curled sidelocks behind their ears. I thought, what a change! What connection was there between *mizrahi* Judaism and ultra-Orthodox fanaticism? Where had the hundreds of years of tradition disappeared to? What happened to the religious tolerance and acceptance, which regarded everyone, believers and non-believers, as legitimate members of the Jewish faith?

What a glorious failure, I thought. As a person coming from Morocco I regarded the success of the Shass movement as a distortion of history. As a secular Israeli, I was extremely worried by the movement's growth, especially because its leaders were busy trying to recruit young *mizrahis*. The movement that had emblazoned on its shield the rehabilitation of the *mizrahi* tradition had become a movement of mass religious recruitment.

I thought about the ultra-Orthodox Ashkenazi rabbis I had seen in my childhood. They wore black and had long beards and walked through the Jewish neighborhoods of Meknes. They visited the synagogues and schools to lure Jews to their yeshivas in Europe and the United States. After the Holocaust there was an urgent need for new students to replenish the ranks of Torah scholars who had been killed. Morocco seemed to the Hassidic movements like a good place to find and recruit new young scholars. I remember a fanatic, insular rabbi named Ze'ev Heilprin who walked around my neighborhood in Meknes as though he had been born there, although in fact he had been born in Lithuania and had previously lived in Jerusalem. He tried to teach his students from Morocco a new method of studying the Torah. While students in other yeshivas studied for the sake of learning, in his yeshiva they studied for the sake of studying. Even in Meknes there was a dispute between him and Rabbi Massas over the issue of Jewish work on the Sabbath. Rabbi Heilprin claimed anyone who worked on the Sabbath should be ostracized for having defiled its sanctity. Rabbi Massas suggested that a special *minyan* be organized for them so that they could also pray on the Sabbath. He said that expelling them from the Jewish community would distance them and their children, while openness would bring them closer to Jewish tradition.

I followed Shass during the early nineteen eighties, at the beginning of my journalistic career. One day I covered a mass Shass event held in Saker Park in Jerusalem. Tens of thousands of people, obviously enjoying themselves, had crowded into the park. With its rising political power, Shass had achieved a new status, more glittering. During Shass' early days the party members had found it difficult to support their families. I used to see them in the stores in the Jerusalem neighborhoods of Shmuel HaNavi and Sanhedria, two of their strongholds. During the day they searched for bargain prices and basic, cheap foodstuffs, and in the evening listened to the rabbis preaching the return to religion, especially Rabbi Reuven Elbaz. A few years passed and Shass activists discovered that politics was a cornucopia. They had six or eight or ten Knesset seats of their very own, without having to share the loot with the ultra-Orthodox Ashkenazi.

The day of the Saker Park event the rabbis waited for the arrival of Ovadia Yosef, whom they called the "crown upon our heads," and the comet who was always right next to him, Arieh Deri. The rabbis wore expensive suits and fashionable ties, carefully-trimmed beards and expressions of extreme smugness. Many of them were important or well-connected figures who had managed to find their way to the stage, where Arieh Deri's father and brothers sat with Rabbi Ovadia's sons and the people close to him. As time passed a hierarchy was established within Shass, most of it determined by unashamed, untamed, unrestrained nepotism. The relatives of the senior figures rose to the top by virtue of their connections with founding families. At the beginning men and women mingled and sat together at party functions, but as the years passed Ashkenazi ultra-Orthodoxy managed to recreate Shass in its own image. Except for speaking Yiddish, the ultra-Orthodox *mizrahis* adopted almost all of the outward hallmarks of those they accused of racism and discrimination.

In other words, Shass had brought an identity crisis to *mizrahi* Judaism, robbing it of its moderate religious approach and tolerance and replacing them with religious fanaticism. Knitted *kippot* were replaced with black satin and velvet ones. Young *mizrahis* left the national religious education system and attended Shass yeshivas. The open, politically congenial neighborhood where my parents lived was swept away in a Shass-ist flood. Voters who traditionally supported the Hapoel Hamizrahi religious Zionist party deserted it for the ultra-Orthodox parties. At the synagogue where my father prayed, women were asked not to linger in the open space leading to the prayer hall, lest they distract the male worshippers.

As the years passed I saw the same change in the development towns. I asked Avi Lazimi, a friend who was the principal of an elementary school in Migdal HaEmek, what it was like for the Jews in Morocco. He had come to Israel with his family in 1963, when he was eleven years old. The family was sent to live in Nazareth Illit, which had just been founded. "I remember our life in Casablanca like yesterday," he told me. "Like most of the Jews in the city we were considered traditional. We had a saying in Arabic, 'a little bit goes to God and a little bit goes to His servant.' We had a religious tolerance that is completely lacking in Israel. They killed it here, and made sure it stayed dead. I don't remember anything concerning religious belief ever being forced on us. On Saturday morning we went to the synagogue and after lunch we went either to the beach or to the movies. We lived in both worlds with perfect harmony. I call myself secular, but like all the Moroccan Jews I respect faith, fate and miracles. To this day my wife won't light a fire on Saturday. If someone comes to visit us on Saturday and wants a cigarette, she asks him to light it outside but she won't tell him not to smoke. I don't remember black robes and not even beards. Even in Israel it wasn't like that. We were new immigrants and went to live in Nazareth Illit. The community leaders were public representatives. They wore fancy suits and most of them didn't have beards. They were community leaders and taught in the schools. None of them went around with a black ultra-Orthodox robe or a hat. They represented the Moroccan Jews of that time. I am sorry to say that today Nazareth Illit is unrecognizable, so is Migdal HaEmek, where I live now. Religious tolerance and moderation are dead and the *mizrahi* rabbis have divorced themselves from their Moroccan past for the sake of Ashkenazi fanaticism."

In the nineteen nineties the *mizrahi* turn towards ultra-Orthodoxy peaked to the point where in the 1999 elections Shass won seventeen seats. The public opinion polls were against them, but Shass was about to effect an unprecedented electoral revolution. The commentators relied on Arieh Deri's criminal conviction and subsequent imprisonment to predict the imminent demise of the party. Even Haaretz, the paper I worked for, printed a headline like the Chicago Daily Tribune's "Dewey Defeats Truman." "Requiem for Shass," screamed the headline, prophesying that in less than two months, when the elections were held, Shass would be much weaker.

The day after the court handed down its verdict in March 1999 I visited the development towns in the south to write an article about Deri's conviction. I discovered that the requiem would be held for the justice system, which was considered as having convicted him because he was Moroccan. In Kiryat Gat, Kiryat Malachi and Sderot everyone was certain that the only purpose of the trial had been to diminish the standing of the *mizrahis*. There could be, they were absolutely certain, no other explanation. The trial and conviction were an Ashkenazi plot to regain political power. I spoke with dozens of people, and dozens more gathered around to voice their opinions. On the one hand I was Ben Simon the Moroccan, one of them, but on the other I was Ben Simon who worked for Haaretz, the newspaper of the enemy. That duality, enforced on me without my request or consent, meant I again had to decide which side I was on. I came to take notes for an article and found myself a defendant in a kangaroo court. They wanted to know what I thought about the conviction. I knew exactly what they thought and I was concerned that if I voiced my opinion, I would be considered the Moroccan who had betrayed ethnic solidarity. Kiryat Gat voted for Shass. Anyone who in the past had voted for a different party promised to vote for Shass this time. Because of the trial, of course. It channeled all the complaints of all the immigrants from Morocco into one conviction of one politician, who compared himself to Alfred Dreyfus.

"Tell me the truth!" demanded the watchmaker, who had a store in the commercial center of Kiryat Gat. I used to visit him every time I came to town. He wrote poems and liked to read them to me. He had always loved poetry, he told me, and hoped one day to find a newspaper that would print one of his poems. It never happened. He sent them in by mail, but he hoped in vain. The distance from there to the conclusion that the media were anti-*mizrahi* was short. Deri's trial had come at the right moment to inflame his log-standing sense of being a victim of discrimination. "And all I'm asking for is the truth," he said somewhat more loudly. "Was it a fair trial or were the charges made up?"

I knew that what I said would determine my fate in Kiryat Gat for the rest of my life. I looked at him and delayed answering. "I want the honest truth," he yelled, "don't you see what they did to us in Israel? Don't you see where they sent us? Don't you see how much racism there is against us? Look around, do you see something worthwhile for a *mizrahi* to live for? The truth, Mr. Ben Simon. We love you because you are a Moroccan, one of our own. But don't be naive. The Deri trial put all Moroccans on trial. They hate him because he is a *mizrahi*. They say we ruined their country. What can you do? I'll tell you what we're going to do. We'll go with Shass. But not because we're religious. I am completely secular. I barely pray on Saturday. But they hate us, so we are all Shass. Explain that to your Ashkenazi newspaper. So I'm asking you, the honest truth, weren't the charges against him made up?"

At other such gatherings a polite effort was made to differentiate between me and the paper. Maybe they wanted to spare me, maybe it was done out of ethnic solidarity. In any event, the watchmaker was still waiting for my answer. I didn't get the impression he was going to stop waiting any time soon. There were dozens of people in the coffee house next door, all waiting tensely to see what I would say. Unfortunately, my tongue had become paralyzed.

The day before I had gone to the Jerusalem district courthouse to cover Deri's sentencing. There I happened to meet Yitzhak Cohen, a Shass Knesset member. He looked upset. He was upset. He hadn't slept all night. He linked his arm through mine as though we were cousins and we walked through the ground floor of the courthouse. Shass Knesset members always treated me like one of the family. Whenever I met them in the Knesset corridors they kissed me on both cheeks. My colleagues in journalism, who sat around the tables of the Knesset cafeteria, found it difficult to understand such familiarity. "What are you, related?" they always asked me. They saw me as one of their own, but the Shass Knesset members also saw me as one of their own because I came from Morocco.

I will never forget them the love they showed me when I was elected to the Knesset. The day I was sworn in I walked around the Knesset as though I were the guest of honor at a party, waiting for the moment the ceremony would begin. Hundreds of guests, most of them relatives of the new Knesset members, filled the place to bursting. Everyone congratulated everyone else, kissing and embracing and shaking hands. Some winked at one another. Shass representatives whom I knew as a journalist fell upon me and showered me with emotion as if I were a long-lost son. The depth, width and breadth of the ideological differences between us was something I had never bothered to hide. Nevertheless, their chosen representatives never forgot for a second that I was a *mizrahi* like them. They took every opportunity to remind me that everything else notwithstanding, I was still '*dialna*', "one of ours" in Moroccan Arabic.

"As I am sure you know, they brought us to Israel to be hewers of wood and drawers of water," Cohen explained to me, his armed crossed. "Not only us, you and your family, too. They brought us to Israel because they had no choice. The turning point came for us when Rabbi

Ovadia and Ariyeh Deri brought us out of the slavery into freedom. Ariyeh's alleged crime was that he challenged the Ashkenazi oligarchy, so they decided to finish him off. What is on trial here is the *mizrahi* revolution, nothing less. If he falls, we all fall. You too. I promise you, no one will help you."

And not just Yitzhak Cohen. All the Shassniks said founding the movement had liberated the *mizrahis* from the shackles of the Ashkenazi establishment. They regarded Shass as an anchor of salvation after years of oppression and discrimination. Months before the sentencing Yitzhak gave me another angle from which to view Shass. It was after I had written an article for Haaretz criticizing the movement. "There is no difference between me and you," he said with a smile. "The greatness of the *mizrahis* is that we are mid-stream people. We came to Israel with many different lifestyles and we have an openness the Ashkenazis don't have. Take me, for example. On the Sabbath eve or on holiday eves I sit with relatives who come from all kinds of backgrounds. In the first place, all of them served in the army. So did I, of course, and so did all my children. At family events my sister's son sits next to me, he is a helicopter pilot and completely secular. My niece is secular and is a clinical psychologist, and I have other relatives who represent the entire spectrum of Israeli pluralism. Some are secular and some are religious. Some have right-wing opinions and some have left-wing opinions. In *mizrahi* Jewish culture we don't exclude people or disqualify them the way Ashkenazi Judaism does. We don't force our ideas on people the way they do. Our party was founded because of blatant, intolerable discrimination. We brought with us to Israel a tradition of tolerance, acceptance and respect. To a great degree we were forced to become ultra-Orthodox, because we were prevented from living lives of self-respect."

The watchmaker was losing patience. I plucked up my courage and mumbled that Deri had been convicted by a district judge of *mizrahi* heritage, and that the verdict left no doubt as to the fact that Deri was a politician who had taken bribes and received other benefits. The harder I tried to strengthen my argument, the less interested people became in what I had to say. Obviously, they had been expecting, or hoping, for me to say something else. They were certain my answer was based on fear of what the Ashkenazi media would say about me. They were doubly certain I had sold my soul to the Devil to remain in the clique of journalists. They were even surer I was lying, and their unavoidable conclusion was that I was sinning against my Moroccan heritage.

They identified with Shass and were going to vote for it, but none of them called himself ultra-Orthodox or even religious. "Traditional" was how they viewed themselves. As followers of the Jewish tradition they had brought with them from their countries of origin. None of them called himself secular, and when asked about secularism, they immediately recoiled because to them it meant disrespecting traditional values. They also did not consider themselves religious. They were going to vote Shass because they identified with the injustice they felt had been done to Ariyeh Deri. They identified with his being a *mizrahi*, not with his being religious.

Even after four decades in Israel I found it hard to find an exact way to describe how I related to religion. I was not religious and I was not secular. My life in Morocco, where it had never been necessary to define myself as anything but a Moroccan Jew, had fashioned my worldview. They more Israeli I became, the more I felt that Israel's greatest tragedy was not allowing more space for the hundreds of thousands of North African

Jews to maneuver. The model of Jewish identity, already split in Europe between those who tended towards secularism and those who continued the Orthodox Jewish tradition, was unsuited to the Jews from North Africa. The strict, intransigent division between religious and non-religious was foreign to their experience. The struggle between the founders of the country, who aspired to Israeli-universalist values, and the Jews who wanted Jewish values along the lines of "the nation shall dwell alone, and not be reckoned among the nations" [Numbers, 23:9], was not something the North African Jews wanted. Hundreds of years of coexistence with Muslims had taught them a different lesson.

The tragedy visited upon them when they came to Israel was that they became hostages in the cultural war waged in the first days of the state between those who supported secularism and those who supported religiosity. The immigrants from Morocco and other Arab states witnessed the struggle as it was played out in front of their eyes in the *ma'abarot*. Young students, who had just landed in their new country, saw secular teachers shove religious teachers from classrooms and religious teachers pester secular teachers. Even at the beginning, the state divided education into categories, but the Moroccan children didn't really belong to any category. They had studied at Alliance schools, which provided a wide range of secular subjects as well as Torah and languages. The Alliance school network had been founded in 1860 to get Jewish children out of the *cheder* where only Hebrew and religious subjects were taught, and to turn them into modern Jews with the skills to integrate into the new world.

Apparently, the war for the identity of the new state was even stronger than security worries at the time. Religious groups broke into the *ma'abarot* and immigrant camps and distributed printed propaganda against the Mapai government's "unified education" – which also didn't watch from the sidelines. There were instances of violence and hooliganism. They barely spoke Hebrew, but they were already fighting over the image of the new immigrants. Would they be Jewish or Israeli? Would they be New Jews or Old Jews? One of the flysheets distributed by religious groups to new immigrants read as follows: "The rabble-rousers and the instigators who with their Satanic plots and evil intentions are planning to seduce you away from G-d in heaven and want to seduce your pure, innocent children and teach them to violate the Sabbath, eat non-kosher food, not to lay *tefilin* and not wear prayer shawls."

Hatsofeh, the newspaper of the Hapoel Hamizrahi, reported on "hunting for souls in the immigrant camps" and "kidnapping souls in the immigrant camps." The government was preoccupied with the issue of educating the younger generation of new immigrants and even Prime Minister David Ben-Gurion intervened in the controversy, which threatened the continued existence of the first government. "It has been brought to my attention that the stories of rape and the forced cutting of sidelocks have no basis in fact," he wrote to several rabbis, "and there is no foundation for the accusations that anyone wants to choke religious education in the camps or anywhere else."

If I hadn't stayed in the Religious Youth Village, it is almost certain I would have been sent to a secular boarding school, where there would have been no reference to religion or tradition. Or in other words, Israel fashioned a public space with two poles: blind faith in and adherence to religion on the one hand, and blind rejection and abhorrence of religion on the other. And I, almost like all the other Jews from North

Africa, was adrift in the middle. How does one live in a country which refuses to accept compromise as a way of life? The immigrants from North Africa did not have the strength to renew their tradition. A country that cried out for the creation of a moderate Judaism, equal for all, failed miserably and was left helpless in the face of ultra-Orthodox fanaticism and secular fanaticism. The end was unconditional surrender, and many immigrants found a haven in ultra-Orthodox Ashkenazi Judaism.

My friend Dr. Yigal Ben Nun, who studies Moroccan Jewry, told me that unlike me, who had been sent to a religious school, he had chosen a completely secular life as soon as he arrived. In Morocco he had graduated from the Lycée Lyautey, a secular high school named after Morocco's first French governor, General Louis Lyautey. The school was French and attended by Jews, Muslims and Christians as the most natural thing in the world. "There was no religious-secular separation between us," he told me. "We were all the same. I had Jewish friends who smoked on Saturday and Jewish friends who didn't. There was no problem. Everyone lived the way he wanted to. We were all traditional and we all went to the synagogue on Saturdays and holidays. That was the beginning and end of our Jewish tradition. I don't remember a single instance of religious coercion. Everyone lived according to what seemed best to him. The rabbis were part of that openness and even encouraged it. It was only in Israel that I discovered religious coercion. Unhappily, Shass' move towards ultra-Orthodoxy was manufactured completely in Israel, it had no roots in Morocco."

That was why it was particularly jarring that we had lost the religious tolerance of North Africa. Combining religion with politics brought it even lower. Even as a boy at the Religious Youth Village I felt they were strongly connected. Most of the visitors who came to speak to the students belonged to the Hapoel Hamizrahi movement and they all came for the express purpose of strengthening our faith in the party. Even religious youth villages were turned into party branches. So it is not surprising that when the settlement project in Judea and Samaria began to form, representatives came to speak to us about the *mitzvah* of settling the Land of Israel.

When I left the boarding school I took off my *kippah* and entered the secular world. There was nowhere else for me to turn. Those were the only two options open to me. But I rediscovered the religious tolerance of Morocco in France, of all places.

When the second intifada broke out in 2000 Haaretz often sent me to follow the dramatic changes occurring in France. From a thriving, secure, self-confident community, the Jews in France were being menaced by groups with ties to radical Islam. The emigration of the Jews of North Africa to France in the middle of the twentieth century led to an unprecedented flowering of the local Jewish community. It strengthened the community and made it a member of the club of great Jewish communities around the world. Until they came, three out of every four Jews in France had come either from the region of Alsace or from Eastern Europe. When they came, the ratio was reversed and four out of every five Jews came from North Africa.

The new emigrants caused a revolution in the lives of the Jews of France. When they arrived they tried to recreate the Jewish way of life they had known in North Africa. Theo Klein, one of the leaders of the Jewish community, told me that the coming of the North Africans added *joie de vivre* to the gloomy outlook of the community. "When the masses of Jews came from the Maghreb," he said, "they brought us warmth and vitality and a kind of religion that we hadn't known before."

One Saturday in the fall of 2005 I dropped by to visit the Centre Communautaire de Paris, located not far from the Galeries Lafayette, one of Paris' largest department stores. René-Shmuel Sirat, the former chief rabbi of the Jews of France, invited me to join him in the Sabbath prayer. Although I was secular, it was an invitation hard to refuse.

"When should I come?" I asked.

"If you want to be present for the entire prayer, come at eight," he suggested. "If you only want to be present for some of it, come around eleven, before the portion of the Torah is read."

After we agreed on a time, he told me which Metro station was closest to the synagogue. "There won't be a problem with that?" I asked.

"Why should there be a problem? It will honor me if you join the Sabbath prayer. I will save you a seat next to mine."

I mentioned the matter of traveling on Saturday.

"Never mind," he said, "it's not important, the main thing is the Sabbath prayer."

It reminded me of Rabbi Massas from Meknes, who found nothing wrong with going to the swimming pool after the Sabbath prayer.

Rabbi Sirat had integrating religion into modern life down to an art form. He was admired by both Jews and Arabs. During the seven years he served as chief rabbi he toiled ceaselessly to bring Jews, Muslims and Christians together, and to forge bonds between rabbis, imams and priests. Both before and after him, no rabbi was so accepted by people of other faiths, or so frequently invited to mosques and churches. During the years in France when there was no tension between Jews and Muslims he was invited to the Ramadan prayers to speak before worshippers in the Great Mosque in Paris.

He was born in Algeria and emigrated to France. Of the 800 thousand Frenchmen who left Algeria after the bloodbath of its war of independence, more than 100 thousand were Jews. Even though two of his bothers were killed in tragic circumstances, he remained optimistic about human nature. His older brother was murdered during the Algerian war of independence in 1962 on his way to Friday evening prayers at the local synagogue. Another brother was killed by a drunk driver as he was walking on the Champs Élysées in Paris. His appointment as chief rabbi of France marked openness and tolerance that radiated throughout the Jewish community. He was a religious figure well-versed in the ways of the world and believed that Judaism had to march forward hand-in-hand with progress and modern life.

I arrived at the synagogue just before ten in the morning. I rang the bell at the entrance and the door opened. I had come unprepared, without prayer book, *tallit* or *kippah*. A man came out and gave me a prayer book, *tallit* and *kippah*. "Welcome," he said with a smile. I saw Rabbi Sirat in the seat of honor next to the Holy Ark, looking at the congregation. I was invited to read the weekly Torah portion. That was how they treated an invited guest. Since my days at the Youth Village I hadn't read aloud from the Torah. Here, in Paris, among a congregation whose members might have been secular or religious, I felt at home. The combination between the two that the Jews of Morocco had managed to preserve in France made it easy for me.

As we left the synagogue some members of the congregation offered to give me a ride back to my hotel. They saw no contradiction between praying on the Sabbath and driving on the Sabbath. That openness filled me with pride and longing for other times. It pained me to remember the change that had occurred overnight in Kiryat Shmuel, where my parents lived. Ten years previously the ministry of transportation had unsuccessfully tried to open the main street separating Kiryat Shmuel from Kiryat Yam on Saturday. Kiryat Shmuel was closed hermetically, streets leading in and out had sturdy steel chains hung cross them, making the neighborhood look like a ghetto. The state had to bow to protests from the ultra-Orthodox and those who were becoming ultra-Orthodox, and to the threats from the coalition. Kiryat Shmuel remained closed from Friday evening until Saturday when the Sabbath ended. Ariel Sharon's secular government surrendered unconditionally. And thus the fate of a pleasant, tolerant neighborhood was sealed, after my parents had been sent to live there in the nineteen seventies with other immigrants from Morocco. In those days the Moroccans were open-minded and the neighborhood was open-minded; those who protested joined the ultra-Orthodox Ashkenazi demand to close the street.

For me, this whole affair symbolized the failure of the immigrants from North Africa. They came with a tolerant religious lifestyle and over the years turned into intolerant ultra-Orthodox in every respect. Ultra-Orthodox *mizrahi*.

Reconciliation

"Daniel, you have to come back to Rabat as soon as possible." André Azoulay, advisor to King Hassan II, speaking from the palace, could barely get the words out. A few minutes previously I had been called into the lobby of the hotel I was staying in in Agadir. I was informed that I was wanted in the royal palace in Rabat. The director of the lobby took me into his office so I could take a royal phone call with the respect it deserved. "This is hard for me to say, but keep it a secret. You can't tell anyone about it," said Azoulay.

"No problem."

"First promise me."

"I promise."

"His Majesty passed away a few minutes ago. In a few hours there will be a formal announcement. I'm telling you, leave Agadir before the chaos begins. They will probably close the airports, and the roads will be clogged."

I looked around the lobby and didn't see anything out of the ordinary. Tourists in bathing suits were on their way to the beach and the swimming pool. The two restaurants were full and waiters in white *galabiehs* moved among the tables taking orders. The large TV in the lobby broadcast the Friday prayer, also perfectly normal.

It was 1999, and the first royal death since King Hassan had inherited the throne from his father in 1961. Almost four decades of rule had made people think the king was immortal. Most Moroccans knew no other ruler but Hassan. I had no idea how news of his death would be received by people who called him *Sidna* or *Mullana* ("our master"), or what would happen next. Would there be riots? A military coup? Was it the end of the monarchy that had given Moroccans the rights of a democracy? What about the interim period, before a new ruler was appointed? Was his son, Sidi Mohammed, the crown prince, sufficiently mature to take the reins? The Moroccans were used to seeing him, but didn't really know him well.

I went out into the street. It was noon and Agadir looked like any other southern tourist town that attracted hundreds of thousands of Europeans every year, everything routine. There was a picture of the king wherever you looked, and he never looked more alive and more present in the lives of his citizens. I kept walking through the hotel district. There were soldiers hanging around with nothing to do, policemen directing traffic just as they always did. Clearly no one had been told anything.

Agadir, which lies at the foot of the Atlas Mountains, had been the site of a tragedy. On February 29, 1960, twenty minutes before midnight, an earthquake with a magnitude of 5.7 almost completely destroyed the city. More than a third of its 40 thousand residents were buried alive. Almost 2,500 of the city's Jews were killed. King Mohammed V mourned the ruined city, saying, "If destiny decided the destruction of Agadir, its rebuilding depends on our faith and will."

And so it was. Agadir was rebuilt and its population increased tenfold, and it became one of the most popular tourist sites in the world. The French built their holiday houses there and turned it into a Morocco's number two tourist attraction, after Marrakesh.

I returned to the hotel an hour later after having seen nothing unusual in the streets.

The previous day André Azoulay had invited me to his office. I had been in Casablanca on a mission for the paper, and the king's advisor had been looking for me at my hotel. The telephone conversation with the palace had thrown everyone off balance. It was late morning and I was at the pool. All the hotel employees followed me around feverishly. I heard my name called on the public address system and hurried to the lobby. The hotel directors were almost breathlessly tense. "Sir," said the head of reception, "the royal palace wants to speak to you." He extended the receiver and I found myself talking to André Azoulay, who told me an official vehicle was on its way to bring me back to the palace in Rabat.

From that moment my status soared among the hotel employees. It wasn't every day they got a phone call from the palace. Everyone smiled an extra smile and made sure I lacked for nothing. Returning to my room I discovered an enormous bouquet of flowers and a dish of local delicacies. A bottle of Champagne was waiting in an ice bucket on the table. The general excitement didn't surprise me. The power of King Hassan II was extraordinary.

In less than an hour an official vehicle was parked outside the hotel in Casablanca, surrounded by a crowd of dozens of the curious, both adults and children. The license plates had no number, just simple two words, Palais Royal, in both French and Arabic. Just seeing the word "royal palace" was sufficient to excite the whole street. Casablanca was less than 60 miles from Rabat, the capital. On the drive we saw dozens of traffic policemen on the lookout for speeders. We were driving at almost double the legal limit, but when the policemen saw our car they were quick to jump to attention and salute.

The royal palace looked exactly like the colorful pictures in the travel brochures. The royal family lived in its wings, as did the families of the king's advisors and members of the court. It was a picturesque village in the center of the capital city. Of all his dozens of palaces located throughout the country, the king preferred to spend most of his time in Rabat. His glory and status in the eyes of his people were unaffected by his legendary wealth and his extravagant lifestyle. He invested much of his personal fortune in businesses abroad, especially in the United States. On one visit abroad he returned with one hundred luxury cars, thousands of ties and hundreds of expensive knickknacks. In his palace he lived the life of the *Thousand and One Nights*. Exposés in books and newspapers in France claimed he had collected hundreds of mistresses on his trips in Morocco and other countries and housed them in wings of the palace. According to Le Monde, he had a penchant for dressing them in costume.

The car stopped at the entrance to the building housing Azoulay's office. There were hundreds of uniformed royal police milling around and black-suited security personnel in every corner. Obviously, the king took no chances. The walls had been decorated by master mosaic makers. The hundreds of decorators who had toiled on the palace had produced an architectural masterpiece. The floors were entirely covered with extravagant rugs.

I was received by a secretary, who greeted me in Moroccan Arabic and with a smile. Everyone spoke French mixed with Moroccan Arabic. Azoulay, the most famous Jew in the country, walked towards me. He smiled and took me into his office. He pointed at a framed picture on one of the tables, of the king shaking hands with Prime Minister Yitzhak Rabin. Azoulay was in the background between them, smiling a small, restrained smile.

No other picture could better symbolize the life of Azoulay, the Moroccan Jew who had reached the pinnacle of his country's Muslim regime. He was in his seventies at the time, and his Judaism, of which he was so proud, was fully harmonious with his Moroccan identity. He saw them as one inseparable entity. Many Moroccans considered him the most powerful figure at court. Social scientists measure political power by physical proximity to the leader. Azoulay was one of the people closest to the king. His own office was only a few dozen yards down a corridor from the king's.

Everything was quiet. The security personnel and

palace servants walked around on tip-toe. According to reports in foreign news media, the Israeli Mossad participated in maintaining the security of the king and the royal family.

Nine years had passed since the king had appointed Azoulay as his economic advisor, after he had been head of the Middle Eastern branch of a bank in Paris. The king was interested in the conflicted arena of the Middle East. He was convinced that good for the entire world could come out of the region, or evil for the entire world. For years he preached, consistently and with single-mindedness, reconciliation between Jews and Muslims, and welcomed whatever brought prosperity and progress to both. He always thought that if the Arabs, with their money, and the Jews, with their brains, could join forces, they could change the face of the Middle East.

Azoulay had a similar dream. He pointed proudly at a picture of Shimon Peres hanging on one of the walls and at a picture of the king and Yitzhak Rabin enjoying one another's company. His eyes filled with tears as he looked at the pictures. "His Majesty admired Rabin. After he was murdered he found it hard to function. He couldn't believe Israelis could sink so low."

The election of Ehud Barak as prime minister in the summer of 1999 breathed new hope into Morocco. Azoulay said the king had been overjoyed. Once Benyamin Netanyahu had been defeated, the Moroccans felt there would be a rapprochement with Israel. It was difficult, he said, to describe the cries of joy heard in many homes when Barak's victory was announced. A senior government official hold him that the local television stations were following the news from Israel as though the elections were taking place in Morocco. "The lights were on in the palace all night long," said Azoulay, "we were all sitting there, watching, it was fantastic. Moroccans had always thought the army was Israel's strong point, but after the elections they said, 'Now we know democracy is Israel's strongest weapon.' "

Azoulay showed me the album he had put together of pictures chronicling Morocco's special relations with Israel. Many of the pictures had not been made public for security reasons. One of the palace workers entered the office with a pot of Moroccan tea. Azoulay poured tea, took a sip and said, "You have to understand, the Arabs in Morocco view the election of Ehud Barak, and especially the ousting of Netanyahu, as a rare opportunity for regional peace. That is the king's ideal, and I think his son the crown prince will also work to achieve the vision."

I asked him about the fate of the "special relations" between Israel and Morocco. He was about to answer when the office telephone rang. He lifted the receiver and his pale face became paler. He kept nodding as he listened. Sometimes he looked at the window, at the king's office. My presence obviously made him uncomfortable. On the other side of the line was Driss Basri, the minister of the interior, a particularly influential person. He was the bringer of bad news: the king had just collapsed in his living quarters. He was having trouble breathing. Basri told Azoulay to call the king's personal physicians and others as well. "We have to be prepared for the worst," he said. Azoulay's eyes were red. He could not imagine that the same night King Hassan II would breathe his last.

That ended our meeting. I did not go back to Casablanca, instead I went to spend the weekend in Agadir. I thought about the special relationship Morocco had with its Jews. Hundreds of thousands of them had pulled up stakes and gone to Israel and Europe and only a few thousand remained, the rest strongly missed by their Muslim neighbors. Two thousand years of Jewish-Muslim coexistence had bred a unique, tolerant Moroccan temperament. The same question was always asked when I met with government officials and local media personnel: where did the Jews who left Morocco for Israel find their political extremism and how did they become the main stronghold, not to say fortress, of the Israeli Right? The people I talked to interpreted their voting for Right-wing parties, especially the Likud, as anti-Arab. It is hard to describe how deeply they were hurt and offended by reports in the French and Israeli media describing Jews from Morocco as hating Arabs and has having learned that hatred in Morocco.

"We lived with Arabs and we know they can't be trusted," Jews from Morocco always told me to justify their suspicion and skepticism about peace. Foreign correspondents who covered Israel customarily described Jews who had come from Arab countries as tending to vote for the Right more than Jews from Europe. The French press was full of reports about their extremism in the Israeli-Arab conflict.

The day before I met with Azoulay I was sitting in the office of Khalil Hachimi Idrissi, editor of the weekly French-language Maroc Hebdo. Not long before, he and other Moroccan public figures had been invited to visit Israel by the Israeli foreign ministry. Idrissi, who was in his forties and spoke fluent French, was impressed by the immigrants from Moroccan he had met in the southern part of the country, in places like Ashdod, Ashqelon and Beersheba, but also in the smaller towns. He was particularly impressed by the emotional connection they had with the country of their birth. They spoke about Morocco with love and longing, and listening to them brought tears to his eyes.

He saw, or more accurately, wanted to see, the immigrants from Morocco as a bridge reconciling Israel and its neighbors. The Israelis he met spoke French and Moroccan Arabic, recalled memories of life with their Arab neighbors and their childhoods, and said they hoped that before long Jews and Arabs would again live in peace "the way we lived with the Arabs in Morocco." He was impressed by their tolerance.

"You won't believe it," he told me, "but when we talked politics they all said they had voted for the Likud. Actually, it was a paradox I didn't understand. How could anyone be so connected to Arabic culture and still support extremist politics? Everyone said it had no connection to the Arabs, but it was because of their hatred for the Israeli Left. I asked what the connection was. They said the Left had claimed ownership of peace. And because they were against the Left, they also didn't support its peace. They said only if the Right could make peace would they follow. I have to admit it made me very sad. I have visited communities of emigrants from Morocco in many countries around the world. They are all known for their moderation and tolerance. Except for the Moroccan community in Israel. They kept telling me that the Arabs in the Middle East were not like the Arabs in Morocco."

The election of Ehud Barak in 1999 and having David Levy and Shimon Peres as ministers in the government made Idrissi more hopeful. All the newspapers in Morocco praised the wisdom shown by Israeli voters in toppling Benyamin Netanyahu. Idrissi wrote an editorial saying he hoped Morocco and Israel would institute full diplomatic relations and that other Arab states would follow their example. Like many others, he admired King Hassan for the prominent role he assumed in trying to broker a détente between Israel and the Palestinians and the Arab world. He had a picture on his desk of the king taken during a state visit to France a few days previously for the Bastille Day parade. The king looked unwell. His eyes were half-closed and his lips were slack. For months there had been rumors he had cancer that was slowly, relentlessly, ending his life.

I met with Idrissi on July 21, 1999, in Maroc Hebdo's editorial offices in Casablanca. He praised the king's tolerance and never imagined his was fighting for his life. Two days later the king would pass away. "Daniel, my friend," he said, "you Israelis have to stop talking about security and defense all the time. You don't live alone in the Middle East. You have to focus on regional cooperation and stop talking about having to be the strongest country. What good does all that talking do you? What is peace for, if not to create a new life founded on regional cooperation. Stop talking about 'we Israelis' and start looking at yourselves as part of the family of the Middle East."

In every meeting with Israeli public figures who were born in Morocco, the king urged them to bring their innate "Moroccan tolerance" to the fore. He had no qualms about criticizing the Israeli Right wing and the Moroccans in Israel who had tied their fate to it. He refused to receive Israeli Prime Minister Yitzhak Shamir, and refused the request of Israeli Prime Minister Benyamin Netanyahu to visit Morocco. Three years of the Rabin administration, which had been a pinnacle of Israeli-Moroccan relations, were wiped out. The Oslo Accords, the peace agreement with Jordan and openness to the Arab world were regarded in Morocco as turning points in Middle East history. Then in 1995 Rabin was assassinated and after Peres finished his term as prime minister the axe fell and Benyamin Netanyahu was elected. The king mourned Rabin's death and was disappointed by the election, whose results indicated Netanyahu had the massive support of the Moroccans in Israel.

King Hassan never missed an opportunity to influence Israeli elections. In every pre-election speech, Labor Party leader Shimon Peres invited him to pay a state visit to Israel. Peres and the heads of the Israeli Leftist camp were fully aware of the great love the Moroccan immigrants had for the king, and were certain that a meeting with his former subjects would make exceptional political capital for the Labor Party.

The 1981 elections were held in an atmosphere favorable for both the Labor Party and its head, Peres. What could they do to ensure the Moroccan vote? Drop in on Morocco, obviously. So, Peres arranged to be invited for a state visit and a meeting with the king. His particular hope was that having his picture taken with the king would make a good impression on Moroccan voters. The king never hid his political dealings, and told the Moroccan media he wanted to send a message to "my subjects in Israel," as he called them, to vote against Israeli Prime Minister Menachem Begin.

Hassan received Peres at the palace in Marrakesh on March 18, 1981. He did everything in his power to make the visit pleasant. Before Peres left the king promised, "I will do everything I can to help you." He told every Israeli visitor he met how disappointed he was the Moroccans voted for the Likud. He viewed the Israeli Right as an obstacle to peace. "My dream is for peace between Israel and the Palestinians," he told one delegation. "If there is peace and a Palestinian state is established, it will be a blessing for everyone in the region. The Middle East will become an oasis of peace and prosperity..."

Yehuda Lankri was a member of an Israeli delegation that met with the king. He had begun his public career in the leftist Mapam Party, deserted to the Likud and was elected to the Knesset on the Likud ticket. He had an emotional meeting with the king in 1999. The king's face reflected his terminal illness. He welcomed his guests in Moroccan Arabic, saying, "This is your home." For Lankri, who was born in Morocco, the king symbolized the Moroccan tolerance that had been twisted and deformed in Israel. "The king," he later told me, "regarded the delegation of Moroccan Israelis as continuing the long-standing Moroccan tradition of tolerance. I have to admit that he expected us to bring that tradition to the Middle Eastern experience. We always personified tolerance. But the oppression of our first years in Israel crushed that. Alienation took me from Mapam and brought me to the Likud, and made countless others support the Likud. I saw myself as wanting to be a bridge to peace with our neighbors. I believe that if the Israeli establishment hadn't oppressed us, the lives of people who came from Morocco would look different today."

The king himself said the same thing in an interview with the Egyptian weekly al-Musawar. He said, "I asked Moroccan Israelis who were Likud Knesset members why they had joined Menachem Begin's party. They said the Labor Party discriminated against them and didn't give them equal opportunities. Begin, on the other hand, made them feel proud of their heritage, treated them with respect and like equals, and appointed them to key government and military positions..."

Could traumatic experiences when coming to Israel have drastically changed the nature of an entire ethnic group? Could their rage with the founders of the country for the way they were treated be passed down from generation to generation? Was their turning to Orthodoxy a result of the traumas of the nineteen fifties? Could the humiliation they felt they had received at the hands of the Left make them regard the Right as a place where they were welcome? Did they hate the Arabs because they hated the Left? How could an entire people who were supposed to serve as a bridge to religious and political tolerance turn into a bastion of religious and political extremism?

Those questions trouble me still. I was reproached with the anomaly of being Moroccan and identifying with the Left at every turn. When the paper sent me to cover Likud meetings I was treated like one of the family. Being Moroccan absolved me, to a great extent, of being Leftist. After the embraces and kisses I was always asked, "What are you doing working for them? Come to us. You will feel at home here. No one will discriminate against you or offend you. The Likud is our home. There are quarrels and conflicts, but it's all in the family."

They made sure to tell me that they would accept any far-reaching political compromise for the sake of peace, as long as it was the Likud that reached the compromise. They made sure to tell me they had voted for every peace agreement brought before them. They regarded the Left as attacking the state's Jewish values. They regarded the Right as an insurance policy against any damage the Left was capable of doing to the identity and image of Israel.

One conversation in particular sticks in my mind. It was so shocking I felt I was a journalist inside a hermetically sealed box with my back to reality. It occurred in 1996, the day after Shimon Peres lost the election to Benyamin Netanyahu. Twenty years later, it is still with me. I had taken a taxi from Mt. Scopus in Jerusalem to Tel Aviv to join the television broadcast about the election results. The driver, a man named Yoav, was ecstatic. A post-earthquake atmosphere hung in the air. The election results had surprised winners and losers alike, and divided Israel into two camps, those who rejoiced in victory and those who mourned in defeat. Yoav, who lived in the Pisgat Ze'ev neighborhood of Jerusalem, rejoiced. Four years of Labor Party rule had been good to him. He had moved from a small, crowded apartment in a slum in the southern part of the city to a new apartment in a new neighborhood and had received a generous, low-interest loan as part of a "living improvement" program. His children went to good schools and participated in after-school activities with "children from good families, Ashkenazi, I am happy to say, thank God, I have no complaint."

"You know," he said, "this is the happiest day of my life." On the rear windshield there were still two stickers, one reading "Netanyahu is good for the Jews" and the other, "Netanyahu [will win], with God's help." He still couldn't believe Netanyahu had won. "Believe me," he said, " I never believed it would happen. I was certain the Left would win this time. With the help of God, believe me, it was with the help of God."

Under the rearview mirror dangled a small, framed picture of Rabbi Kadouri, "the greatest Kabbalist of our generation," as his followers called him. I asked Yoav if he was religious. "No," he said, in a semi-apologetic tone of voice, "but I have great respect for religion." He opened the glove compartment with his right hand and took out a black *kippah*. "You see, I always have this ready, if by chance a rabbi gets into my taxi. Because I respect religious people and because I respect our religion. So what's the big deal if I wear a *kippah* to show respect for our rabbis? Is that any reason to look down on religious people? It's disgraceful that it has come to such a pass in our country. People ashamed of their religion."

An IDF roadblock delayed traffic on the main road near Modi'in. "Netanyahu will get rid of this too, with God's help," he said with absolute assurance. "This whole mess is Peres' fault. He gave the Arabs everything they wanted and always caved in. And what did he get in return? Terrorist attacks and more terrorist attacks. I ask you, how can you drive a taxi if there is a roadblock every mile? And in your own country. Understand one thing, the Arabs won't try anything with Netanyahu in charge. Their luck has changed."

There was a long line of cars waiting to pass through the roadblock. Yoav was restless. "You look sad because of the elections," he said with a smile. "Listen, you have no reason to be sad. Take me, for example. I voted for Netanyahu and Shass. One ballot for each. Understand what I'm telling you. Bibi will make peace with the Arabs. And don't get the wrong idea. I am in favor of peace with all the Arabs, but not the peace of Shimon Peres and the Left. At least Bibi will make peace with honor. He won't just give them what they want for the sake of giving. I know the Arabs. They don't like appeasers and people who try to suck up to them like Peres. They have honor as well, and they like it when people respect them."

I asked him why he had voted for Shass. He asked me back, "Tell me, where are you from? Are you Ashkenazi or *mizrahi*? If you are a *mizrahi*, how can you ask me such a stupid question? Excuse me, yes, you amaze me. I told you I'm not religious, OK. But I support our religion because I believe that without Jewish values we have no business being here. We can go back to where we came from. Tell me, this is a real question, why did we come here? To be like America, a country of criminals and whores? I'm sorry to have to say this, but Shimon Peres and his comrades lost their connection with Judaism. I have great respect for Peres and I think he is a great statesman, but tell me, why does he have to suck up to Clinton and the king of Morocco and King Hussein, to say nothing of Arafat? I'm telling you, what hurt me most of all was that Peres thought he would win because of the votes of Israeli Arabs. What are we, losers? Not worth his attention? He doesn't need the Jews any more? Whose country is this? Ours or theirs?"

By the time we got to Tel Aviv, Yoav was practically shouting. The setting sun was reflected in the widows of the tall buildings. "I can't stand this city," he said. "What does it have? Nothing but pubs and coffee houses and bars for homosexuals and lesbians. That's all Tel Aviv cares about. Just having a good time. Believe me, I'm a liberal, but why do there have to be so many clubs for homosexuals? You know when all this started? When the Left came into power. Those people think they're allowed to do anything they want. They think people like me are retarded and primitive."

Suddenly he stopped the car and said with repressed fury, "You know what else made me mad about the elections? The television debate between Peres and Bibi. That finished me off. Did you see how Peres belittled Bibi and treated him like garbage? Who does he think he is? When the moderator asked him to ask Bibi a question, why didn't he? He's willing to talk to Arabs but not to Jews? Bibi isn't a Jew? He doesn't love his country? I'm fed up with their arrogance and condescension. You know, I was born here and I grew up here and in the army I was in a combat unit. But I feel like I don't belong to them. Why do I have to feel like they don't want me? I know it's because I'm a *mizrahi* with dark skin. Does that make me not as good as them? Now do you understand why I'm happy Peres lost? Because all those condescending Ashkenazis got what they deserved. They thought the country belonged to them and that they knew everything, and now it turns out they don't know anything."

Not too long after that I happened to meet with Peres

THE IMMIGRANT

in his office in Tel Aviv. He asked how I explained the defeat in the 1996 elections. Two months had passed and he refused to be consoled. I told him about my taxi ride from Jerusalem with Yoav. I reminded him about when he had attended the most recent Mimouna celebration[24] in Saker Park in Jerusalem. Tens of thousands of people had crowded into the park. It was less than a month before the elections and the polls predicted a win for the incumbent Prime Minister, Shimon Peres. Peres came to the park to celebrate the holiday with the Moroccans. A raised stage had been erected for him. And then the unexpected happened. Some of the people started booing him. The more he tried to speak to them honestly, the more protestors joined them, booing and whistling. Peres looked upset and offended. He tried to speak louder and the protestors drowned him out. Trying to calm them, he said he had just met with the king, "your king," he stressed. Everyone understood he was talking about King Hassan II of Morocco. Instead of appeasing them, he had only made them angrier. The Mimouna of 1996 left no doubt in anyone's mind that the Moroccans would never vote for Peres.

He thought for a minute, then said, "I know many people hate us," he said, his voice getting louder with every word. "They hate us because we are in favor of peace. They hate us because we're modern. They hate us because we're Ashkenazi. They hate us because we're taking Israel forward. They hate us because they want to be like us. And who influences that hate? The stupid, senile, backward rabbis and religious gurus who want to return to the ghetto."

And back to Morocco, Sunday, July 25, 1999. By

---

24. A North African Jewish celebration held the day after Passover, marking the return to eating leavened food.

morning world leaders had begun arriving at the royal palace in Rabat. After they debarked, the planes returned to nearby airfields. The members of the new royal family, of King Mohammed VI, sadly received their condolences. The king isolated himself in the mourning hall in the palace. When the plane bearing American President Bill Clinton landed, he came out to receive him personally. His father's funeral was to be held in the afternoon, and millions of Moroccans had already filled the streets of the capital to mourn the king.

On orders from the king's advisor, André Azoulay, I had left Agadir a few hours after the official announcement of the death of King Hassan. The airport was empty when I arrived. I joined a group of high-ranking officers on their way to join the cortège. I found myself, an Israeli journalist, on a Moroccan plane full of army officers.

The plane carrying the Israeli delegation to the funeral circled above the airport for a full hour, waiting for Bill Clinton's plane to disappear over the horizon. André Azoulay, wearing a traditional while Moroccan robe, received visitors from abroad. Standing next to him was Mullay Rashid, the new king's brother, and Driss Basri, the omnipotent minister of the interior. Passengers debarked from other planes. Almost two hundred people got off the Israeli plane. Everyone who could had pushed his way onto it. However, of all the Israelis, the Moroccans waiting at the airport were interested in only two: Ehud Barak and David Levy. A few weeks previously Barak had appointed Levy to the post of foreign minister, after Levy had helped him form a joint ticket for the 1999 elections. The Moroccans took that as a sign Levy had reconnected to his Moroccan tolerance. Over the years they tried to bring him to Morocco for a state visit, but Levy refused. He kept refusing until King Hassan died. The Moroccan media often reported on Levy's unique position on the Israeli political scene and hoped he would become Israel's first Moroccan-born prime minister.

Barak had been *persona grata* in Morocco from the time he was an IDF officer. He often visited the kingdom to help the Moroccan army fight the Polisario Front, a rebel national liberation movement whose objective was to end Moroccan presence in the Western Sahara. Units of the pro-Algerian underground often infiltrated into Moroccan territory and exposed the Moroccan army's inability to defend the country's borders. Barak and other officers advised the king to construct a border security fence to keep them out. King Hassan was familiar with Barak's army career and admired his courage. While he usually never met with anyone below the rank of head of state, he enjoyed listening to Barak talk about security and strategy. When Barak was elected prime minister in May 1999, the king sent him an invitation to visit in the fall. His death changed the plan.

Barak got off the plane first, smiling at people as though he had arrived at a party. After him came President Ezer Weizman, Shimon Peres and after them, Foreign Minister David Levy. It was his first visit back to the country where he had been born and raised.

I watched Levy for a long time when we arrived at the palace. Members of the Israeli delegation offered their condolences to the mourners in English. When Levy's turn came, they spoke to him in Moroccan Arabic, saying "Welcome to our country." The Moroccan minister of the interior shook Levy's hand. Levy was tense. Obviously, the unexpected visit to his "first homeland" had shaken him strongly. He looked around as if not particularly interested, touring in some Scandinavian country without having read the guidebook. It was a combination of extreme emotion mixed with almost catatonic restraint.

He answered in French. Hundreds of Israelis fell upon the refreshment tables set up inside the palace with typical enthusiasm. Levy stood apart on one of the balconies, drinking Moroccan tea from a gilded glass. I stood next to him, looking at the man who had come to Israel when he was 20 years old and paved the road for many after him who had made their way in Israeli politics. He looked stony, like the Sphinx. I spoke to him; he didn't answer. He just kept looking around, silently. Hundreds of world leaders passed by, kings, presidents, prime ministers, foreign ministers. Peres kept shaking hands. Weizman didn't know what to do with himself and walked around aimlessly. Barak ate. Levy was struggling to contain the enormous emotion filling him.

A long line of leaders had formed along the wall leading to the mourning hall where the new king sat. The Israeli delegation cut to the head of the line and went to console the king. Azoulay asked me to fetch Barak because the king was waiting for him. I located him near one of the tables, looking for another interesting dish to eat. The heads of the Israeli delegation were waiting for him. On his way to the king, Barak stopped a moment next to the king of Saudi Arabia, who was leaning on a cane, and wondered if he should surprise him by offering to shake his hand. He asked me what I thought. In the end, he decided not to.

King Mohammed VI rose to greet him and held him in a long embrace. They obviously knew and liked one another. Weizman sat next to the king and looked at the interior decorations. Barak, who had only been prime minister for a month, thin and wearing a black suit, talked to the king about his late father and the challenges facing Morocco. The king, 36 years old, wearing a light yellow robe and a red Moroccan tarbush, listened and nodded occasionally.

THE IMMIGRANT

André Azoulay sat on the sidelines and could barely hide what he felt about a group of Israeli leaders sitting contently in perfect harmony with a Muslim leader who was called "the exalted Muslim, the emir of the faithful," a title he had inherited at the death of his father. This Moroccan Jew, a man of the world, was in love with the country of his ancestors and wanted to be buried there when the time came. He always found a way to arrange meetings between Israeli leaders and the royal house. He always stressed the importance of peace between Jews and Arabs, the height of his aspirations. The members of the Israeli delegation were wearing suits, but he wore a Moroccan robe, in which he felt most comfortable.

Not far away, in one of the palace wings, sat the heads of Moroccan Jewry, waiting for the funeral to begin. They had spent their entire lives fostering their two loves, Israel and Morocco. More than anyone, they hoped a diplomatic bridge between the two countries would be built soon. They loved hearing Hebrew spoken in the streets of Casablanca, in the Old City of Fez, in the fish restaurants, in the famous market of Marrakesh. Tens of thousands of Israeli tourists, most of them born in Morocco, brought an atmosphere of reconciliation to Morocco like the one that had existed before the Jews left.

In the evening I spent some time with Serge Berdugo, the head of the Jewish community, who was about to leave Rabat and drive to Casablanca. The Israeli delegation was planning to return to Israel, a four-hour direct flight. Morocco mourned the dead king and opened its arms to the new one. "If only you reached an arrangement with the Palestinians, the entire Arab world would be open to you," sighed Berdugo. He was a successful businessman and a scion of a dynasty of rabbis from Meknes. He had been minister of tourism in

Hassan II's government and a special ambassador sent on various missions around the world. Members of his family had left Morocco for France, the United States and Israel. He preferred to stay in the country he loved. He wanted to make sure everyone knew Morocco had not just a past full of longing, but a future full in promises.

"We Moroccans," he said, "understand and have an emotional attachment to everything in the Middle East. We have lived with the Arabs for two thousand years and learned to live with them as with family. We speak their language, love their poetry and are an integral part of their rich culture. Our advantage is in our balanced temperament and the tolerant way we view the world. We don't have the fanaticism of the Jews who came from Europe. There was no anti-Semitism here and no hatred for the Jews like in Europe. What I am trying to say is that that our past has no emotional trauma. That allows us a worldview based on reconciliation. The day will come when Israel elects a prime minister of Moroccan heritage. Then maybe the dream of Hassan II will become reality, may God have mercy, and Israel and the Arab world will live in peace."

The noise of a plane circling above us forced him to stop talking. He put his head out of the window of the black Mercedes we were sitting in. He smiled at me. It was the Israeli plane taking the delegation back to Israel. "That's what I mean," he said emotionally, "that you can fly in and out of the Arab world freely and naturally. When that happens, it will be the greatest victory of the concept of Zionism."

He pushed his seat back and leaned his head on the headrest. "It makes me so emotional I want to cry," he said, and closed his eyes.

Epilogue

The car that drove us through the busy streets of Casablanca made its way to the Oasis quarter. More than forty years had passed since I left the École Normale Hébraïque and passed through its gates for the last time. The car stopped at front gate and the Muslim gatekeeper asked how he could help. I explained I had spent three years at the school and nostalgia had brought me back for a visit. We spoke a combination of Moroccan Arabic and French, as is customary to this day. "Are you a tourist?" he asked.

Beyond the iron gate I could see the offices of the boarding school, close to the entrance. The headmaster of the school was summoned. "Le directeur va venir tout de suite."

Amram Lévy, who was head teacher when I was a student, walked towards me. He took a good look and identified me. We embraced for a long time. "Monsieur Knesset member, this is a great honor for us," he said in French.

Epilogue

The same thin frame, still wearing a tailored suit, the same carefully combed hair and the same gait, headmaster since he inherited the chair of the legendary Émile Sebban. He was then second in command, but the power of Monsieur Sebban overshadowed everyone, including Monsieur Lévy, as we called him then. The news that Monsieur Sebban had retired spread like wildfire throughout the Alliance Israëlite Universale network in Morocco and beyond. Dominant personalities like Émile Sebban, who changed and fashioned the fate of thousands of young people, were not found every day.

Monsieur Lévy, speaking slowly and carefully, accompanied me along the corridor leading to the classrooms I had sat in so many years ago. I studied for three of the four years I was supposed to before graduation. At the end of the fourth year I would have gone to the high school. I remember how we looked at the high school students, longing to join them. To us they seemed like adults, mature and ready for the world. We knew that when they finished the twelfth grade we would never see them again, they would disappear as though the earth had swallowed them. The earth in France. They would pull up stakes in Morocco and replant them in France, where their new lives were waiting for them.

Monsieur Lévy walked with me to the classroom where I had studied before I parted from my friends. There were fifteen students sitting there, exactly as we had sat. The chairs and desks had been replaced and the ink wells were gone. The children looked so young. Some of them wore kippot, others were bare-headed. Boys and girls sat together. As soon as we entered they sat up straight and in chorus welcomed us, "Bonjour, monsieur." They listened as Monsieur Lévy told them about me, that I had been a good student, and then what seemed like a unique achievement, "Daniel is a member of the Israeli parliament," he added. The children applauded. He walked over to a seat where he said I had sat forty some-odd years previously. He remembered; I, somewhat less. Just seeing the classroom was an emotional experience for me, and memories came flooding back.

The lesson we had interrupted was about Hebrew literature. I was introduced to the teacher: "Please," said Monsieur Lévy, "meet Muhammad. Muhammad, this is Monsieur Ben Simon, a former student." We shook hands, and Muhammad spoke to me in Hebrew with a strong French accent. He had a BA in Hebrew literature from the University of Casablanca and had fallen in love with Agnon, Brenner, and Holocaust author Aharon Appelfeld. He told me he preferred classic Hebrew literature to modern Israeli novels.

Given the lack of Jewish students, the Alliance network had agreed to enroll children of other religions. For the first time since its founding in 1860, Muslim children were studying at Alliance institutions. For years, upper class Muslim families in Morocco had wanted their children to study at the École Normale Hébraïque, with its unprecedented success rate: for as long as the school has been in existence, EVERY SINGLE ONE of its graduates has received a BACCALAURÉAT CERTIFICATE, THE BEST RECORD NOT ONLY IN MOROCCO BUT IN FRANCE AS WELL. AND NOW THE TIME HAD COME. THERE WERE ALMOST NO YOUNG JEWS LEFT IN MOROCCO. THE DIRECTOR TOLD ME IT WAS ALMOST CERTAIN THAT THE CURRENT TWELFTH GRADE WOULD BE THE LAST WITH JEWISH STUDENTS. "I WON'T BE HERE EITHER," HE SAID IN A LOW VOICE, "I'M GOING ON ALIYAH TO ISRAEL NEXT YEAR, TO LIVE IN NETANYA NEAR MY FAMILY AND FRIENDS."

I asked him if he felt the end had come for the Jewish presence in Morocco. He nodded, finding it hard to hide his sadness. "I think it's over," he said. We walked around

Epilogue

the school yard. There were so few students it was no longer a boarding school and everyone went home in the evening.

Thousands of École Normale Hébraïque students had graduated over the years and emigrated to new lives in France. Almost all of them viewed it as their next logical station. They thrived and prospered, and living in France was a glorious chapter in their lives and in the life in France. France to its credit, opened its doors wide to the Jews of Morocco, regarding them as its sons and daughters. It gave them everything necessary to assimilate, integrate and succeed in their new country. Therefore it was no wonder that after two generations children of Moroccan heritage reached unprecedented heights in French society and culture. Their contributions to engineering, medicine, literature, architecture, entertainment, the arts and economics are enormous for such a small percentage of the population. And so the question is asked again and again, and again and again there is no real answer, why did they succeed so famously in France and fail so miserably in Israel?

In 2017 I returned to Morocco to visit my old boarding school. The signs that an era had come to an end were clear. The voices echoing from its classroom for so many years were no more. It had turned into a mirror image of Moroccan Judaism. There are still Jews and Jewish institutions in Morocco, the disagreements are over how many. Optimists say more than a thousand, pessimists, a couple of hundred.

Before I went into the school I glanced at the villa across the street, where the school's royal couple had lived. Monsieur and Madame Sebban. The entrance was neglected and overgrown with weeds. I asked the gate keeper about the family. He said Monsieur Sebban had passed away and his wife hadn't been seen for a long time. However, he had recently heard voices, but he didn't know whose.

I walked over and rang the bell. There was no answer and I hadn't been expecting one. It was just an instinctive act on my part. When I was a student I never would have dared to approach the villa, let alone ring the bell. The image of Monsieur and Madame was sufficiently formidable to deter the bravest student. I was about to turn away when I heard a frail voice call out from the second floor,

"Qui c' ést?"

I looked up at the second floor. Dusty shutters covered the window. I answered, " C' ést moi," without specifying who exactly "moi" was.

"Attendez un moment," came the response.

I was certain I had spoken to a maid, a local woman who looked after the house in the absence of its owners. Then the door opened, and before me stood a small wrinkled figure who looked at the assembled throng, myself and the Israelis who had accompanied me on my visit to the school.

Behind the face of the old woman I could recognize Madame Sebban. It was actually she. Her hair was thin and she was stooped over. I hadn't seen her for almost fifty years. And now, here she was, standing in front of me.

"I remember you," she said, "you are Monsieur Ben Simon."

"Yes, I am. You have a wonderful memory."

"It's one of the few faculties I still possess."

"You know I was in the same class as your son, Ariel."

"I do know. You know he died?"

"Yes, I do."

"At least he didn't die in pain."

Epilogue

Now she lived alone. Her husband was dead, her son was dead. Her other son lived in Paris. She divided her time between an apartment in Casablanca's Oasis quarter and her son's home in France. We knew her as Madame Sebban, we never referred to her by her given name, Marcelle. She invited us in. I told her it was the first time I had ever entered what in our day was considered a fortress. The description surprised her. "There was no reason to be afraid of us," she said with a smile. Even now, after so many years, I was in awe of her. During an era when discipline was a central factor of our lives, she and her husband symbolized our fear. What I remembered was the way they looked at us and the fierce expressions on their never-smiling faces.

While we were trading stories about days gone by in the boarding school, I began telling her about how my life had turned out in Israel. She knew I had spent many years as a journalist and knew I had written several books. "I remember, you wanted to be an author even when you were young," she said. And smiling, "I'm not sure my recollection is accurate, Monsieur Ben Simon," she said, still using formalities after so many years. I would never dare call her Marcelle, and she would never be so familiar as to call me Daniel. That's how it had been, and that's how it remained.

And then she reminded me of that meeting in her husband's office so many years ago. She still recalled how her husband, fearing for my future, had tried to dissuade me from immigrating to Israel. I had a sudden flashback, a fleeting memory. There had been a fourth person in the room when I had been summoned for the discussion between Monsieur Sebban and the aliyah representative. Monsieur Sebban, as I have indicated in this book, was not happy about the meeting, knowing it would not end as he would have wanted, as had apparently happened several times before. The aliyah representative wanted to send me to Israel. Madame Sebban remembered that her husband was clearly against it, arguing that it wouldn't be good for me and I wouldn't be able to realize my dream of becoming an author.

"Alors, il eut raison?" ("Was he right?") She smiled and waited for my answer.

I was astounded. Astounded that she remembered after so many years, astounded that she asked, disconcerted that I had no answer. I didn't know what to tell her. Such a simple question, but answering it would mean telling her the story of my life in Israel. All the happiness and all the moments something inside me was about to break. My instinctive reaction was to tell her that no, he had been wrong. In the final analysis, my life turned out as I had wanted. But I couldn't say that to her. She waited patiently for my answer.

"Madame Sebban, je ne suis pas sûr. Je ne sais vraiment pas." ("Madame Sebban, I'm not sure. I really don't know."). That was all I could say.

www.ingramcontent.com/pod-product-compliance
Lightning Source LLC
Chambersburg PA
CBHW070139100426
42743CB00013B/2755